FIRE SALE

A GUIDE FOR CANADIAN REAL ESTATE INVESTORS AND SNOWBIRDS

FIRE SALE

HOW TO BUY U.S. FORECLOSURES NOW!

Philip McKernan
Author of *South of 49*

John Wiley & Sons Canada, Ltd.

Library and Archives Canada Cataloguing in Publication Data

McKernan, Philip
       Fire sale : how to buy US foreclosures / Philip McKernan.

ISBN 978-0-470-96412-5

       1. Residential real estate—Purchasing—United States. 2. Real estate investment—United States. 3. House buying—United States. 4. Foreclosure—United States. I. Title.

HD259.M387 2010   332.63'240973   C2010-903695-6

Production Credits
Cover Design: Natalia Burobina
Interior Design and Typesetting: Pat Loi
Printer: Friesens Printing Ltd.

Editorial Credits
Editor: Don Loney
Production Editor: Pamela Vokey

John Wiley & Sons Canada, Ltd.
6045 Freemont Blvd.
Mississauga, Ontario
L5R 4J3

Printed in Canada

1 2 3 4 5 FP 14 13 12 11 10

ENVIRONMENTAL BENEFITS STATEMENT

John Wiley & Sons - Canada saved the following resources by printing the pages of this book on chlorine free paper made with 100% post-consumer waste.

TREES	WATER	SOLID WASTE	GREENHOUSE GASES
76 FULLY GROWN	34,795 GALLONS	2,113 POUNDS	7,225 POUNDS

Calculations based on research by Environmental Defense and the Paper Task Force. Manufactured at Friesens Corporation

Contents

Acknowledgments

"You are who you meet."

—Philip McKernan

Like any good real estate deal, it takes a great team to make a book like this happen.

We all need people to support and believe in us and Don Loney, my editor at John Wiley & Sons Canada, Ltd., has encouraged and believed in me ever since he spotted me on stage in Toronto and suggested I write a book. I remember being nervous about whether I really could do it. I told Don that I had dyslexia and was really impressed when he remained overwhelmingly supportive of the project. Don represents a talented and committed team at John Wiley & Sons, and I am honored to be represented by such a publishing house.

Joy Gregory, whose talent in crafting a manuscript while simultaneously keeping a team of experts on track, is another gift. We are honored to have had her as a major part of the team.

My wife Pauline and I arrived in Canada three years ago with nothing other than a suitcase and a dream, and reaching that dream would not have been possible without the incredible welcome we received from the Canadian people, and in particular the community of the Real Estate Investment Network. They opened their arms, homes and hearts to us and we will never forget that.

I am lucky to have been able to attract a lot of great people into my life and the team of real estate experts who helped me research and write this book is no exception. I would like to extend a special thank you to Jim Sheils, Brian Scrone, Tom Wheelwright and James Burns who committed to this project when it was just a concept. They are more than well versed in their field—they are good people and I am grateful to have them in my life.

Philip McKernan

Introduction

I can help you make money

"Fear is the assassin of dreams."
—Philip McKernan

People who pick up a book like this often do so with a healthy dose of skepticism and a wee bit of fear. They're curious about what the book purports to offer, but they are also afraid that, even with a book to guide them, they will not be able to take any actions that make a difference to the strength of their current or imagined Canadian real estate portfolios.

I want to put those fears to rest by encouraging you to take a different approach to your decision to pick up this book. First, I can assure you that anyone who picks this book off the shelf already knows two very important things:

1. The US real estate market is still reeling from the devastating consequences of an economic maelstrom that's widely recognized as the Subprime Mortgage Fiasco, and

2. The very fact you picked up this book shows me that you know there's money to be made by investing in real estate south of the 49th parallel.

What are you going to *do* about it?

The only question, then, is what are you going to do about what you already know? Let me introduce myself. I am Philip McKernan and I moved to Canada from Ireland because I saw the great opportunities this country presented to real estate investors and to residents who sought a great quality of life in general. Having lived in Europe for many years and having visited 60 countries around the world, I found myself living in Canada when the US market was shaken by the economic fallout of a global recession that started in late 2008.

Needless to say, living in Canada gave me a bird's-eye view of an American real estate market experiencing historic upheaval. And let me be clear: while I am not greedy, I know a good opportunity when I see it and there are incredible opportunities in the US market for individuals looking to invest in residential real estate. I also recognize the potential pitfalls that accompany investing in any international market. There is a significant shortage of credible resources about how best to invest in the US. There's lots of information coming from people with a financial interest in US investments, but remarkably little from impartial third parties.

The fact that I do not sell real estate makes what I have to teach even more valuable! Realizing that, I jumped at the opportunity to build a credible team in the US and to start learning everything I could about what Canadians need to know before they invest in American property.

And by "jumped at" I mean that I set out to meet people who could help me with my personal portfolio and teach me what I could teach others. I pride myself on attracting brilliant people and see this book as a great opportunity to share my new team's wisdom with you.

I am also wise enough to know that it's the team that created my success, not me. Using their knowledge and experience, I am now ready to help other people invest in real estate in the United States and avoid making some of the mistakes I made in the early days when I set out to buy property there.

This book is the culmination of my quest to invest in American real estate and help other Canadians do the same. It features the great ideas I gleaned from people like Tom Wheelwright, who is a tax expert and a real estate investor and great speaker based in Phoenix, Arizona; James Burns, a highly-respected asset protection and tax attorney from California; Jim Sheils of Jacksonville, Florida, an author, speaker and international real estate investor; and Brian Scrone, another Florida-based real estate investor who has purchased hundreds of cash-flow investment properties.

With their help, this book delivers the definitive fundamentals you need to buy foreclosed (or distressed) properties in the United States. Its pages teem with the unbiased and reality-based information you need to structure a real estate deal in the US, and all of this great information comes from a group of experts who invest in real estate themselves.

Education cultivates confidence and confidence leads to action

So stop being afraid—and start reading! To simplify a complicated subject, the book has been divided into four general topic areas, beginning with the fundamental question of what distressed property is and how you should buy it, through to renovations and management, tax planning and legal considerations. The book concludes with a selection of general information topics you should know about before you invest in the US, followed by a challenge to enter this market with what I like to call the "right mindset."

Together, we'll look at the basics, like what you need to know about the connection between your emotions and bad decisions, the importance of curb appeal and what constitutes a "bad neighborhood" in the US. From there, we'll move to more sophisticated subjects and review the ways you can maximize depreciation deductions and reduce taxes. We'll even get into the legal strategies you should avoid. With 95% of all legal litigation cases in the world emanating from the US, you will not want to skip that section.

I know this topic is daunting, and some investors will be put off by the sheer complexity of the different moving parts. I encourage you to persevere. You can learn to invest in US real estate, and it is something you can learn to do well. What we have before us right now is an opportunity that we may never again see in our lifetimes. It is a "perfect storm."

Now, let's get started . . .

What Distressed Property Is and How to Buy It

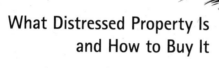

PART

1

"In the absence of clarity, take action."

—Philip McKernan

Part 1 owes much to the contribution of Jim Shiels, an American author, speaker and international real estate investor who specializes in the acquisition of foreclosures. Jim's passion for teaching has taken him all over the world. I'm thrilled to be able to share this straight shooter's advice in this section on distressed properties and acquisitions in the US foreclosure market.

1

Learn to Properly Identify a "Distressed Property."

What You Really Need to Know to Identify This Market

It may not be a term you are familiar with, but the whole notion of what constitutes a "distressed property" has strong roots in the real estate investment world. As this whole book focuses on the distressed property market, I want to make sure we're all on the same page when it comes to understanding exactly what a distressed property is. Simply defined, a distressed property is

> *a property where either the physical condition of the property is distressed or the owner of the property is in a financially distressed situation. In some cases, the property and owner are both distressed. The level of distress often motivates decisions to sell and can intensify the potential for price discounts.*

At least one of these two factors (physical condition or owner distress) must be in place for a property to be considered distressed. By the same token, the simultaneous reality of both factors definitely increases the odds for a better deal.

What Causes Distress

Property owners may not want to deal with a particular property for a variety of personal and financial reasons, causing the property to fall into the distressed properties category. Death and divorce are two of the most obvious reasons.

In recent years, the No. 1 contribution to the growth in the number of distressed properties on the US market is financial hardship. Here, the owner cannot afford the property. In many cases, these owners bit off more than they could chew when they purchased the home. They may have bought at subprime mortgage rates without a plan to reduce their debt before the rates rose, or lost employment income during the latest economic recession. Regardless of what happened, they've found themselves in a situation where they are behind on their property loan payments.

Once that happens and the properties are in distress, these homes may end up in a short-sale situation (where the owner and lender endeavor to sell the property as quickly as possible). Others will be foreclosed upon, meaning the bank assumes ownership in lieu of missed payments. In either situation, the banks involved are now in a distressed situation to sell the property.

This is where I see the greatest opportunities for solid investment deals.

Banks as the New Volume Seller

The fallout of the recent real estate market correction has made "foreclosure" the new buzzword for distressed property sales south of the 49th parallel. To profit from this situation, you must understand what's really going on in this market.

First, you should recognize that right now in the United States, banks are the biggest volume sellers of homes. And make no mistake, they are very motivated to sell these homes, often at significantly reduced prices.

To capitalize on those deals, however, Canadian investors need to be able to assess a market and determine whether the potential for a price discount on a particular piece of property is enough to warrant buying that property. I am going to look at the whole issue of "bad" versus "good" neighborhoods in Fundamentals #6 and #7. For now, you need to understand that if an area has low inventory levels and steady sales at steady prices, you'll have to look harder to find bargain distressed properties. Properties in those areas won't likely be available at a deep discount.

 SOLD

Aim for facts over hype! Contrary to what the media headlines might make you think, lots of US markets have very few distressed sales. What's touted as a "bargain price" in that area may not be much of a bargain at all.

Don't neglect your responsibility for market due diligence just because the sign says "Foreclosure."

Given all the media excitement over the foreclosure market, the need to look beyond market hype is one lesson Canadian real estate investors sometimes find difficult to put into action. Let me give you an example. Joe is a successful real estate investor in Virginia Beach, Virginia. He has bought hundreds of properties in his career and he owns a very large rental portfolio in that area. Last year, Joe came down to Florida to visit one of my US real estate investment experts. He wanted to tour the region and see some of the properties the Florida-based investor was acquiring.

He was amazed at the discounts that market-savvy investors were getting. "Fifty cents on the dollar!" he kept saying in disbelief. "Unbelievable! Distressed properties in my area are going for 85 cents on the dollar . . . even higher!"

The purported difference between these two markets in the same country intrigued the two investors and they both asked a few questions. It turned out that because Joe's area in Virginia had remained steadier during the market correction, the level of motivation for distressed sellers was much lower in Virginia Beach versus Florida. Without that motivation to sell, the discounts being offered were not the same.

Florida, on the other hand, had experienced higher foreclosure levels and higher inventory levels and was attracting fewer active buyers. In its purest sense, this was market supply and demand at work!

Resist the Temptation to Think You're Different

I know that some of the Canadians reading this story about Joe will think that maybe Joe just didn't know what he was doing in Virginia Beach. Others might think they can go into a market like Florida and make a good real estate investment buy having done almost no due diligence. I appreciate your self-confidence, but urge you to think again.

The basic truth of this situation is that Joe from Virginia Beach is a very good real estate investor and he's on the "inside track" for distressed property sales in his area. Believe me, if there's a deal in Virginia Beach, Joe knows how to find it and how to get the best discounts available.

He was taken aback by the situation in Florida only because he hadn't yet done his due diligence to see the remarkable differences between those two distressed markets. And those differences really are dramatic. A deal that costs you 50 cents on the dollar in Florida will almost always need a significant rehab. When you're paying 85–90 cents on the dollar in Virginia Beach, that investment might not need as much work. (And if it does, you may have paid too much!)

Compare Apples to Apples and Oranges to Oranges

I want Canadian real estate investors to know they can go into the American market for distressed property and make money. But pay attention to market fundamentals and understand that they differ from state to state, city to city and neighborhood to neighborhood!

What's Behind the Discount?

This brings up another interesting point. Investors who are willing and able to rehab a home that is in a distressed condition can really score some great discounts. And those discounts are especially common in areas where banks have a lot of inventory.

This situation exists because banks do not want to be in the business of home renovation for the investment market. That's a problem for banks because, at least for now, they are the world's largest seller of distressed property. The banks do not like to own property because that's outside the core competency of their business model, which is to make interest profits off the money they loan out. In fact, distressed property ownership equates to underperforming real estate investments and it greatly affects a bank's lending ability and its overall stock value.

The need to improve their lending ability and stock value makes it imperative for banks to clear out this real estate inventory as quickly and as efficiently as possible. But they also have another concern: banks, like property owners everywhere, have learned that the longer they hold onto underperforming properties, the greater the chance that the condition of the assets will deteriorate even further.

Besides all that, banks as property owners also find themselves on the hook for property taxes and property insurance, meaning the distressed property will cost them real money as long as it's in their portfolio.

Moreover, bank representatives typically freak out when they see roof damage, plumbing leaks, overgrown front yards and the like. Why? Because if they're not in the business of managing real estate investment property, they're certainly not in the business of renovating homes. The bottom-line message is that when a bank decides how to price the house, their motivation to offer a deep discount peaks if all they have to market that property are ugly pictures of a house in disrepair.

Understand the bank's motivation to sell distressed property at a discount, especially if the property is physically distressed as well. Recognize, too, that a bank's motivation to discount prices drops as their inventory declines. This is why it's important to look at the US market for distressed properties today versus next year!

So, There's Money to Be Made

Part 2 of this book is going to look at the key issues with managing property renovations for the buy-and-flip and buy-and-hold markets. I've made that a priority because I know that Canadian real estate investors recognize that property rehabs are a proven way to make money in real estate, especially when big discounts are being offered.

Before we get to that, however, I'm going to take a closer look at what this "distressed property" market is all about. I want to help you understand how the American foreclosure system works and to walk you through some of the other investment fundamentals you need to know about if you want to embark on a wealth-building strategy that aims to capitalize on what constitutes a truly historic set of circumstances now at play in the US real estate market.

The best distressed property deals I am seeing are in markets that got hit in the downturn that started in 2006, but have positive underlying fundamentals that make them a good long-term market to invest in.

The best deals I see also require some renovation and repair work, so I recommend that you consider property rehabilitation a critical part of this game.

2

Understand the Fundamentals of the US Foreclosure Process.

Why Foreclosures Equal Market Opportunity

If you're a Canadian who's been thinking about investing in real estate, you're probably a Canadian who's been thinking about investing in residential home foreclosures south of the 49th parallel. And why not? American residential real estate foreclosures are a hot topic in today's investment circles, and wealth gurus on both sides of the border are asking their students to take a serious look at foreclosed real estate in the United States.

Before you take that step, I want to share with you a little bit more about how the US foreclosure process works and to explore the fundamental market facts that make it worth your time and money. In an attempt to keep the discussion "real," I also want to explode one of the great myths that surrounds this market.

Foreclosure Defined

Generally speaking, a US residential real estate foreclosure involves a situation where a homeowner holds legal title to a property and the bank places a lien on the house for the amount owed. The lien remains with the bank/lender; the borrower holds title. In the event of a default on the loan, the bank notifies the borrower and requests that the borrower make back-up payments. After 90 days, or three missed payments, the bank has the legal right to begin the foreclosure process and take back the house in lieu of missed payments.

Depending on the state, the actual foreclosure can take anywhere from 112 days to two years. In today's economy, the process can take even longer because the banks don't really want to take back more houses. This reluctance is not a business-as-usual approach to how banks usually sell foreclosed property!

Foreclosures have always represented an opportunity for real estate investors. Some investors in Canada and the US have specialized in this sector. The current foreclosure market is different because of the number of properties under foreclosure.

The Homeowner Has Rights

If you are buying houses that have been foreclosed on in the US, you should know that the homeowner has some rights. First, the bank cannot take back a house unless one of the following conditions is met: the house goes into a foreclosure auction or the borrower voluntarily deeds the house back to the bank in lieu of a foreclosure. As the foreclosure auction is more common, I focus on that here.

Foreclosure Auction

In a foreclosure auction, the bank auctions the house at the local county courthouse for the amount it wishes to receive. If no one bids on the house, or if the opening bid set by the bank is too high for any bidders, the bank gets the house back and then will list the property with a local real estate agent. Such properties—those owned by a lender, usually a bank—are placed in a class called Real Estate Owned (REO).

Size and Immediacy

From an investment standpoint, the current foreclosure market is important because of its sheer size and the immediacy of the crisis. If you're new to the US foreclosure market, you may be wondering how long this situation can last. According to my research, this market is just starting to heat up. Statistics cited by US foreclosure market insiders predict four million foreclosure filings for 2010, and banks are on track to take back more than one million homes. That could be the tip of the proverbial iceberg. Given the economic climate and employment woes, the current epidemic of US foreclosures could be exacerbated by even higher numbers of loan defaults in the months to come. Insiders tell me that 24% of all US homes are currently over-leveraged. That is, 24% of the homes Americans own are worth less than what those homeowners owe on the loan or loans taken to buy those homes.

The Big Picture

That stark tidbit of reality sheds light on the tough situation a great many American homeowners are finding themselves in as housing prices continue to fall because people aren't buying homes. And let's face it, if people don't have money, they're not buying property. In what can only be described as a kind of vicious economic cycle, some of them may, however, be putting their houses on the market.

 SOLD

From an investor's position, a strong foreclosure market means some homes not in foreclosure will sell for bargain prices simply because so many of the neighbors have defaulted on their loans. Ahh. Supply and demand. Now there's a residential real estate fundamental that matters!

Since numbers tell the story better than any market insider or wealth guru, let's take a look at some US foreclosure stats from April 2010. At that point in time, the top three US foreclosure markets were Nevada, at one in 33 homes, Arizona, at one in 49 homes and Florida at one in 57 homes.

Myth Buster

Those numbers are shocking. But as you will learn in Fundamental #4, numbers tell only part of the story. Indeed, the two fundamentals after that, on "bad" and "good" neighborhoods, will give you some valuable perspective on why some US neighborhoods have weathered the economic downturn and residential housing market corrections much better than others.

In the meantime, I want you to remember that the very *worst* state in the entire United States of America is running at a foreclosure rate of **3%**. That's high when compared to the normal historic rates, which sit at less than 1%. When I ask Canadians to estimate the rate of foreclosures in states like Nevada, however, they routinely cite figures of 15%, 20% and 30%. Some go even higher—and those estimates are dead wrong. The actual number in the worst state is 3%. Period.

From an investment perspective, that means a lot of American homeowners are still paying their mortgages. And that means that while foreclosures equal investment opportunities, you shouldn't expect to be shooting fish in a barrel!

SOLD

Do your homework and avoid market hype that gets in the way of sound investment decisions. Residential real estate foreclosures can present great investment opportunities. But the only recipe for success begins and ends with due diligence that includes real market analysis. Always get the facts *before* you act.

3

Commit to the No. 1 Rule.

Then Get Your Options Straight.

In mere moments we'll take a look at the three ways you can go about buying a US property in foreclosure, but first, I want to stress how important it is that you understand the No. 1 rule about foreclosures. That rule states

Not every foreclosure is a good deal!

Commit that rule to memory. Believe it or not, some Canadian investors turn their backs on the whole US foreclosure market because the first few deals they look at turn out to be dogs. Don't be so short-sighted. Foreclosed real estate properties in the residential real estate market do present investment opportunities and this market is not going away anytime soon. But not every foreclosure is a good deal. Always put your faith in market fundamentals—whether the property you are looking at is in good standing or in foreclosure.

3 Ways to Buy

Now that you've recommitted to taking a good look at the market fundamentals of how a property fits your investment portfolio, let's look at the three stages at which you can set about buying foreclosed properties. They are

1. Short sale

2. Auction

3. Real Estate Owned (REO)

Each of the three stages occurs at different times in the foreclosure process. All three have their pros and cons and smart investors will use that information to decide if a particular foreclosure merits their investment cash.

Short Sale

The first stage is the short sale. Here, the bank agrees to settle for less than what's owed on the loan. In terms of opportunity, this is the first time an outside buyer can get involved with a foreclosure process. At this point, the troubled homeowner is generally behind in his mortgage payments and has put the house on the market with a real estate agent. The asking price is typically less than what the mortgage is on the property, so the bank will need to approve the offer. In cases like this, the bank will appoint a "loss mitigator" to handle the file. This is the main point of contact from the bank.

Among the pros of the short sale is that an investor would be able to get full access to the property. From a property analysis perspective, this is critical. As well, as the bank is still involved, an investor may be able to get financing for the property versus paying cash. There is also the opportunity for a discounted price and, if the deal proceeds, the buyer will have a clean title on the property.

On the negative side, banks in short-sale situations can take a very long time to make a decision. (Loss mitigators are typically buried in files.) Some potential buyers leave the short-sale situation thinking their efforts were in vain and feeling frustrated by a situation where they felt "strung along" for months. In some cases, the loss mitigator may forgo your offer and bring the house to auction instead. This is especially frustrating if the bank takes the property to auction at a lower price than your short-sale offer. (And yes, that happens, sometimes just because a particular file was lost in the pile. This is one area where it's very important that an investor's due diligence includes making sure that a bank's loss mitigator knows who you are and what you're prepared to offer.)

Making the Short Sale Work

If you are going to buy in a short sale, make the real estate agent involved in the sale ride the loss mitigator very hard. This is a situation where the squeaky wheel gets the oil. If you do not stay on top of the file, it might be overlooked.

Tip: An experienced realtor who has a track record of getting short sales completed is a plus!

Auction

Stage two of the foreclosure process is the auction sale, where the house can be bought at the courthouse steps. In this situation, the bank has had enough. It is not accepting short-sale offers and has proceeded with the paperwork to set an auction date for the property at the local county court-house. This gives an investor the chance to bid on the property and pay cash. The bank sets the opening bid amount.

The No. 1 benefit of the auction scenario is the potential for huge price discounts. As well, you'll leave the auction knowing if you got the property (no waiting!) and it's possible there will be less competition than at the short-sale stage.

But the disadvantages are real. First, you must pay cash for an auctioned property, usually at the time of the auction or within 24 hours. As well, you won't get clear title and there may be serious title issues lurking in the background, including additional liens. You will also have only limited access to the property before the sale and you may have to deal with a very unhappy resident if he or she still lives on the property.

Making the Auction Work

If you plan to buy at an auction, you need cash and you need to do your homework. You must make sure there are no other liens on the property and that you are bidding on the right mortgage. Once you buy for cash at the auction (also called "buying on the steps"), all sales are final. That means you will inherit any problems with the property.

Tip: Auction sales are a very local game and its players are usually full-time local investors who target this niche. Because the due diligence can be intense and mistakes can be costly, respect that auctions are serious business.

Real Estate Owned

At this third stage of a foreclosure, the home has gone through the auction process and there were no bidders, so the bank gets the property back. The property is assigned to an "asset manager" at the bank and that person hires a local real estate agent to list the property for sale the same way other properties are listed. This is now called a Real Estate Owned (Bank REO) or bank owned property, meaning the real estate owned property is now owned by the bank. This is now considered to be bad debt on the bank's balance sheet, so the lender wants to get rid of it.

Real estate agents working in the REO field can have some great deals, and working with these agents can be very rewarding. Always remember that banks prefer cash and they usually want to close an REO deal quickly to get the bad debt off their books. (They also do not want to be in the property management business.)

On the plus side, REOs offer large discount potential. With a real estate agent involved, investors can get full access to the property. As an added bonus, REO property is vacant, so investors will not have to deal with the emotions of the people who were living in that house. Buyers will also get clear title and the entire process is much faster and more predictable than the short-sale process. Investors who like doing business in the REO stage of the distressed property market may access repeat business if they have good relationships with high-volume REO real estate agents.

The quick close and the fact you usually have to pay cash for the property are two key disadvantages of the REO. As well, there tends to be more competition for these homes.

Making the REO Work

You can make money here—in fact, one of my US investor colleagues focuses on the REO niche market—but you need to research and track the REO listings constantly. You also need to build a good working rapport with an REO agent.

Tip: This is one niche where relationships really matter. If you can't keep current with REO listings, you'll need to find someone who can. You also need to know agents who target this market.

To Review

Foreclosures are a great niche market for real estate investment deals. But not every foreclosure is a good deal. I've met investors who are willing to sacrifice due diligence and solid fundamentals just because the property is called a "foreclosure." My main point here is that you need to cut through the media hype when it comes to overplayed terms like "foreclosure." Here's what you really need to know:

1. A foreclosure is a house that is owned by a bank.

2. A bank, just like other distressed sellers, will sometimes list their homes for a high sale price hoping that someone will bite. This can happen at the short-sale, auction or REO stages of the foreclosure process.

3. Each stage of the process has different pros and cons. Learn them.

4. Investors can and do pay more than they should for foreclosed properties.

5. Investors can and do end up with major renovation headaches when they buy foreclosed properties without seeing them first, or before they've done any real property analysis.

6. The best offense is a great defense. Know your numbers and have a clear strategy that you can execute to make money with the property.

7. You can nibble, but don't bite until you've done your homework!

PROCEED WITH CAUTION!

Forewarned Is Forearmed

Three things can happen when a Canadian investor starts looking at the US foreclosure market. Some investors will make money. Others will lose money. Members of the third group will throw up their hands in despair and leave the market when it turns out that every foreclosure is not a great deal.

One sage investor tells me that to avoid giving up too early, market newcomers should know three things. They are:

1. If you look at 10 houses, five will be dogs and priced too high.

2. If you look at 10 houses, three will be "okay" deals, but not "great" deals.

3. If you look at 10 houses, two will be really good and absolutely worth your time and effort.

When he finally finds a house with potential, this investor will likely make an offer—and it will be less than what the bank is asking for. Remember: the bank is a distressed seller!

Look for Local Market Data.

National Housing Averages Make as Much
Sense as the National Weather Average

Real estate investors use numbers to make sense of markets. But that business strategy only works when the numbers you use are relevant to the market you want to buy into. Canadians looking to buy property in the United States must be particularly wary of national housing averages. These numbers can be used to mislead you towards a false understanding of a particular property's investment potential. Even when they're not misrepresented as a way to help make a sale, the value of a national housing average is suspect. In fact, investors who try to make sense of this "information" are actually wasting their time.

Think About It

If you think about it, the national housing average makes about as much sense as a national weather average. While it's nice to know that Canadians enjoyed a moderate 10 degrees Celsius on a certain day in April, that "data" means nothing to the Albertans who were shoveling out their cars from underneath mounds of fresh snow and nothing to the Torontonians who were putting up with record winds and torrential rains.

Indeed, the information is meaningless and that doesn't change when you switch countries and look at a "national" weather report that includes New York, Cleveland, Los Angeles, Jacksonville and Minneapolis. Put all of those numbers in a pot, stir them around and presto, you have an interesting statistic for a media story and nothing of value to the people who want to use that information to make work and recreational decisions.

That's right. None of those people will have any sense of what the weather is like in their own backyards. And when it comes to making information relevant, real estate markets are kind of like weather reports. Markets have (and always will be) geographically specific. Weather patterns, just like market drivers, can differ wildly from one area to another.

Aim for Relevance

As a real estate investor, you want the best information you can find regarding investment opportunities. In other words, you need market-specific information to help you calculate the potential of a particular property. Without that relevant data, your choices lack direction.

In 2009, residential real estate markets in Stockton, California, experienced one of the steepest drops in value across the US. Those numbers may be statistically in line with what happened at the national level. A closer look, however, shows neighboring cities a few hours west of Stockton experienced healthy growth through the entire market correction. While national housing statistics would lead you to conclude that *every* market in the US has discounted properties for sale because *every* market in the US lost value in the last crash, the Stockton example illustrates how that is absolutely not the case!

By the same token, an oversupply of houses in certain areas of Phoenix, Arizona, does not necessarily have any impact on an investor's attempts to fill his or her rental properties with tenants in Jacksonville, Florida. The fact that property values in Miami dropped almost 50% also does not translate into a scenario where you can buy a house for 50 cents on the dollar in San Francisco.

What's going on? The fundamentals for each market are totally different. Not every market went through a huge correction and therefore some markets will not have the huge discounted property sales that you read about in the paper. Moreover, even when a particular market experiences a significant correction, the fact that "cheap" properties are on the market does not guarantee that market is a good place to invest.

Look at your own city and your own neighborhood. Market variances are a fact of life in every real estate market. As an investor, you need to know how to figure out what the numbers *mean*. It's your job to get past the "fluff" and pay attention to what really matters. The media will bombard us with statistics, but we can still keep our eye on the prize!

5 Market Fundamentals

There are five fundamentals that drive individual real estate markets:

1. Economic Growth

2. Population Growth

3. Affordability

4. Desirability

5. Supply and Demand

These fundamentals provide necessary relevance for what really matters when choosing the right market to invest in. Remember: information is power and once you commit to these fundamentals, your investment strategy will be powered by information that matters.

 SOLD

When you are assessing the investment potential of real estate property, aim for five of five and never be satisfied with anything less than four!

1. Economic Growth

Zero in on the local economy and find data for local economic indicators of

- Job activity/employment
- New company growth
- Military growth
- Various economic resources
  - Is the area dependent on one industry or job source?
  - Are there opportunities to buy rentals close to an important job source? (The farther you are from a significant employer, the more troubled the market during an economic downturn.)

2. Population Growth

What is the local population doing in terms of growth? Certain US markets have been shown to be shrinking in population at a steady pace. Other markets are growing and that's predicted to continue for years to come.

Much of that predicted growth is due to baby boomers retiring and deciding to spend their money in warm-climate states like Florida, Arizona, Nevada and California. Several of the areas popular with baby boomers were hit hard in the market correction. What's that noise? Sounds like opportunity is knocking!

3. Affordability

The lack of affordability is a big cause of the recent downturn in certain markets. But some of the markets with the most "affordable" housing also have shrinking populations, no jobs and, by default, not much opportunity for real estate investors.

Understand the difference between cheap and affordable. Affordability is a hot topic in the US right now and consumers are looking for affordable housing to rent and buy.

4. Desirability

Real estate investors are not buying properties they will live in. They are buying properties in desirable areas that others will want to live in. Always be realistic about what a property offers a renter in that market.

- What's the property close to?

- Why would someone want to live there?

- What does it offer in terms of lifestyle, warm weather and proximity to amenities (groceries, recreation, sports, beaches, restaurants, historic areas and the arts)?

5. Supply and Demand

During the economic boom of the mid-2000s, some American cities were overbuilt. That's right. There were not enough people to fill all of the houses that were being built, even when the economy was firing on all burners. Other areas experienced significant devaluation when populations were depleted by job losses.

Your goal is to enter a market that has a positive balance of supply and demand, or is moving in that direction because of economic and population growth alongside factors like affordability and desirability.

The need to consider all five market fundamentals has never been more important. Industry insiders, for example, consider Las Vegas to be an overbuilt market. But investors who turn their backs on that market based on the supply and demand market fundamental may be missing the rest of the Las Vegas story. While inventory may be high, this city's resale volume has hit record highs and the inventory is dropping.

Also be sure to investigate what type of property is deemed to have high vacancy rates in the area you are researching. In some areas, condos are in oversupply but single-family homes priced below the median value are in undersupply.

An Extra Word on Vacancy Rates

Vacancy rates also hold a wealth of important information for real estate investors who are trying to determine the potential of a market. This information is typically available from a quality real estate agent or property manager. But always go beyond the surface data. Real estate agents and property managers do not have a vested interest in your ability to make money, but they do have a vested interest in their own business goals.

If you learn that the vacancy rate in a particular market looks pretty good from an investment perspective, you need to take that information and look at what's behind the numbers. Find out what kind of properties people are renting. Are there areas that are tougher to rent? I've seen areas where the market vacancy rate has been pegged at more than 10%, but trusted investors tell me their properties run at about 2%. This probably speaks to high demand for the type of property they own and a practical commitment to excellent property management.

 SOLD

Once you know the vacancy rates, review the five market fundamentals to see what else they can tell you about a residential real estate market's investment potential. If a quality tenant has several properties to choose from, what kind of property is she most apt to select? What can you do to make your property No. 1?

More Market Facts

Market fundamentals are critical to your assessment of a market, but they don't tell you anything about a particular property's investment potential. Here, I recommend that real estate investors calculate one more figure into their decision-making toolkit: the 1% marker.

The 1% Marker

Once you know that the market fundamentals tell you a real estate market bears a closer look, you need to go looking for what successful investors call the 1% marker. This is a simple and effective way to assess a potential deal. Here's how it works:

Using the purchase price and cost of initial repairs,
look for a 1% gross a month in rent.

Say you bought a house for $100,000 and it's ready to rent. Rent is $1,000 a month, which equals 1% of the purchase price. That's good. Similarly, if you buy a house for $90,000 and allocate $10,000 for repairs to get it rent ready, at $1,000 a month for rent, this deal still meets the 1% marker rule of thumb. That changes for both scenarios as soon as the rent drops below $1,000.

What's the 1% marker telling you? As long as your property is subject to fair taxes and insurance, a 1% marker means you can cash flow a property. It can be difficult to find a property that hits the five fundamentals and the 1% marker, but never turn your back on what the 1% marker is telling you.

Avoid the Snake-Oil Salesman.

Seminar Fakes, Lender Scams and Housing Rip-Offs

It would be nice to write a real estate investment book and never talk about the risk of fraud, but doing so would be impractical. While there is no guarantee that you won't encounter the proverbial snake-oil salesman in Canadian real estate deals, you must be especially wary of fraudsters when working in another country, including one as geographically and culturally close to Canada as the United States.

From this perspective, I see seminar fakes, lender scams and housing rip-offs as three subject areas that merit special attention. All three are alive and well in the US and all three could present a serious danger to your investing efforts. If you know how to identify them, however, you can avoid them and their ill effects.

Let me stress that when it comes to dealing with people and money, there is no room for complacency regarding fraud. So while I can't explore every aspect of the fraud issue, I do encourage you to be vigilant and to pay keen attention to some of the most powerful warning signs I've learned about through my own investing and that of my US-market insiders.

Seminar Fakes

This is one area that few real estate investment insiders want to talk about. From where I sit, savvy investors who want to create long-term wealth need help standing up to what I'll call the 800-lb. gorillas that are ruining the wealth-creation industry.

I can honestly say that paying for specialized knowledge can be one of the best investment decisions you'll ever make—as long as you take the information you've paid for and put it into action. That is, *if* you get the information you've paid for.

Believe it or not, some of the real estate seminar industry's most popular experts have never bought a property or done investment business in the areas where their seminars are offered. These are professional marketers, not professional investors, and they grab onto popular theories and techniques to position themselves as experts in real estate solely because they can make money at it.

One of the US investors I work with has a special saying when he talks to me about why investors should want to work with people who have real-world experience. In his words, "If you don't know how to skate, don't take me out on the ice."

The big problem with these gurus is that because they haven't done deals, they can't possibly know what you need to understand to do those deals. Unfortunately, their pitch is sometimes so good that investors leave their seminars thinking they have valuable information. That enthusiasm quickly deflates when they try to put their new knowledge into practice and realize that without specific investment strategies, they are woefully unprepared to take action (and their wallets are a lot lighter!).

PROCEED WITH CAUTION!

Just Because They Talk Big...

Some hucksters are really good at convincing seminar-goers that they know what they're talking about. But if they haven't done what they're teaching, they cannot offer insight into how you can avoid the mistakes and pitfalls they've encountered. Some try to give the impression that it's so easy they've never made mistakes.

Let me be brutally honest here. Every investor makes mistakes. And speakers who can share their tales from the trenches have the most to offer.

People who've listened to me talk say some of the most powerful lessons they've learned from my presentations come from my willingness to share my mistakes. I've had the same experience with the people who have taught me about real estate investing. By learning about what they did wrong, I've been able to avoid a few pitfalls and focus on what works.

So how do you find the right seminar teacher? Here are three things to keep in mind:

1. Always Go for Real-World Experience.

The best seminar teachers I've learned from over the years were real people. They were down to earth, authentic and straightforward. They taught from personal experience and what they talked about on stage had substance. These teachers did not hold themselves above their students, nor were they cheesy or obnoxious. They spoke with sincerity versus taking a sales-pitch approach. They did not brag about material riches, but taught from their successes and failures. They were also quick to give credit to those who had helped them along the way.

The best seminar speakers talk from personal experience. They can answer your questions forthrightly—or willingly point you in the direction of someone who can.

Be on your guard for arrogant seminar speakers. If they know everything, have had nothing but success, and did it all on their own thanks to a superior intellect and fancy techniques, don't be impressed. They're not likely giving you anything of value. A less politically-correct description is they are full of you-know-what!

Gurus put their pants on one leg at a time—just like the rest of us—but some industry "experts" are nothing of the sort. They will take your money without remorse and without taking any responsibility for the poor quality of the program they've offered.

2. Value the Easy-to-Understand Explanation.

Real estate investment is not rocket science. Be wary of seminar speakers who make the subject confusing. They want you to think you don't "get it." That's essential to their sales pitch: if you stick with me and keep buying my programs and seminars, you'll understand (wink, wink!).

Be suspicious of speakers who "talk around" a subject when people (also known as paying customers) ask questions. One of my US colleagues, who has been buying distressed real estate for about 10 years, says he was once almost asked to leave a seminar because he was giving away too much valuable content. Can you believe that?

3. Look for Content.

Content matters, and if you're paying for the information, it really matters! You don't want to pay to hear inflated success stories with very little detail, or pay to listen to sales pitches that always involve buying a bigger, more expensive program with the promise of "bonus" content. If you go to a seminar and the speaker delivers nothing but a sales pitch, expect the same thing from their other programs—and back out of the room with haste.

These are the "carrot-on-the-stick" gurus. They may offer tidbits of valuable information, but you will pay dearly for it with time and money. These seminar leaders will take a subject that can be taught in one or two sessions and make it a 10-session event. They will make you believe that real estate investing is fraught with complications and only those who sign up for every one of their programs will be successful.

Seminars that are low on content and high on the newest sales pitch often try to convince investors they have some fancy "system" that is the secret way to huge profits, guaranteed (by the way, there's no such word in real estate investing). These seminar leaders simply love complexity and encourage you to think that's the way it has to be (at least until you understand what they are talking about).

And the sales pitch isn't only for more seminars. If someone is telling you that you need a fancy phone system, special software programs, websites, expensive marketing, huge letter campaigns and the like just to get started in foreclosures, run away!

"Content," by the way, is not something you can measure by the size of the seminar binder. Content is real and practical insights, tools and street-smart information that you can put to work in your own investment business.

 SOLD

A little education can go a long way. I tell people that when it comes to avoiding seminar fakes, they should go with their GUT feelings. For more on this, see Fundamental #46 in Part 6. The foreclosure market is attracting a lot of attention among financial educators. That popularity attracts sharks. Be prepared to ask the tough questions. Be prepared to expect substance for your cash. Be prepared to do the research to find the seminar that's right for you.

Lender Scams

Getting people to lend you money to make real estate deals happen can be essential to your success; I talk about using joint venture money in Part 5. But be careful who you borrow money from. Here are three of the main things to watch for when it comes to protecting yourself from common lending scams.

1. Be Wary of Up-front Requests for Money.

If anyone asks you for money up front as a prerequisite of finding you money for your deals, they're not legitimate. No one who can honestly access funds for your real estate deals will need to be paid up front to "find" the money.

This is a very old scam and it plagues the world of private financing. If you're one of the many international investors who turn to the private financing market, remember this warning!

2. Get a Good Faith Estimate.

A good faith estimate (GFE) is provided to you by your lender and will put in writing all rates and terms. By having these details in writing, you can avoid the "bait and switch" lender scam. This fraudster will try to trick you into a higher-interest loan or into terms different from those in your verbal agreement. Getting a GFE in writing may not guarantee the rate, but it will help keep the lender honest.

3. Read Your Loan Documents and Ask Questions.

Never sign anything you don't understand. When you work with knowledge-able and experienced advisors, you can call on them for advice you can trust.

Housing Rip-Offs

Housing rip-offs are a scourge on the US real estate market these days and international investors, including Canadians, are among those at greatest risk. Indeed, international buyers are the ultimate target of the housing rip-off artist.

Most of these scams look pretty much the same. Every aspect of these deals will be promoted based on one main theme: the property is cheap with high cash flow.

In a common application of the housing rip-off, you'll be offered a house for $20,000 to $30,000 with great rent rates. No wonder investors are interested! But if you scratch below the surface of this deal, you typically see that the plan is a house of cards. More specifically, most of the homes are located in cities with terrible fundamentals. Others will be located in the "bad" neighborhoods of an otherwise good investment area and many will have serious structural issues that jack up the cost of the renovation, putting your investment's success at risk. That is, the potentially positive indicators you could get from population, economic, desirability of location, and supply and demand data are all pointing in the negative direction. In the end, affordability is the only positive indicator.

Fundamental #2 looked at the market fundamentals of the foreclosure process. It emphasized the fact that where other market fundamentals are lacking, affordability is an investment deal-breaker. This is especially true if these homes are in terrible areas and in terrible condition.

 **SOLD**

Housing rip-offs are often promoted by "house groups." They claim to have a plan to renovate entire neighborhoods. Again, do your due diligence. These groups do not usually have an experienced and professional reno crew, nor are they backed by tested and proven management. This is a good way to lose your investment, fast.

Beyond a price that might knock your socks off, these investment scams often employ similar language. For example, they typically claim to involve the ever-so-sexy "bulk deal." Other times, they allude to their special connections with banks as the reason they are able to access homes at such great prices.

Once you look into the property, ideally after you've reviewed the fundamentals, you'll see that while anyone could buy these homes, very few people ever want them. Vacancies are high, tenant turnover is high, repairs and maintenance are through the roof, management is tough to find and the area lacks resales.

Some of these scam artists will try to convince you that what makes these deals special is their location in a "great transition neighborhood." Again, put your fundamentals to work. History tells us that when economic times are bad, the quality of life in a bad neighborhood will get even worse.

Another good indicator of a housing rip-off scam is that the group trying to convince you to buy these crappy houses located in crappy areas will not have any of their own money invested there! Their goal is to collect the money—and head for the hills. One of the most frustrating angles to this scam is the fact that when things go wrong, no one from this housing group will be available to take your call. This is in stark contrast to the beginning of the deal, when you will find them always available, promising the sun and the moon.

Look into claims of what might make a bad neighborhood turn around. Be suspicious. If you can't back up claims, don't believe them.

PROCEED WITH CAUTION!

These Are Volume Sellers

The people behind the housing rip-off scam are not trying to sell you a house because they think it's a good deal. They just know it's easier to find several potential investors with $20,000 than one with $90,000. Because their buyers can pay cash at such a low price point, the crooks can be in and out of a neighborhood at top speed.

Their goal is to sell more houses, not better houses! Fall prey to this scam and you'll be in a neighborhood of inexperienced investors, all of whom now own the wrong house in the wrong neighborhood.

Know the Sure Signs of a Housing Rip-Off

Anyone who's spent any time in the American foreclosure market knows housing rip-off scams are out there—and avoidable. Here's what you need to be on the lookout for when a house group is trying to reel you and your money into the wrong property.

1. The cheap price is all they promote. The deal focuses on affordability. This way, the investors typically won't need to finance the deal. The scammer can get you into a bad property faster and easier and then skip town with the money.

2. They promise high rent returns. Estimated rents are just a theory, so do your homework. These properties tend to be located in areas with above-average vacancy rates, higher repair averages, higher tenant turnovers, higher damage claims, higher crime rates and more. Once you do the math, you'll know that the promise of extra cash flow is all smoke and mirrors. This property isn't going to make you money. It's going to cost you money.

3. The homes are always run down and located in bad neighborhoods. They are always marketed as affordable fixer-uppers in "transition neighborhoods." If there's high crime, high vacancy, no first-time homebuyers and a wealth of investor-owned property, then the neighborhood is a long way from transitioning towards gentrification! (See Fundamental #6.)

4. The sales pitch will claim the house needs very little work to become "rent ready." That's often code for "the home is so run down that it's uninsurable."

5. The people behind the deal talk big numbers. "We buy 20, 30, 50 houses a month." The smart investor knows to ask if that's a good thing. If you're buying 50 homes a month, you're renovating 50 homes a month. You're also looking for 50 good tenants a month. Can you see where I'm going with this? Without some major support, these numbers spell nothing but trouble. When the area implodes, investors will be left holding the pieces.

 SOLD

My US colleagues tell me that housing rip-off scams leave a lot of international real estate investors in their wake. Market-wise investors know that greed is a bad source of motivation. When a deal looks too good to be true, it probably is.

6. The investors talk about how they are investing in several markets. Again, that's not always a good thing. I encourage Canadian investors looking at the US market to proceed with caution and to focus on one market, at least until you gain some real-world experience. Good investors know they need to pay attention to ensure their business strategies work. If the people you are dealing with are in 10 different markets, then they need 10 different teams on the ground and every one of those teams must be able to perform. Think about how complicated it would be to put that together. Now use that skepticism to avoid getting taken in. I know of one "guru" who is running bus tours for Canadians in five different US cities. While there is nothing wrong with this *per se*, I do wonder how focused he is.

7. The investors claim they have rent-to-own tenants ready to go and buyers basically lining up to buy you out of the property within a few years. They will also will tell you they can get a "government Section 8 tenant" to move in. (Rent is subsidized for Section 8 tenants.)

What they won't tell you is that tenants who qualify for assistance through the US Department of Housing and Urban Development (HUD) have lots of choices about where they live. Remember what I said happens to a bad neighborhood in an economic downturn? It gets worse. People will always move to a better area when that choice is available. And in today's US market, it's available.

8. The house group selling these homes will not own any property in the area.

9. They can talk the talk, but they've never walked the walk. The house group will not have a track record. Since market fundamentals are all about the track record, this is a problem.

Questions to Ask

As part of your due diligence, it makes sense to ask a few questions when you come across a great deal. The answers to these questions will help you identify a housing rip-off.

- How long have you been investing in the area?
- Do you have rental property in the area?
- How do you handle property management?
- Where do you find your contractors? Have they been tested?
- Can I look at some testimonials and references from actual investors and property managers your housing group has worked with in the past?

 SOLD

Other real estate investors can help you make money. You should not let them help you lose money. Never confuse "affordability" with a deal that's too good to pass up.

So here is where I pitch how credible and great my training is, right? Wrong! While this fundamental may appear to knock every guru from Alaska to Tampa, please let me point out there are also some very credible people in the training and seminar business.

6

Recognize That a Bad Area in the US Is Very Different From a Bad Area Elsewhere.

You're Not in Calgary Anymore . . .

A few years ago, a Canadian real estate investment guru shared my story in a book about successful real estate investors in Canada. Then, as now, I can be described as a student of the global village. I am a native of Dublin, Ireland, but my business ventures have taken me all over the world. Long before I relocated to Canada to focus on my speaking and training business in my new country, I spent my days searching for the planet's finest wines and coffee beans. These days, I'm routinely traveling to cities in Canada, United States, Europe and Australasia to look at and talk about real estate investing and the importance of the right mindset in achieving entrepreneurial excellence.

I'll admit there are some cities in Canada with which I am not all that familiar. But I would learn more about them if I was going to invest there and I urge Canadians doing business in the land of their southern neighbors to bone up on what makes some US cities, or parts of those cities, remarkably different from their Canadian counterparts. Guess what. It's got nothing to do with the weather!

A story I heard years ago about two tourists heading to the zoo in New York illustrates this point beautifully. It seems the tourists got off at the wrong station and were spotted by a police officer doing patrol. When asked what they were looking for they replied, "the zoo." The police officer looked at them and said, "You're in it, now get the hell out of here."

Define Your Bad Area

The most important point I want to convey here is that a "bad" area in a US city is very different from a "bad" area in a Canadian city. Canadian real estate investors ignore this at their peril. And I am not the only one who notices the difference!

An American upon whom I rely for US investment advice tells me he once got to tour some Canadian cities with a good friend who is also a very successful real estate investor and owns an impressive portfolio. As they drove around and looked at properties, they came to a neighborhood where the Canadian owned several investments. The Canadian warned his American friend that they were entering "the dangerous part of the city." He wasn't trying to be dramatic, he just wanted to give his US colleague a kind of heads-up about the community they were about to enter.

My American friend acknowledged the comment and their conversation returned to a discussion of what was happening in that city's overall real estate market. After a few more minutes passed, the American broke the stride of the conversation and asked, "Hey, when are we going to the bad area of town?"

His friend looked at him in disbelief, saying they were in the midst of the bad neighborhood. "Can't you tell?"

This story illustrates a primary difference between the American and Canadian cultural experience. "It wasn't even *close* to what I expected when he told me we were going to the 'worst' part of the city," says the American.

The tremendous discrepancy in their understanding of what constitutes a bad neighborhood comes from the fact that the two men hailed from radically different environments. Whereas the Canadian investor grew up in Calgary, Alberta, the American investor grew up 30 minutes outside of New York City. The worst neighborhood Calgary had to offer was no comparison to a bad neighborhood in many of the US cities the American knew. Not even close.

I think this experience holds true for most Canadians and Americans. The basic truth is that a bad neighborhood in the US is much worse than what Canadians are accustomed to. In fact, if Canadians coming south think that a bad neighborhood in a Canadian city matches a bad neighborhood in the US, they are going to get one hell of a nasty wake-up call.

Be Real

Anyone who knows me knows that I don't share this information to put American real estate investments in a bad light. I merely want Canadians who are thinking about doing business there to know they will have to do some basic research about specific markets.

That basic research should shed light on some of the fundamental differences in demographics that affect the quality of life in a neighborhood. The raw population data is striking in and of itself. Whereas Canada has some 35 million citizens, the US population hovers at around 309 million people.

Those population differences aside, there is little to be gained from debating the various reasons for demographic differences in American versus Canadian rates of crime, poverty, etc. In fact, I tell Canadians who want to invest in US real estate to steer clear of talk about gun laws, drug legalization, racial stress and political parties. You are investing in real estate, not transforming the American political and socio-economic system!

Know What You Need to Know

What Canadian real estate investors do need to be able to talk about is how they can identify the right US neighborhoods to invest in. This can be especially critical when you are investing with others. While some people may be willing to invest in a bad neighborhood in the US, I would recommend against it. But to really protect myself, I would also need to make some decisions about what constitutes a bad investment neighborhood for me.

And here, I would put to work in my own business the experience of people I trust. For example, one of my American real estate investment specialists tells me that in Jacksonville, Florida, he refuses to invest with partners in a neighborhood that is owned solely by landlords and that has a strong history of drugs, prostitution and violence. Period. That rule works for him and keeps his investors happy. In fairness, this same specialist has tried to make a go of "all investor" landlord-owned neighborhoods. But once burned, twice shy. He now knows that first-time homebuyers can stabilize a market. Where first-time homeowners are absent, the market is more susceptible to a crash. (For more on how this works, read the next fundamental.)

Weigh Risks and Returns

Canadians who do not understand the incredible differences between a bad neighborhood in Canada and one in the US should take a closer look at what happened in Jacksonville during the economic boom pre-2008. Back at that time, the niche areas my investor colleagues focus on today were selling to first-time home buyers for an average of $140,000 to $145,000. As of April 2010, these same properties were selling for $20,000 less.

Something entirely different happened in communities populated solely by investor-landlords. In the boom times, homes in these tougher neighborhoods were selling for $80,000 to $85,000. At the time, these homes were considered cheap. As of April 2010, these same properties sold for $10,000 to $15,000 and sometimes even less.

Canadian investors who want to understand the US market and the peculiarities of the bad neighborhood must look at what was behind such a drastic change. Fundamentally speaking, investors *fled* these lower-priced markets during the downturn. They also stopped buying properties in these markets. With more homes on the market and no buyers wanting to purchase them, property values went into a freefall.

Now, guess who really got hurt on these deals. For the most part, it was uneducated out-of-town investors. Not realizing the key market demographics at work, they had bought houses in terrible condition and located in dangerous neighborhoods where no one really wanted to live, and where there was no workable strategy for market improvement (where gentrification was a dream, not a plan). These investors bought into the notion that there was a lot of money to be made thanks to cheap prices and high cash flow. Unfortunately (and unbelievably) they never saw the fundamental flaw in an approach that ignored a key economic reality of the investment market: your property must be located in an area where people want to live.

 SOLD

Market-savvy Canadian real estate investors must commit and re-commit to understanding the market they want to invest in.

Want to hear an even sadder investment story? What happened in this segment of the housing market in Jacksonville, Florida, also occurred again and again across the United States in very similar markets that were dominated by landlords. Real estate investors from across the US and around the world were attracted to the action and a lot of them jumped right in. The smartest investors did not, because they knew these markets had a fundamental flaw. They watched other investors make highly emotional decisions based on low housing prices, but wisely refused to follow the lead of these uninformed investors.

Please take the information in this fundamental as a warning. Canadians investing in US real estate can and should appreciate that there are a lot of cultural similarities between the two countries. But not everything is the same. Once you cross that border, even words like "good versus bad neighborhood" merit closer scrutiny.

PROCEED WITH CAUTION!

10 Warning Signs That Indicate a Bad Neighborhood in the US

If you're not sure whether a neighborhood is good or bad from an investment perspective, add this checklist to your due diligence process and do a little independent fact checking, including asking around. If several points on the following list hold true, you should probably back away from the neighborhood, and then run!

1. Property management is hard to find.

2. Good tenants are hard to find.

3. There is a high rate of tenant turnovers and an even higher vacancy rate.

4. Investors report higher maintenance and repair bills compared to other neighborhoods.

5. The neighborhood can be dangerous to visit for property checks, maintenance and repairs, with reports of high crime and violence.

6. When you compare changes to property values, prices in this neighborhood dropped faster and farther than in adjacent, "better" neighborhoods.

7. Your insurance broker quotes higher insurance rates because of the property's poor condition.

8. A check of resale values shows prices on the decline.

9. Urban crime statistics show higher rates of problems related to drugs, prostitution and violent crimes.

10. More investor-scam deals are performed in these neighborhoods.

Look for the Stability of a Good Neighborhood.

Why It's Good to Follow First-Time Homebuyers

Now that you have a sense of why Canadian real estate investors need to avoid bad neighborhoods in the US, you should be looking at why a combination of homeowners and renters makes for a better investment neighborhood.

First and foremost, look at the facts. Quality market research shows that the problems plaguing investor-landlord communities in the United States are largely absent in neighborhoods where first-time homebuyers are purchasing homes. And this isn't only happening in the good times. Throughout the recent market correction, as prices plummeted in neighborhoods that were dominated by renters, neighborhoods that were attracting a number of first-time homebuyers were characterized by more stable housing prices.

This happened (and will continue to happen) because first-time homebuyers are concerned with terms and condition, not price. This simple fact keeps sales comparables stronger in areas that are attractive to first-time buyers. For this reason alone, several members of my US investment team recommend that investors deliberately look for neighborhoods that have a mixture of homeowners and renters.

The Benefits of Market Stability

Market stability affects more than housing prices. Having a mix of homeowners and renters in a neighborhood also tends to have a positive influence on property management. Since the people who want to live in these neighborhoods are less transient, they are more likely to take care of the properties they inhabit. Tenants in these neighborhoods also tend to want to own the house they are renting. This is rarely the case in the more troubled areas.

You may be wondering why so many investors continue to look at unstable housing markets as a major opportunity and ignore the real risks involved with investing in them. I think it comes down to the difference between investing with facts and investing with wishes.

People who've met me know that I spend a lot of time talking to people around the world about entrepreneurship and real estate. In that role, I am constantly challenging individuals to be honest about their business and personal goals and what they are doing or not doing to meet them. On the real estate front, for example, I tell people that real estate represents the single best asset class in the world for creating long-term wealth. I also tell them they need to be very specific about what they must do to make money in this sector.

So, when people come to me and say, "I've got $80,000 to invest in the US market and I think I am better off buying four $20,000 houses than I am buying one $80,000 house," I resist the temptation to tell them they're dead wrong. My more diplomatic response usually goes something like this:

"Maybe. But let me ask you this. If someone you know has a horse manure sandwich and they cut it up into little pieces to make it taste better, is that what happens? Does it taste better because they want it to taste better? Or does it still taste like horse manure?"

Always think your investment strategy through from start to finish. It's true that in the current market you can buy a house in Detroit for $20,000 or less. But some areas have up to 50% (no this is not a typo) unemployment.

Again, it's all about facts versus wishes.

What's Your Investment Plan?

I personally know investors in the US who make almost all of their real estate investment money in neighborhoods dominated by landlords and renters. But rest assured these investors are a very particular breed.

First, often they are extremely seasoned investors. They are not guessing what might work in a particular neighborhood; they know. Second, they also *live* full time in the city where they are investing in these tougher neighborhoods. This gives them constant access to the property and how it's managed. These investors also tend to invest in a large volume of these homes and deliberately stay very involved in day-to-day property management. Where they are not involved in the day-to-day management, they have very strong relationships with quality management and repair services. If this all sounds easy, you're not listening. Here are three things to think about. Canadian real estate investors

1. Do not typically know what these neighborhoods are really like, because they are substantially worse than their Canadian counterparts

2. Do not live in the cities where these neighborhoods exist (and may not even want to visit very often)

3. Probably do not want to buy large volumes of these properties or be highly involved with their day-to-day management

 SOLD

Investors who enter "tough" markets must know exactly what they're getting into. They must also make these investments with proven management already in place so these houses stay rented to paying tenants and repairs are kept under control.

A Final Word of Caution

Why am I so adamant that Canadian real estate investors understand how bad neighborhoods can affect their portfolios? I am passionate about this subject because I don't like to see people invest without knowing all of the facts. I have seen too many international investors get in over their heads when they buy the wrong house based on the largely emotional attraction of a cheap price. To reiterate the points made in Fundamental #6, your dreams of a high-rent return are seriously compromised in neighborhoods with high crime, high turnover, high repairs and terrible resale prospects. To make things worse, these deals are often made by shyster salesmen who won't return your calls after you buy one of their nightmare properties.

To identify a shyster pitch, look for what's behind a salesman's use of words like "transitional neighborhoods" or "gentrification." Both are supposed to mean neighborhoods moving towards improvement during good economic times. But in the current market, there are good deals to be had in good neighborhoods that do not need gentrification—they are already good neighborhoods!

I know that some people who buy property in a bad neighborhood will make money. But the odds are against you. As the great Warren Buffett says, "Price is what you pay; value is what you get."

SOLD

One of my US real estate investor friends tells me that he buys investment property in neighborhoods that he can walk into at 10 p.m. on a Friday or Saturday and not feel afraid. The fear-free walk cannot be your only point of due diligence, but it is the kind of no-nonsense advice investors should put to work when they're assessing the value of a particular property in a particular neighborhood.

PROCEED WITH ENTHUSIASM!

The last fundamental gave you 10 items for your bad neighborhood watch list. Here are a few things you can do when trying to weed out bad neighborhoods and select good ones.

1. Visit your investment market.

2. Drive through the neighborhoods at different times of the day or night.

3. Check local crime statistics.

4. Search local newspapers for neighborhood names.

5. Spend some time talking to local real estate professionals including real estate agents and property managers.

6. Focus on neighborhoods with both renters and homeowners.

8

Choose Your Exit Strategy Before You Make the Deal.

Are You a Gambler or an Investor? Pick Your Game Early

Two things are very clear in the current US market for foreclosed residential properties. First, anyone can buy at a discount, and second, it's what you do after you've made the deal that really matters.

The need to have a solid exit strategy in place as you make an investment deal is old news to experienced investors. They plan to make money when they buy and they know that a deal is defined by its exit strategy—their plan for how and when they will sell the investment and take their profit. If you do not have an effective exit strategy in place for the property, you stand to lose money, even if you acquired the property for pennies on the dollar.

I know that prediction takes a lot of new investors by surprise, so let me be clear about how important an exit strategy is. In a market like this, it's very easy to get caught up in the deal and not think through the process. That is an abdication of solid due diligence. To drive this fundamental home, I'll share a story based on dozens of phone calls one of my US investor colleagues has fielded in recent months. He's been buying distressed investment properties for years and he says the calls go like this:

> *"Hi there! It's me, your newbie investor friend and guess what? You were totally right about what's going on in the US market for distressed property! I just bought an incredible deal at a huge discount. It was a foreclosure sale and the price was incredible. The single-family home is located in the kind of neighborhood you told me to look at and while it's got a few cosmetic issues I'll need to clear up, it's structurally sound. The HVAC, roof, plumbing and electrical systems are in great condition,* too, so I figured I've saved some real money there."*

"That's wonderful news. What are you going to do with it?"

"Do with it? I'm going to renovate first and then..."

* See Fundamental #17: Do the Big 4 Renos on a Rental Property—Now.

My colleague tells me the phone goes quiet at this point. After a few moments of awkward silence, some novice investors will insist a plan doesn't really matter "since I got the property so cheap!" Others will dismiss the question as an issue they'll deal with as work proceeds on the property upgrade. Some will stumble with a response as they start to appreciate the magnitude of the question they've just been asked. All three have a problem, but at least the last caller is starting to see the forest for the trees!

I'm here to tell you it does not matter if you're buying real estate investment property in your own backyard or in a foreign country—you need to have an exit strategy. If you cannot fix it up and sell it or rent it out, it is not an investment, it's a gamble. And that's the case if you got it for 10 cents on the dollar or 50 cents on the dollar.

 SOLD

An exit strategy provides a course of action that's designed to make you money. When you buy a "deal" you invest in that exit strategy. Anything less is speculation. It can pay off, but speculators generally lose more money than they make. Why take that chance in a market where knowledgeable investors are telling you there is money to be made without the extra risk?

Identify Your Exit Strategy

There are three real estate investment markets where you can make money: the fix-and-flip, the long-term rental and the wholesale market. In the latter, you buy deeply discounted homes to sell to other investors.

When you're choosing an exit strategy that focuses on one of these market niches, remember that while each can make you money, their potential differs depending on what stage the real estate cycle is in for that market. (See Fundamental #10: Become Knowledgeable About the Real Estate Cycle.)

In light of the current market situation, I'm going to zero in on the part of the real estate cycle where the investment opportunities are driven by two factors: discount prices and high foreclosure rates.

We know those two factors contribute to your ability to find a good deal. At this stage in the market, all three exit strategies can work, assuming you have a buyer or renter who wants that property. But there's no question one exit strategy is especially well-suited to these market conditions and that's the buy-and-hold exit strategy.

Before we look at why the buy-and-hold strategy is particularly advantageous in this market, I want to dig beneath some of the common misconceptions I hear about using the wholesale and buy-and-flip markets at this stage in the real estate cycle. A lot of inexperienced investors (or those who don't pay close enough attention to market fundamentals) tell me their exit strategy is based on the wholesale market. They plan to flip the property to another investor (one who'll do the actual property upgrades) and while they'll only make a few thousand dollars on the deal, this strategy quickly frees up their time and money. Others tell me their exit strategy involves buying a discounted property, fixing it up and flipping it back onto the resale market.

Both are workable strategies. Both can also be more difficult to put into play than the shortsighted investor might think. For one thing, both strategies require a buyer. No problem, since this is a buyer's market, right? Wrong! Because you are selling into a buyer's market, your position is naturally compromised. There may well be money to be made, but it's risky because buyers are inundated with choice.

 SOLD

The buy-renovate-and-flip-market is a serious business because every month your investment stays on the market is another month its mortgage stays on your books. Understand that staged homes sell 50% quicker than non-staged homes, so seriously consider staging your home for the retail sale market. Hire a professional staging company or, if you have an eye for decorating, do it yourself.

The biggest thing to remember: less is more! Keep the furniture and decorations to a minimum so potential buyers see livable space and not clutter.

Why Buy-and-Hold Makes Sense

Once a market-smart investor realizes the risks of selling into a buyer's market, she may develop her deals a little differently. In this current market, the best exit strategy is the buy-and-hold market. That potentially means years of dealing with property managers and tenants. If the deal is structured correctly, it should also mean years of cash-flowing revenue. But most importantly, down markets go up, so investors who buy and rent properties will also benefit from their property's appreciation. Here, the exit strategy looks ahead to a time when prices are rising and fewer houses are on the market.

My main point is that the buy-and-hold strategy is successful when applied to neighborhoods with a stable tenant market and steady demand for rental properties. I think this strategy also exemplifies what smart investors talk about when they say they are after the "patient money." What they advocate meets market fundamentals because they buy at a discount in a buyer's market, rent the property for a good cash flow, allow the market cycle to do what it has always done and then sell when the market shows clear signs of being a seller's market. In fact, that's where some investors discipline themselves to be even more patient. Instead of selling early in the seller's market of the real estate cycle, they hold on to their properties longer than planned because inflation has kicked their rents so high they don't want to give up the healthy cash flow.

 SOLD

If you can make more money by revising your exit strategy, then go ahead. Just avoid having to change your strategy so that you lose less!

A Closer Look at the Wholesale and Fix-and-Flip Options

The wisdom of patient money aside, some investors will stick to the wholesale or fix-and-flip markets and it's clear that both can make you money. But be careful. These markets are often perceived (and aggressively marketed) as "easier" because they appear to demand less commitment (you won't have to deal with property management issues). Reality paints a different picture. The historic number of distressed properties on the market means there are more houses than buyers. Be honest about what that means. The opportunities are there, but buyers—including investors— can afford to be pickier. Unless your properties are deeply discounted and located in prime neighborhoods, you will have trouble finding buyers as there is a much greater chance they will be able to find better deals in better areas.

To make wholesale deals work, you need a business strategy that includes a good relationship with a group of investors. You also need to know reliable Real Estate Owned (REO) agents (who typically work for lenders) and others who can find you these deals, cheap. You'll need up-to-date information about the auction schedule and when different inventory will be auctioned off and, ideally, a way to find out when homeowners want to discount a property for a quick sale to ward off the foreclosure process.

Even with all that background work, the investment facts remain the same. If you pay too much for a distressed property and set the wholesale price too high, you might get stuck with the property. As it's currently more difficult for Canadians to finance the wholesale deal, carrying a property for longer than anticipated can cause big problems for your next deal, too.

Canadians who want to get into the wholesale and fixer-upper retail market should also be aware that the most successful wholesalers and property flippers live in the markets where they work. This gives them critical and timely access to buyers and sellers.

 PROCEED WITH CAUTION!

Location. Location. Location.

If you don't plan to live in the market where you're buying real estate investment property, think twice about the wholesale and fix-and-flip niches. Once you get a reliable team on the ground, these markets can be quite manageable, but other investors and those selling distressed properties will not wait for you to fly in when local investors have properties to buy and sell.

Recognize that financing is more difficult on the wholesale and residential retail markets. If you decide to fix and flip homes into the first-time homebuyer market, you will need to understand how federal assistance mortgages work.

Historically speaking, Federal Housing Administration (FHA) loans have allowed lower-income Americans to borrow money to buy a home when they could not afford a conventional down payment. Veterans Affairs (VA) home loans play a similar role for veterans, active duty personnel, reservists and National Guard members and some surviving spouses. Canadians in this market must understand that FHA and VA financing are the most active loans in the nation right now.

Besides understanding that your market targets people who qualify for FHA and VA loans, you will need to fine-tune your marketing plan to meet the needs of the first-time homebuyer. While you may think it's enough to market on price, these buyers are not familiar with the market and respond much more quickly to information about "how much down and how much a month."

My US market insiders tell me that property condition in the current fix-and-flip market is also very important; to make a sale, the property must be stellar and stand out from competing inventory. As the success of this exit strategy hinges on the quick sale, you may also need a more aggressive marketing program that uses everything from lawn signs to what the industry calls "bandit signs," which are eye-catching signs posted in high-traffic areas.

Working with a top-notch real estate agent is another way to push your house to the market. In addition to costing you a commission (arguably a good use of someone else's time!) you will need to be in close contact with that agent to make sure your house is being marketed aggressively.

Pick Your Partners Carefully

There's no question that a hot market attracts money. Before you hand over any investment cash, make sure you know what you're getting! Some investors already doing business in the US market have proven track records and do high-volume business. That's a good starting point. Also look for good contacts with local investor groups and buyers—you want to make sure your partners have a team on the ground before you invest with a particular company.

Again, this is a buyer's market. It's relatively easy to acquire and upgrade property, and if you've got an influx of cash, you can do a lot of deals. But do you want to get into a large-volume market that makes your money swim against the real estate cycle current? Absolutely not. You want to partner on deals that sell and that requires people on the ground and familiar with that market. What works in one part of Arizona may not work in another part of the same state, let alone California, Florida or Nevada!

Choose an Exit Strategy That Makes Money

A smart investor once told me that no man is bigger than the market. E.W. Howe summed it up a little differently when he wrote, "no man's credit is as good as his money." I like these quotes because they address two of my central points about investing in the US distressed property market. First, you can make money here, and second, you can lose money here. I'm all about staying on the positive side of the investment ledger.

To do that, I swim with the current. In the real estate investment market right now, that means focusing on the buy-and-hold side of the market. It's a niche where I can develop a volume business with less risk, all because the market fundamentals are so positive. As long as I'm paying attention to where I'm buying, there is no shortage of renters. As long as I'm attentive to how much I'm paying, there are good opportunities for cash flow. With good management and some patience, my "patient money" properties can develop future wealth, and so can yours.

9

Know Your Financing Options.

Financing 101: Options and Obstacles

Financing is another investment fundamental Canadians need to understand as they research the US foreclosure market. While a lot of Canadians are bringing their own capital to this market, others are wisely looking at financing as a way to put someone else's money to work on their deals. Where can you find money and how does it work? That's what I want to talk about in this fundamental.

The news is not all good. If you're looking for financing, you'll soon find that the US options for Canadians and other foreign real estate investors wanting to buy US property are scarce. For Canadians, that American money is available if you're planning to buy a second home for personal use; investment property financing is much harder to find.

This surprises me—and a lot of other investors—since the same lenders that deny dollars to international borrowers also say that foreign investment can revive American real estate markets. To understand what's going on, Canadians should know a bit about what's behind the massive downturn in the American real estate market.

It all goes back to the Federal National Mortgage Association (FNMA), known as Fannie Mae, and the Federal Home Loan Mortgage Corporation (FHLMC), known as Freddie Mac. These stockholder-owned corporations were set up by US Congress in the late 1960s. They were to purchase and provide some security for mortgages and ensure funds were consistently available to the institutions that lent money to homebuyers. In essence, these were two government-backed mortgage agencies and they held almost all of the mortgage loans in the US.

The banks that you may be trying to meet with now (Wells Fargo, Bank of America and Chase Manhattan, for example), sell their mortgages to FNMA and FHLMC. Fannie Mae and Freddie Mac made the rules about what type of loans were acceptable and they didn't buy mortgages from lenders who didn't stick within their guidelines. That hasn't changed, and since Fannie and Freddie currently hold that international investor loans are too risky, lenders won't lend foreigners investment money.

Fannie Mae and Freddie Mac argue that international investor loans are too risky if the borrower doesn't have a US FICO score (credit rating). They also take issue with the complications of verifying foreign income and assets and argue that if an international borrower defaults, it's too hard to chase them for recourse on the loan.

That rationale ignores the validity of reliable credit ratings available in countries like Canada. It also dismisses the potential to decrease the risk of default by requiring international investors to put down more money. (An investor with 50% down has some real skin in the deal and is less likely to default. That's how basic investment math works.) Fannie and Freddie's approach also discounts the fact that today's US housing prices reflect such a significant market downturn that many properties are substantially undervalued. The ability to buy an investment property at such deep discounts protects the investment risk. Lenders could also implement a faster foreclosure process against non-US residents.

The legitimacy of these arguments aside, that's not what is happening in the US market, where Americans with a "fair" credit rating can borrow money for their primary residence and put down 3% (or less).

This is a message Canadian investors need to speak to when they're working in the US investor market. The more Americans hear this message, the greater the likelihood that the people at Fannie Mae and Freddie Mac will wake up and realize that they can't claim foreign investors can save the US real estate market without supporting those same investors with financing.

Looking ahead, I suspect financing options will improve in the future because that's what happens when a real estate market cycles back after a correction. If US money is critical to your deal, however, you've got a problem. My American market insiders tell me changes to the foreign investor lending rules aren't likely within the next two years.

Portfolio Loans

In the meantime, though, how do you get some US financing for your deals if your options with mortgages bought by the Fannie Mae and Freddie Mac group do not look promising? Portfolio loans (mortgages held for the long term, usually by smaller local banks) represent a small percentage of housing loans not sold to Fannie and Freddie. Since they are not trying to sell mortgage paper to Fannie and Freddie, they do not have to follow their guidelines.

This is a good place to start your search for a US investment loan. Begin with smaller local banks that do portfolio loans in the area where you are looking to invest.

To be straight, a lot of them will turn you down and probably for the same reasons the FNMA guidelines suggest. But I recommend you be diligent. Find smaller local banks that work outside the FNMA box and start building relationships with people who may be able to look at your deals on a case-by-case basis. If you're serious about accessing US financing, be very professional. Make sure you know what you're asking for and be prepared to show these banks how you'll deliver their money, with interest.

Private Money

Private money, also known as hard money, is another option. Private money lenders do loans to foreign investors. When compared to bank financing, these funds can be easier to get and harder to pay off, so be careful.

Finding sources of private money is relatively easy. Private lenders can be found in most of the big markets through advertisements, real estate investment association clubs, real estate agents and title companies who work with investors. As always, relationships are important, so ask around and find out who knows whom.

Keep in mind that a private lender will tend to lend based on the deal itself versus the borrower. This is why private money is almost always higher in fees and the interest rates can be double or triple what a bank charges. In the current market, foreign investors can expect to be charged borrower fees plus interest rates between 10% and 17%.

With a sound exit strategy, private money can be an ideal way to finance a fixer-upper in the short term. (Remember, even if you can get bank financing, most banks will not loan money on a house that needs major renovation work. With the right deal, this is where private money can help.) However, carrying the property with such a high interest rate for too long can hurt cash flow or resale profits. As well, most of these loans stipulate a one-year term, so a good exit strategy is vital.

One good thing about using private money is that it can provide good leverage to get you into a property and give you time to "season" a property. "Seasoning" is the term banks use to describe a property that's been owned for a certain period of time. A seasoned property can make a bank feel more comfortable about loaning on the property. For a property to be considered seasoned a bank usually wants to see that someone has owned it for one year or more. (A few banks will consider six months to be a sufficient seasoning period.)

This is important because you may be able to use private money to secure a property after it has been seasoned for a year and then refinance the home with a local bank that does portfolio loans. But that refinancing "possibility" is not a detail you can leave to chance, especially when you will most likely need to repay that private loan after 12 months. Remember, hard-money lenders are not afraid to take your property. If the term of the loan is only one year and you can't pay it off when that year is up, the private money lender can choose to extend the loan for you or take the property back. So if you plan to use private money with this strategy in mind, start interviewing local banks before you use the private money and make sure you have a backup plan in place to pay off the private loan. That may also be possible through an equity line of credit on a Canadian property or by using cash reserves you have on the sidelines.

PROCEED WITH CAUTION!

Can You Buy It Back?

If you're looking for US financing for your American deals, proceed with caution. Your plan to get the money has to include a plan to pay it back, especially if you're using private financing.

You do not want to pay premium interest rates on a private loan for 12 months—and then lose the property as well.

Leverage Your Canadian Successes

Another viable option involves leveraging off a lowly-geared (low debt-to-value) property you own in Canada. Here, you use that property to take out an equity line or a second mortgage and apply that money to financing a property you buy in the US. As long as the property you buy has a healthy cash flow, it should cover the debt service for the money you borrow. (You could also leverage a US mortgage, although that's going to be more difficult to access in the first place given the Fannie Mae/Freddie Mac rules.)

PROCEED WITH CAUTION!

Cash Is Better Than Debt

Robust real estate investment markets are no excuse for putting your Canadian assets at risk, and market veterans with integrity would never encourage you to over-leverage any property—because hard cash is always better than new debt.

Again, do not confuse money-making strategies with "sure things." In real estate, as in life, there are no sure things!

Become Knowledgeable About the Real Estate Cycle.

What Time Is It on the Real Estate Cycle Clock?

The current buzz of media stories and investment gossip about the US distressed property market was predated by a whole lot of attention to real estate market booms, busts and bubbles. If you pay any attention to the real estate investment market, you know the "three *b*'s" garner a whole lot of attention when people are trying to figure out what's going on in the market. What they're really looking for is information about *why* a market is acting the way it is at a particular moment in time. Why are prices so high or so low? Why are so many homes on the market? Why are there more buyers than sellers or vice versa?

I want you to think differently. Instead of asking why a market is acting a particular way, I think you should be asking where a market is at in the "real estate cycle." This information answers all of the questions I mentioned above in terms of how a market is behaving. Better yet, it will guide your investment acquisitions and fine-tune your exit strategies!

 SOLD

> Think of the real estate cycle as a circle of activity that spins in one direction. Fortunes are made and lost as the cycle revolves, but there is money to be made at every point. This is possible because smart investors invest with the cycle's momentum. They go with the current to reap bigger rewards and minimize their risks.

For example, the real estate cycle offers insight into what happened in the US market to contribute to the current situation where we have record numbers of distressed properties on the market. The cycle doesn't predict when a change might occur, but those familiar with how it works will see indications of an impending shift from recovery to boom or boom to slump. History shows that a lot of people familiar with the real estate cycle were asking questions about the US real estate market by 2006. They wondered how long the boom was going to last and, by default, what events might precipitate a market crash and how bad things might be when the boom ended.

A US investor I know tells me she suspected a crash was near after she was consulted by Kieran Trass and Greg Head, leading real estate cycle experts. After their assessment of the Phoenix market, she called a meeting with a group of investors in Scottsdale, Arizona. She provided them with real estate market analysis about why the real estate cycle was shifting and why they should reposition their portfolios before there was a significant downturn in prices.

The fact that this meeting took place in 2006 tells me a lot about the wisdom of the real estate cycle. It also underlines the fact that real estate investors need to take the cycle seriously so they can apply this information to their portfolios.

What Is the Real Estate Cycle?

The real estate cycle (which occurs on both sides of the Canada/US border) was first identified more than 70 years ago by Homer Hoyt, the man now called the grandfather of the real estate cycle concept. In 1933, Hoyt analyzed a century of movement in Chicago's land values and documented his findings in his book, *One Hundred Years of Land Values in Chicago*. In the book, Hoyt documented how a recurrent succession of causes and effects impacted land values from 1830 to 1930. In sum, he recognized a "big picture pattern" at play and detailed how that pattern affected the real estate market.

Subsequent studies support Hoyt's contention of that recurrent succession of causes and effects impacting land values. We now understand that the real estate cycle follows a consistent pattern that moves through three basic stages of what's called the Real Estate Cycle Clock. These stages are recovery, boom and slump.

Source: Kieran Trass

The clock's timing can be somewhat irregular and even volatile, but the fundamental pattern remains the same; that is, the recovery, boom and slump pattern always repeats itself, but the time frame of each phase in the cycle is not consistent with previous cycles. The timing is based on the simple laws of supply and demand. By knowing what factors affect those forces you can find genuine predictive value in the real estate cycle, making understanding it one of your real estate investment fundamentals.

Before we look at how to recognize these three phases, I want to talk about some of the factors that contribute to the movement from one phase to another. They are known as the key drivers and market influencers.

Key Drivers and Market Influencers

Key drivers propel the real estate market through the various phases of the real estate cycle. Some of these key drivers are volatile and others are more stable. Regardless, it is the "collective impact" of key drivers that a real estate investor has to watch. While no single key driver can move the real estate cycle through a complete phase on its own, the right combination of drivers can have a major impact. The key drivers can be divided into three categories: demographic, financial and emotional.

Demographic

- Net migration/population growth
- Real estate vacancy rates
- Employment
- Real estate construction
- Number of people per household

Financial

- Real estate return on investment (ROI)
- Rents
- Incomes
- Real estate financing availability
- Gross domestic product

- Real estate values
- Real estate affordability

Emotional

- Number of days to sell real estate
- Gentrification
- Real estate listings
- Real estate sales

Demographic changes, such as population growth, can quickly increase demand for real estate. Other key drivers are the result of financial changes such as an increase in the level of rents, which affects the financial viability of real estate investment. Other key drivers, like the number of days it takes to sell real estate, can induce panic buying when buyers are driven by the fear of missing out during the boom phase of the real estate cycle. If population growth, an increase in rent levels and panic buying occur simultaneously, their impact on the real estate cycle is more immediate.

Market influencers are factors that affect the perception of the length of a specific phase of the real estate cycle. It is important to understand that these market influencers are often confused with key drivers of the real estate cycle. Unlike drivers, which actually move the real estate cycle from one phase to another, market influencers affect the immediate levels of supply and demand in the real estate market. Their impact, however, is temporary.

Real estate investors need to recognize how the temporary nature of market influencers impacts the cycle by giving a false impression of where a cycle is moving. Market influencers do not drive the real estate cycle from one phase to the next, but create the illusion of that happening. The great news about market influencers is that they can set up a window of opportunity for prudent investors. These opportunities arise as a direct result of the confusion created by the market influencers in terms of what is really happening in the market.

 SOLD

Students of the real estate cycle can capitalize on the short-term effects of market influencers because they recognize how temporary blips in the market create short-term opportunities to acquire property or execute an exit strategy.

Classic market influencers that can temporarily shift a real estate cycle include the following:

- Interest rates (the cost of finance)
- Ease of borrowing (the availability of finance)
- Confidence in real estate as an investment vehicle
- Inflation
- Legislative amendments (taxation and/or local authority)
- Investment alternatives

Boom, Slump and Recovery

The three phases of the market cycle, boom, slump and recovery, can be identified by specific things that happen in the market during these periods, and investors can use that information to figure out where a particular market is at on the Real Estate Cycle Clock.

The Boom

The boom phase tends to be the shortest phase in the real estate cycle (although anomalies do happen!). At this phase, capital growth is the name of the game. There are more buyers than sellers in the market and this forces up prices. Property values also increase—slowly at the start of the boom and then gathering impressive speed as this stage progresses. The boom phase nears completion once prices reach their maximum.

During a boom, the public is very positive about buying property. Booms are characterized by a high volume of sales and quick-selling properties. As properties are snapped up soon after they go onto the market, the boom phase sets the stage for relatively fewer listings.

At this point, the sellers have the negotiating power. More and more people focus on adding value to their properties and this continues until the end of the boom. Rents also increase during the early stages of a boom. As the rents rise, the number of people living in each dwelling also increases as it becomes harder for people to afford to rent.

About midway through this phase, rents peak. That affects the return investors are able to get on their buy-and-hold property investments, and with property values still rising, rents cannot keep pace.

The Slump

In the slump phase, the increase in property values slows and may come to a halt as the supply of property exceeds demand. Sometimes values even recede, although this doesn't happen in every slump, or in every area. By the end of the slump phase, values are at their most affordable levels for that phase of the cycle.

With property supply exceeding demand, buyers now have the negotiating edge. It takes longer and longer to sell property and agents have more listings than in other phases of the real estate cycle. As fewer properties sell during a slump than at any other time, investors will notice that the same real estate agents who happily ignored them during the boom now start to return phone calls. Some of the best property-buying opportunities arise during this period as vendors are motivated and purchasers have an extraordinary amount of control.

The Recovery

As a market enters the recovery phase, the rental population starts to increase, resulting in a shortage of rental property. Property values also begin to rise slowly and investors get a better return on investment as rents rise and vacancy rates start to fall. Interest rates are attractive and financing becomes easier to get as banks come under pressure to lend so they can capitalize on the increased need for borrowing.

First-time homebuyers become more active in this market, but fear still rules with memories of price corrections in the preceding slump. As the recovery phase progresses, experienced investors recognize the potential for increased returns and enter the market aggressively. Inexperienced investors remain cautious, most wanting to wait to see what happens before they take any action.

The recovery phase is also characterized by increased construction of new dwellings as builders and developers start new projects and by many property owners adding value to their properties. Throughout the recovery phase, property values rise but media reports reflect low confidence in real estate as an investment. The end of the recovery phase often blurs with the beginning of the next boom, and it can be hard to tell when the cycle is changing.

Recognizing Cycle Shifts

Investors tuned in to the real estate cycle watch for signs of a shift from one phase to the next and use that information to guide purchase decisions and exit strategies, balancing cash flow and appreciation with long-term wealth building.

From Slump to Recovery: Opportunity Thrives

At the beginning of the slump phase, property values may still be rising, though at slower rates. Property sales volumes fall from their former heights and there is a lower ROI. This is accompanied by increased holding costs. Many investors consider selling a property or two, which signals a further market shift as the increased number of sellers start competing with each other. This further floods the market with properties for sale.

Midway through the slump there is an abundance of motivated vendors who were forced to sell their properties because of low returns and high holding costs. The media bashes real estate and fear rules the day as people worry about short-term equity corrections. Employment levels are low at this stage and financing is harder to get.

As the slump nears its end, unemployment is at its peak, population growth and income levels are at their lowest and rents remain fairly static. At the end of the slump, values are low and vendors are increasingly desperate.

This is the stage of the real estate cycle that wise investors have been waiting for! With very few buyers in the market now, there is less competition for you as an investor. Take note of words like "urgent" in property advertisements. In this phase, it takes longer and longer to sell properties but you will start to see more first-time homebuyers entering the market. Even though the media is still reporting doom and gloom as far as property is concerned, these buyers are focusing on what they can afford.

 SOLD

What motivates first-time homebuyers as a market moves from slump to recovery? With rents holding steady, this market segment starts to do the basic math. They don't ask if they can afford the asking price, they ask if they can afford the monthly payments.

Key Recovery Signs Checklist

- ☐ Increasing population
- ☐ New construction starting
- ☐ More accessible financing

- ☐ Rents beginning to rise
- ☐ Property values starting to increase
- ☐ Increasing returns
- ☐ Property sellers dropping their prices to compete with the rising number of properties on the market

From Recovery to Boom: Concerns Give Way to Prosperity

As the recovery gives way to a boom, investors notice an increase in the rental population accompanied by rising employment and income levels. Rents are going up and property values are rising. This means investors are getting a greater ROI on properties they already own. The returns on new properties are often lower at the start of a boom because increases in rent are unable to keep up with increases in property values.

During the initial stages of a boom, much of the public holds "anti-real estate" feelings due to negative memories of the previous slump, and most fail to quickly recognize that the boom is already underway. At the same time, more people start entering the real estate market, driving up property prices.

By the middle of the boom, the increase in rents reaches a peak and vacancy levels are still low. Values continue to rise and property sells quickly. It is easy to get financing; banks are relaxed about allowing people to borrow to the absolute maximum they can afford. At mid-boom, everyone from the neighbors to the taxi driver is talking about the benefits of real estate investments, as is the media. New investors enter the market, egged on by the general excitement level and an increased awareness of real estate investment seminars.

Unfortunately, greed is the flavor of the day. You will notice a great deal of speculation; buyers are buying property based on plans versus built product. As the end of the boom nears, population growth slows and the ratio of buyers to sellers in the market starts to level out. People also are finding it harder to meet their mortgage payments and this slows down the boom's momentum.

Key Boom Signs Checklist

- ☐ Increasing rental population
- ☐ Increasing employment
- ☐ Increasing incomes
- ☐ Increasing rents

- ☐ Increasing property values
- ☐ High, easy property sales
- ☐ More accessible financing
- ☐ Increasing construction
- ☐ Greed

From Boom to Slump: Buyers Struggle With Affordability

Looking back to 2006, real estate investors who were tuned in to the real estate cycle saw how key drivers and market influencers were pushing a market boom towards a slump. The key driver in this latest US market slump was definitely the credit crisis. That occurred as demand plunged in many over-built markets where housing prices had moved well beyond market affordability. Real estate investors who pulled their money out before the slump are now putting that money back in, in anticipation of the market recovery.

Brilliant. But it's not rocket science, it's the real estate cycle!

Key Slump Signs Checklist

- ☐ Low to no population growth
- ☐ Increasing unemployment
- ☐ Decreasing incomes
- ☐ Oversupply of property
- ☐ Less accessible financing
- ☐ Decreasing or flat rents
- ☐ Decreasing or flat property values
- ☐ Desperate vendors

11

Find the People Who Can Help You Find Foreclosures.

Real Estate Investing Is a Relationship Business

Have you heard the story of the out-of-shape person who approaches a highly regarded personal trainer for some help getting back into shape? The individual tells the trainer that all he needs to know is "the best way to get into great shape."

The trainer tells him, "No problem! I know exactly how you can do it!" The client is thrilled. "Great!" says the out-of-shape person. "What's the secret?"

"Consistent diet and exercise," answers the personal trainer.

"Yeah, okay . . . But besides that?" is the disappointed response from the client.

I share this story because it reflects a common problem I encounter when talking to new real estate investors and people who want to be real estate investors. Instead of focusing on what's effective and proven to work, they avoid the obvious because it all seems like too much work.

Well, here's the deal. Real estate investing takes work even if you've decided to focus on the US foreclosure market, which is rife with opportunity. I know that everyone wants a fancy and sexy shortcut! But I'm here to tell you that those shortcuts usually just run you in circles. So lose the attitude that screams, "If something is not clever, it can't work!" Real estate investing works. But there's no magic.

The Not–So–Secret Way to Find Great Real Estate Deals

The first thing you need to find good real estate investment deals for distressed properties in the US market is good relationships with top-notch real estate agents, wholesalers (individuals who focus on the quick-turn or "flip" real estate deal) and the people you meet through real estate investment associations.

This people-centered approach celebrates the fact that real estate investment is a relationship business. And my strategy here is simple. I can spend my time and money on fancy mailings and other programs that are designed to help me find property deals, or I can use real estate professionals and real estate investment organizations to the same end. Being a kind of "anti-overhead" guy, I'm going with the strategy that puts other people to work.

 SOLD

Canadian real estate investors can find lots of people who are willing to sell them foolproof marketing programs that will bring US foreclosure deals to the front doors of your Canadian offices. Save your money. Use a real estate agent to find deals. It's less expensive, less time-consuming and usually way more effective. It's also likely to work in all markets.

Understand What an Agent Can Do for Your Business

If you plan to buy investment property in more than one market, you're going to need real estate agents and wholesalers in each of those markets. What works in California may not get any response in Florida or Nevada, since effective marketing and advertising programs can vary greatly from area to area.

Your goal is to have an experienced real estate agent and wholesaler provide you with good deals at a discount within the niche type of house you aim to buy. To make that happen, you should definitely look for real estate owned (REO) real estate agents. They've been hired by the bank to resell properties the bank has foreclosed on.

As banks are the most motivated sellers on the market right now, an REO agent will be motivated to make a deal.

 SOLD

Not every foreclosure is a good deal. Make that your mantra!
Never make a deal unless you know how the market fundamentals affect the investment potential of a particular property. You don't want to buy in the wrong area, or buy a home that needs significant upgrades unless the discounted price and market fundamentals tell you the deal makes sense.

One of my US investor colleagues tells me that in one city in Florida, there are a handful of agents who handle the majority of all the REO listings. These agents do volume and are no-nonsense. Because their time is in high demand, you can't expect them to go out to long lunches with an investor the first time you meet.

Know How to Get Their Attention

As a newcomer to the US distressed property market, Canadian investors have to realize that REOs in some areas are inundated with investor queries. Since they are probably already working with a network of investors, you'll need to get their attention if you want in on the deals they're involved with.

How do you do that? One of my US market insiders tells me Canadians can use the following three magic statements to get their foot in the door with REOs.

1. I Will Not Waste Your Time.

Say this when you first meet the REO—and mean it. Tell them exactly what kind of deal you are looking for. Skip the list of questions from the last investing book you read and be natural and friendly. You want to let them know that you know what you're doing and what you're looking for.

People do business with people they know, like and trust. Build that rapport.

Let the REO agent know that you need to buy at a discount to make the numbers work for you and be specific about the type of property you are looking for. (A list of parameters will follow.)

2. I Have the Funds Ready to Close the Deal.

REO agents really dislike it when someone puts a house under contract and the deal doesn't close. Let them know that you have access to cash. It might even be smart to give them proof of funds the first time you meet. This could be a credit statement, a bank account statement or an approval letter from a local hard-money lender.

If you don't have any of this yet, don't worry. Just assure the REO with confidence that you can perform, and then follow through.

3. I Always Give You Both Sides of the Commission.

This point is huge. Money talks. Period. Let the agent know right up front that you are not working with a buyer's agent and you want them to keep all of the commission. REO agents work hard to get their listing from banks and would obviously prefer to keep more commission.

If you are an agent, be prepared to forgo your commission. You will make your money on the deal, so don't compromise your working relationship with an REO.

PROCEED WITH ENTHUSIASM!

Canadian investors who are serious about the US foreclosure market must recognize the value of being able to make and follow through on these three statements. With perseverance and honesty, you can use this strategy to open a virtual pipeline of future profits.

Once you're serious about a market, politely stay in contact with your REOs. If a deal comes up that really fits your parameters, buy it. That kind of follow-through shows you are serious.

Canadian investors sometimes tell me they worry it will be difficult to find the larger-volume REO agents in an area, but they're unlikely to have that problem. As part of your market due diligence, you need to talk to real estate agents and property managers. Ask them who's doing the REO business and look on sites like Realtor.com. We will also be listing agents on www.realestate49.com under the resource section.

I also recommend calling different real estate offices in the area and asking to talk to the broker/manager. Tell them you want to work with an agent who

- specializes with investors, distressed property sales and foreclosures
- has been in the market for at least five years
- owns his or her own investment property

This won't always yield a good referral. But it does get you talking to people who are active in the local real estate market. As you interview them and talk about the market, you'll get a better feel for the area. You'll also start to get the kind of information you need to compare agents.

It goes without saying that you should never feel obligated to buy a house from an agent who you've just interviewed. But do be fair with their time. There is nothing wrong with asking an agent to send you some potential listings to look over. Just don't forget what I said about this being a relationship business. You want to cultivate relationships with people you really want to work with.

Beyond the REO

Agents other than REO agents can also find deals for you. Short sales, where the owner and lender are highly motivated to sell before a formal foreclosure action, abound in this market, and a knowledgeable agent can help you identify good deals and put in offers on them. Short sales can be tricky, so make sure your agent and the listing agent are absolute bulldogs with staying on top of the bank. As I talked about in Fundamental #2, the odds of getting a short-sale property are very low. So if a property really fits your system, make sure the deal goes through.

 SOLD

Investors make their money on deals, not almost-deals. If an agent brings you listings that are far outside the parameters of the deals you've asked them to be on the lookout for, find out what's happening. Either they weren't listening, don't get it or don't care.

Relationships are a two-way street. If one side isn't working, look somewhere else.

Check Out the Wholesaler Market

Wholesalers are remarkably different from real estate agents. The good ones are savvy investors who have close relationships with REO agents and banks. Because they buy volume, and volume has its privileges, a lot of wholesalers are first in line for great deals.

And why shouldn't they be? They buy at the auction steps, they buy REO, they buy short sales. Ideally, they aim to buy deals low, and turn around and sell them right away to other investors at wholesale prices. Most will try to tack on price increases of at least $10,000 higher than what they paid.

One of my US insiders tells me he works with wholesalers who will sell him property at $4,000 above what they paid. That discount is based on the fact that this investor buys a steady volume of property from the same wholesalers—and he always closes his deals. The bottom line is that he gets the house at a price that works for him with very little effort. Again, you can chalk that up to relationships.

Double-Check the Wholesaler's Numbers

If you want to deal in the wholesale market, understand that wholesalers will buy property anywhere in town and they then will sell that property for as much as they can get. It's up to you to decide whether a particular deal works for you. Always do the math and know your market fundamentals because some of their deals are good and some are not.

As with any vendor, real estate investors must never take a wholesaler's word on property values, the costs of repairs and the going rental rates. In fact, if you're doing business in the US you must be wary of the numbers you get from a wholesaler, especially if this market is new to you. In a business where cash is king, a wholesaler does not have to do *your* homework!

Investors must also be on guard for what the industry terms "fake wholesalers."

These are the guys who get listings from real wholesalers, tack on a few more thousand to a deal and try to sell it to you at the higher price. This isn't illegal. But the more middlemen involved with a deal, the higher the end price. If you're serious about the wholesale market, aim to buy from the original wholesaler.

A Word About Accents

I know you don't want to hear it from an Irishman, but Canadians talk funny. Seriously, the Canadian accent is recognizable in the US and as soon as the people you're dealing with realize you're not a local, they may test your market knowledge and try to make you pay extra. I saw this first hand when the Irish flocked to Eastern Europe for real estate deals. It wasn't long before it was widely known that someone with a foreign accent was offered one price while the local got another. To find a reputable wholesaler, ask around. Title companies, real estate agents, property managers and hard-money lenders are high on the list of people you need to meet, so get them to help you learn your way around a local market.

 SOLD

Trust but verify. Every property you look at is being marketed as a great deal. Run your own numbers because it's up to you to decide if they're realistic.

Deal Flow

Once you've established a working relationship with REO agents and wholesalers, don't just sit back. You need to stay in touch with these people and you can't expect them to be calling you. Proactive follow-up is key!

You can also expect to spend a fair bit of time reviewing deals, crunching the numbers on potential properties, inspecting homes and checking various market fundamentals. Like the diet and exercise prescribed in my opening anecdote, this kind of due diligence is what will keep your business on track for success.

In addition, new investors must steel themselves against the flood of emotions that comes on as deals come and go. With experience, you'll learn that potential deals are like windows of opportunity. Some open, some close and some slip through the cracks, but that's okay. Persistence pays off.

A Recipe for Success

Canadians interested in the US real estate market often ask me what experienced US investors are looking for when they buy property. Here's what one of my American market specialists tells me to watch for:

- three or four bedrooms with two baths
- block, brick or new construction
- priced below the median value for the area
- 1,200 to 2,000 square feet
- 1% marker with fair taxes and insurance
- starter-home neighborhood
- mixture of renters and owners
- easy-to-manage areas
- proximity to job sources
- tenants with replaceable income
- rents matching government rent rates (monthly mortgage payment within $200 of the rent rate if the home had been purchased at full market value by a first-time homebuyer)
- the ability to buy at a discount

Benefit From the 5 Profit Centers of Real Estate.

There's More Than One Way to Earn From Real Estate Investing

In real estate markets like this, it's easy for Canadians who want to invest in US distressed property to think they can skip over a few of the investment fundamentals. Easy? Perhaps, but misguided. And that's why I want to talk about profit centers.

A profit center is a source through which you generate a gain. Real estate has five profit centers. They are:

1. Natural appreciation

2. Forced appreciation

3. Positive cash flow

4. Mortgage reduction and leverage

5. Tax deductions

Investors who understand the profit centers of real estate optimize their ability to put different profit centers to work in their portfolios. The more you understand about how these profit centers work, the less likely you'll miss out on an opportunity to profit—or focus on one profit center when another one is better. A sound understanding of profit centers will also help you adopt and fine-tune exit strategies.

 SOLD

Most investments only have one or two profit centers. Stocks typically have a dividend component (periodic cash distribution) and a capital gain component. That's two profit centers. Real estate has five.

Natural Appreciation

Natural appreciation is often called market appreciation. It's the gradual inflation in real estate values over time. Some "hot" markets appreciate faster than others and some do not appreciate at all (but that's rare and usually speaks to other issues, like property degradation or a serious problem with location).

The rate of natural appreciation in Canadian residential real estate over the last 50 years has been just over 6% per year. This is a national average and many markets are above or below this. Still, it illustrates that real estate values generally rise over time.

The main factor driving this is inflation in the value of the land. While buildings depreciate over time, the value of the land increases. Research shows that land typically increases in value faster than the consumer price index (CPI) or general inflation in consumer goods. This makes land (and the property that sits on it) an excellent investment and hedge against inflation.

We also know that the purchasing power of money degrades over time, so having your money invested into an appreciating asset is a smart way to maintain and grow the purchasing power of your money.

 SOLD

Natural appreciation is an investor's dream when you're buying in a down market.

Forced Appreciation

Forced appreciation is one of the most powerful aspects of real estate. This is an increase in value that you create through upgrades and renovations. Forced appreciation is entirely within the property owner's control. Whereas natural appreciation speaks to market forces, forced appreciation is a way to increase the value of your property even during a down market or flat cycle.

But the potential for forced appreciation depends on buying the right property. This is a fundamental truism. If you've bought a brand-new penthouse condominium there may be nothing you can do to improve the property in the short term. The same holds for other "traditional" investments since you can't add a basement suite to your mutual fund and create extra value.

Interest in this profit center is why we hear about so many fix-and-flip investors. It's also why there are so many reality TV shows about renovations. While forced appreciation is an important profit center and can allow you to make a quick buck, a strategy that targets forced appreciation also keeps you from taking advantage of the other profit centers. This is short-term gain that sacrifices long-term wealth.

PROCEED WITH CAUTION!

Some Upgrades Are Better Than Others

Can't decide what to renovate, what to remove and what to repair? Is curb appeal worth more than a bathroom do-over? Will anyone notice an aging HVAC system? Do I have to rehab the roof just because the other rental properties on the street all have new roofs?

Slow down! There are smart ways to pursue forced appreciation. The fundamentals in Part 2 can keep your project on track and make sure your reno choices are designed to make you money.

Positive Cash Flow

As an advocate of the buy-and-hold property investment, positive cash flow is my favorite profit center. Positive cash flow is when my rental income exceeds all of my expenses and I have a cash surplus at the end of each month. If you want to be successful in the current US market for distressed properties, this is the situation you want to shoot for. Positive cash flow is the foundation of a recurring cash influx that will allow you to achieve financial freedom.

Investors who target cash-flow properties will accelerate their wealth. First you focus on buying enough properties to cover your monthly living expenses. Several of my US investing colleagues tell me that's their definition of financial freedom. But you don't stop there. Investors who keep investing in cash-flow properties will eventually have excess cash coming in—more than they can use for their living expenses. Many will take this extra cash and reinvest it into more real estate.

The potential is limitless, but never forget how the fundamentals make a deal work. Expect cash flow to be tight when you buy. If the deal is right, cash flow will increase over time as rents rise with inflation and incomes, but your mortgage stays relatively flat. As the gap between your rent and your mortgage widens, cash flow should increase.

Cash Flow Rocks!

The US market for distressed properties teems with opportunities to buy positive cash-flowing properties. Follow solid investment fundamentals. Buy the deal that works. Adopt an exit strategy that lets you take advantage of cash-flow profits. Hire capable management and keep an eye on the real estate cycle.

Mortgage Reduction and Leverage

When you buy a property and use the bank's money to finance it, this debt is eventually paid off. But it's not you who pays off the mortgage, it's the tenant! This makes a quality tenant the best business partner ever. They look after the place and pay your mortgage for you, but walk away with no financial interest in the property. If your mortgage is amortized over 25 years, then 25 years later you own the property with clear title. Although it is unlikely, the market could stay completely flat over this period and you could earn no cash flow. With mortgage reduction and leverage, however, you still wind up with a piece of real estate that you own at the end of it all.

Real estate, more so than a lot of other investments, also allows for advantaged leverage. If I walk into a bank and asked them to lend me $400,000 to invest in a business or buy shares in a corporation, they'd laugh at me and send me packing. I might be able to find a hard-money lender to lend it to me at a much higher interest rate. But if I walk into a bank and ask to borrow $400,000 to buy a $500,000 property, they're likely to play ball and lend the money to me at a good rate. With advantaged leverage, I put in $1 of my own money and earn a return on $5 because the bank puts in the extra $4.

Tax Deductions

A lot of people find tax and accounting a really dull subject. I love studying tax because that knowledge helps me keep more of the money I might otherwise have to pay to the government in taxes. The many ways to create tax benefits in real estate will be looked at more closely in Part 3. For now, I want to whet your appetite for good tax information. Did you know that

- Depreciation on the property structure can be used to shelter cash flow from tax?

- Interest on your mortgage is tax deductible?

- Renovation work that can be properly classified as "repairs" is subject to accelerated write-off?

- Chattels like appliances and window coverings can be depreciated more quickly and used to offset tax?

And why are tax deductions a profit center? It's because successful real estate investing isn't about the money you make, it's about the money you keep. And when you're calculating cash flow and profit, the money you save on an expense is the same as making more income.

 SOLD

A lot of investors are not interested in studying and understanding tax law. The smart ones counter that by making sure they hire an accountant who specializes in real estate. If you're getting into the US market, make sure your accountant understands cross-border issues. Ignorance won't save you from double taxation, but good planning will!

13

Be Wary of What a Full-Service Real Estate Investment Group Offers.

Stick to the Fundamentals to Sort the Good From the Bad

Full-service real estate investment groups can serve as a great stepping stone into the US foreclosure market, and Canadians who are testing the American investment waters will almost always come across at least one of the groups. I want to be clear. Full-service real estate groups have their place. But they're not all created equal and foreign investors need to do their due diligence before hooking up with a group that could spend their money without giving them anything in return!

Full-service real estate groups are generally made up of individuals with years of experience in the market. This can be especially good in the foreclosure market, as a good full-service group will already have relationships with local Real Estate Owned (REO) brokers, contractors, property managers, etc.

Canadians who don't want to invest on their own can leverage off a full-service team and find their way into the market with considerably less risk. The relationship can also lead to much more effective investing. Since the greatest risks in a foreclosure deal involve finding the right property, upgrading it the right way and getting it back on the market with a qualified tenant and good management in place, a good real estate group minimizes those risks. Their market knowledge translates into finding properties at deeper discounts and offering better pricing on property renovations and repairs. Ideally, they even connect you with a quality property manager and qualified tenant—all in the same deal.

If everything goes right, their service actually costs you nothing because the arrangement takes you from zero to cash-flow investing with speed. But let me be frank. The deal's success really hinges on whether they sell you the house at a fair price. There are great groups out there that will get you a solid turnkey investment property at a fair price. But there are also groups that will rip you off. The good full-service real estate groups can supply you a fairly priced property that is fully renovated and located in a good area with high rental demand. It will have equity and cash flow. The property should also be occupied by a qualified tenant and under a top-notch management group that has been tested and proven.

If this is the investment route you plan to take, be careful. Here are some general rules of thumb you can use to assess the quality of a full-service group.

Good Full-Service Real Estate Groups

As you work through your due diligence on a potential full-service group, you will see that quality groups

1. Usually handle a smaller volume of properties but focus on a quality product. Expect three to 10 houses a month with this quality versus quantity approach.

2. Focus on one market and one type of property. If they are buying single-family homes, they are not buying condominiumized apartments or vice versa.

3. Have been active in their market for years and own investment property in that market.

4. Are happy to have you visit the market and tour their business. They are also happy to supply information and answer questions.

5. Do full renovations to get the property into top shape, including the roof, heating/cooling, plumbing and electrical. They don't do "partial rehabs" to get the property back to a just barely rentable condition.

6. Steer away from bad neighborhoods. Even though they could make more money off their clients there, they are long-term players with integrity. They aim to make money and do right by their clients, so they shun the risks inherent in neighborhoods with high vacancy rates and criminal activity.

7. Have happy existing clients and make testimonials and references available.

8. Have property management that's been tested and proven. They have their own personal investment properties with this same management company.

9. Sell you properties that are occupied by a qualified tenant. That tenant has been fully screened by the property management company and the supporting paperwork can be made available for your review.

10. Provide a homebuyer's warranty on their properties and will go back and fix a repair if something in the renovation process was done incorrectly.

A good full-service company will sell you properties at a discount and with healthy cash flow.

Bad Full-Service Real Estate Groups

The worst thing about a bad full-service group is that they make their money by tricking investors into the market. They are all about the smoke and mirrors, at least until they have your money. The wise investor's response is to focus on due diligence. Commit to finding out if a company merits your business. Commit to walking away if you can't decide.

In general, the "bad guys"

1. Brag about doing big volumes of properties and may be doing more than 20 a month. That's a lot of activity in this market and it should lead you to ask a few questions about how they do it successfully.

2. Work several markets at a time and offer a wide variety of property types. They are probably making their "deals" on price, then finding someone to pass the property along to.

3. Are usually new to the market that they are selling you on. They lack local experience and they will not own any investment property in the area. This is huge! I would predict that this kind of full-service group does not plan to be in the market for very long. They want to take your money and run and we in Canada or the US would call them a "fly-by-night" operation!

4. Don't allow you to visit their market or discourage you from visiting. They are also wary of supplying the information you request. Questions may be deferred or ignored. This is bad news.

5. Are into what the US industry calls "partial rehabs." They may do some cosmetic work inside, but they'll try to tell you that curb appeal doesn't matter in this market. Bigger repairs like the roof, heating/cooling, plumbing and electrical will rarely be done. If you ask about this strategy, you'll get excuses, not any evidence the work wasn't required.

6. Tend to steer their clients into bad neighborhoods with a long history of drugs, prostitution and violence. This is how they buy properties so cheaply. No one wants to live there and the banks just want the properties off their books! That makes the price-motivated investor a sitting duck.

Do not let yourself be a foreign statistic for failure. Put investment fundamentals to work. They reduce investment risk and boost profit potential.

7. Don't have any existing clients available for references or testimonials. Remember your fundamentals. If a group refuses to answer your questions it's because you won't like the answers. Move on.

8. Might tell you they assign little importance to property management because "the tenant will take care of a lot of the details." Others have untested property managers in place. What? You value quality property management and market experience. This group offers neither.

9. Claim to be a full-service group but then try to sell you a vacant property. This defies the sound investment fundamentals that might lead you to work with a full-service group.

10. Do not offer any warranties or guarantees on the work they have done for you (or say they have done for you). Again, this is not a company you want to work with. Feel free to back away slowly, or run.

The Real World

Performing Due Diligence

*A Canadian Investor Delivers Full Disclosure
on How He Analyzes a Deal*

Drew Betts is a Canadian real estate investor who walks the talk of due diligence. He knows the US market for distressed property abounds with opportunities for foreign buyers with equity. He also knows that some of the "great opportunities" on the market spell nothing but trouble and that an extra-hot market demands extra due diligence from foreign buyers, not less!

Here's a close look at a pro-forma cash-flow statement and how Drew uses it to analyze a property to see if it belongs in his portfolio.

Cash-Flow Statement

In his days with a major accounting firm, Drew learned all about what he calls the pro-forma (forward-looking) cash-flow statement. It's a monthly statement of cash coming in and cash going out. Drew uses this statement to figure out if an investment property can make him money. "In real estate, cash is king and a healthy amount of positive cash flow is what we're looking for. Setting up a pro-forma cash-flow statement will help you to screen your properties and weed out the ones that cannot produce cash flow," explains Drew.

The reason novice real estate investors find cash-flow statements difficult is that they tend to make three errors that detract from the statement's validity. According to Drew, the three main errors market newbies tend to make include

1. Not obtaining accurate estimates of rental income

2. Not accounting for all expenses

3. Not budgeting monthly for annual expenses like insurance and property taxes

Monthly Pro-Forma Cash-Flow Statement	
INCOME	
Rental Income	
Less Vacancy Allowance	
Gross Effective Income	
EXPENSES	
Property Taxes	
Insurance	
Condo Fees	
Repairs & Maintenance Allowance	
Property Management	
Utilities	
Marketing	
Bookkeeping	
Total Expenses	
FINANCING	
1st Mortgage Payment	
Additional Debt Service	
Total Financing	
CASH FLOW	
Cash Flow	

On the plus side, every one of those mistakes can be fixed, says Drew. He urges investors to commit to a quality in/quality out approach. If you plan to make economic decisions on the basis of your pro-forma cash-flow statements, make sure the figures you enter are real, insists Drew. To counter the potential for errors and ensure the cash flow statement he uses to analyze a deal has solid information, Drew focuses on cash in (from rent and other income sources) and cash out (from operating and financing expenses).

Cash In: Keep It Real

The first line on the statement is for gross rental income. "This is the full amount of rent you expect to collect and it's pretty much the most important number to get right," says Drew. "Unfortunately, it's also the number most people get wrong!"

To remedy this situation, you need accurate information. Listen to a trusted real estate agent, talk to a property management company and research other properties for rent. Above all, don't think it's okay to guess at this number. As a foreign investor, you are looking for a good deal in the US market, not a good story about a Canadian getting burned.

While market research is essential, Drew never forgets where his information is coming from. "As an investor, you should be working with realtors who specialize in investment real estate. Stay away from the ones for homebuyers and jacks-of-all-trades," says Drew.

He also suggests that real estate investors only work with agents "who actually own and operate investment properties themselves," because these individuals are most likely to have a solid understanding of the rental market and to be better able to advise you on what amount of rent to expect.

He warns investors to be on the lookout for real estate agents who inflate prospective rental amounts. They're not necessarily dishonest, but they know investors are more likely to buy a property—and more likely to pay more for that property—when it looks like it will generate positive cash flow. This gives real estate agents an incentive to be very optimistic about rents and overestimate the actual numbers. It doesn't mean you shouldn't invite and consider their opinions; just keep this built-in bias in mind, warns Drew.

The same thing applies to rental data you get from property managers. "Property managers are excellent sources of rental data, especially if they operate large portfolios and rental properties on a daily basis. They will likely have the most accurate rental numbers on the market."

That experience aside, Drew says investors should realize that property managers have a vested interest in underestimating rents. They tend to be pessimistic and undershoot market rents because they know the property will rent more quickly and more easily if it's under the going market rates. Let's face it, property managers look good when places rent quickly.

The tendency to underestimate a going rental rate will cost the investor much more than it costs the property manager, warns Drew. Say market rent on a property is $1,700 and a property manager advises you to rent it for $1,500. When the property rents quickly, they get their fee faster. But both parties will lose. For example, if the property management fee is 10% of the rent, a $1,500-a-month property will earn the manager $150 a month instead of $170 a month. Over a year, that's a difference of $240. That same lowball rent estimate costs the investor $200 a month in rent, or $2,400 a year.

Drew has a solution. He gets rental estimates from real estate agents and property managers and averages them. This should help you zero in on an accurate number for the "cash in" line.

He recommends that investors look at the rents charged in comparable properties or "comps." This information can be found in the newspaper rentals section, through independent rental surveys and on rental websites. Drew browses these for information about properties currently for rent and finds ones similar to his. He cautions investors to remember to make sure the information is comparable. If you have a half-duplex for rent you'd look at other duplexes, not single-family homes or condos.

He also suggests keeping to similar neighborhoods and amenities to get the most accurate information. Remember, too, that you'll only be able to view "advertised rent." The actual rent after tenant negotiation may differ. This is still a solid source for rental data and Drew likes to find as many similar properties as he can and average their numbers.

Once he's got all this data, he uses the information to set a conservative number for his analytical cash-flow statement. And he always errs on the side of caution! If his real estate agent says $1,800, his property manager says $1,500, and your average from rental comparables is $1,675, "I'd be inclined to estimate somewhere from $1,600 to $1,650."

For this example we'll use $1,650. Enter this number in your budget under gross rental income.

Gross Effective Income: Net Rent

Gross effective income, income after you subtract an allowance for vacancy, is "net rent." "Stability of income is very important in real estate and you have to plan for vacancies before they happen," says Drew. If he was analyzing a deal based on a prospective rent of $1,650, he would subtract a monthly vacancy allowance to account for this. "You will typically take the prevailing vacancy rate for an area and double it to get your vacancy allowance. Vacancy statistics are available for virtually every city by searching online. I prefer to be on the conservative side of things, so I typically use 8% even if the market vacancy is very low," says Drew.

To calculate that monthly vacancy allowance, the investor multiplies his vacancy allowance by the gross rental income. If Drew is looking at $1,650 a month in rent, his vacancy allowance is $1,650 x 8%, or $132. This gets subtracted, netting $1,518 in gross effective rent. "This is what you expect to collect after vacancies, averaged monthly throughout the year," explains Drew.

Operating Expenses: Decisions Are in the Details

Operating expenses are line items that are incurred to run your investment property and investors who ignore or lowball these numbers are asking for trouble, says Drew. With experience as his teacher, his list of operating expenses includes some items that caught him by surprise in his early days of investing.

OPERATING EXPENSES

- Property taxes
- Insurance
- Condo fees
- Repairs and maintenance
- Property management
- Utilities
- Marketing expenses
- Accounting and bookkeeping fees

Property Taxes. Property taxes, if not included as part of your mortgage payment, are typically paid annually. "You need to be budgeting for them monthly, though," says Drew. "Let's say you do up your monthly cash-flow budget and it shows $100 in positive cash flow. You think, 'Great! Let's do this deal.' When you get to the end of the year and have to pay $1,700 in property taxes, however, your positive cash flow is actually cash negative."

Drew finds out how much the annual property taxes are when he analyzes the property. He gets this information from the listing real estate agent or owner, who should have a copy of last year's tax assessment, or the city tax department. "Keep in mind that property taxes are tied to the value of the property, so taxes in the current year could be more than the previous year's assessment if the city tax department determines that values have gone up," cautions Drew.

To deal with that uncertainty, he always includes a buffer for property tax inflation. If last year's taxes were $1,700, for example, and Drew figures property values have come up 10%, then he adds $170 to the estimated property tax amount.

Once he's determined the annual property tax estimate, he divides it by 12 to get a monthly amount and inputs that number into his budget. "With my properties I created a separate 'holding' bank account where I put these funds, segregated from the regular operating funds, until they are needed at the end of the year. This way my cash flow isn't distorted and it's much more predictable and stable throughout the year," explains Drew.

Insurance. As with property taxes, Drew is careful to work insurance costs into his pro-forma cash-flow statements. Drew contacts an insurance broker and obtains an estimate for insurance, then divides it by 12 to get a monthly amount and inputs that number into his budget.

Condo Fees. Investors who own a condo, or a home in a community that has a condo association, will also have monthly fees to pay. Drew's focus on due diligence makes budgeting accuracy a priority, so he always includes these fees in his budgets if they're applicable.

Repairs and Maintenance. Common sense tells us that properties degrade over time, with big items like roofs needing to be replaced every 20 years or so. "Our monthly budget needs to reflect this," says Drew. "Instead of waiting for the roof to go and all of a sudden needing to come up with $15,000, we budget for it in monthly chunks put into a reserve or contingency account." He figures 5% of gross rent is a good number to put in reserve and says investors can adjust this upwards "for older properties that require more upkeep. Keep in mind that you should be putting aside this money even in months where you don't incur any actual expenses. You save this up in advance so it's sitting there when you need it. This way you're running your investment property like a self-contained business, rather than mixing it up with your personal finances."

Property Management. Most property managers for residential properties charge 10% of gross rent and some investors try to save this cost by self-managing. Drew recommends "budgeting for property management even if you intend to manage [the property] yourself. What happens if you want to go on a vacation, if you retire or if you get tired of managing it and want to have the budget to hire a manager?" questions Drew. "Your time has value and you need to account for it."

Making this calculation part of your initial deal analysis ensures the property can support management fees before they're an issue.

Utilities. Drew admits to having made a few mistakes in this area when first investing in real estate. While the tenant usually pays for hydro, heat and phone charges, often water, sewer and garbage pickup are another matter. The owner also has to pay these charges when the property is vacant. "If a property is vacant and you're in an area that is cold, you need to leave the heat on to keep the pipes from freezing. This can be a significant unanticipated expense if you didn't include this in your budget," notes Drew.

To get accurate information about utilities fees, Drew asks the owner of the property for access to past utilities statements.

Marketing Expenses. Because these expenses affect the accuracy of his cash-flow situation, Drew doesn't wait until a lease comes up or the property is vacant to budget for things like law signs, online advertising and print ads. Instead, he budgets monthly for this as well. "This amount can vary a lot depending on what your marketing strategy is, but I put $25 a month into this so I ensure I have a sizable budget to fill any possible vacancy. The cost of one month's vacancy in terms of lost rental income is far, far greater than $25 saved up per month to ensure the chance of a vacancy is minimized."

Accounting and Bookkeeping Fees. Owning an investment property requires additional tax filing at the end of the year. During the year, you'll likely also want to have a bookkeeper in place to take care of the financials. Drew targets around $50 a month.

Financing

The final component of Drew's budget is financing. He encourages investors to talk to their mortgage broker, who should be able to tell them well in advance of purchasing a property what the expected mortgage payment will be. Drew plugs this number into the first mortgage section of his analysis statement. If you are using additional financing, such as a line of credit, to fund the down payment or a second mortgage, put this into the Additional Debt Service section.

And the Final Number Is . . .

With all of these numbers in place, Drew's ready to determine his monthly cash-flow estimate. To do that, he takes the Gross Effective Income number and subtracts Operating Expenses and Financing. This leaves him with his expected monthly cash-flow amount.

"If this number is still positive and healthy after all of your reserves and conservative estimates, then you have yourself a solid acquisition opportunity," says Drew.

Checklist for Entering US Real Estate Markets

Review What You Know About the US Distressed Property Market

What good are fundamentals you "know about" but don't put into action? Use this checklist to focus your property quest and acquisitions.

I've Researched My Market.

My due diligence includes

- ☐ People I've talked to
- ☐ Local websites I've researched

General websites: city website, chamber of commerce, real estate investors' associations

Real estate websites: realtor.com, zillow.com, realquest.com (paid site), mls.com (paid site for licensed real estate agents), nearbuyclassifieds.com, rentometer.com

I Know What's Happening With the 5 Key Market Drivers.

- ☐ Supply and demand
- ☐ Affordability
- ☐ Desirability
- ☐ Population growth
- ☐ Economic growth

I've Got Realistic Property Values From Reputable Comparable Sources.

- ☐ I've talked to at least two real estate agents/brokers
- ☐ I've got comparables and current or active listings

I've Taken Steps to Put the Right People on My Team.

Screening includes

- ☐ Experience/track record
- ☐ Testimonials/references from other investors
- ☐ Asking them about their own investment properties
- ☐ I've created my own expectations list
- ☐ I have a plan of action if those expectations aren't met

I Created a Relationship With a Top-Producing Real Estate Agent/Broker.

They are

- ☐ An investor specialist
- ☐ Currently investing themselves (versus only having sales experience)
- ☐ An REO/foreclosure specialist (this is a plus)

My Fundamentals Value Quality Property Management.

My prospective managers know

- ☐ Local vacancy rates and average days on market
- ☐ The size of portfolio they currently manage and the vacancy rate of that portfolio (many experienced investors want 100 units minimum.)
- ☐ Whether they will handle maintenance in-house or subcontract to outside contractors

They

- ☐ Are managing in the submarkets I want to invest in
- ☐ Have fees within industry norms (industry standards range from 8% to 14% of collected rents, plus a placement fee of half a month's rent)

I have

- ☐ Reviewed lease and management agreement contracts and asked a lot of questions
- ☐ Factored in 25% in contingencies of gross rents (management fees, vacancy rate, ongoing maintenance or repairs)

I Know My Renovation/Construction Costs.

- ☐ My budget spreadsheets were based on national average pricing
- ☐ I'm getting good information from general contractors
- ☐ I know that industry standards for general contractors run 20% to 25% margins, plus materials

☐ I check out sites like homedepot.com to compare prices
☐ I always get three bids

I Am Committed to Understanding the Tax Consequences of My Decisions.

I understand that I need a cross-country legal and tax specialist to help me

☐ Determine entity structures
☐ Set up US bank accounts
☐ Make sure I'm not paying more tax than I should
☐ Avoid double taxation

I Crunched My Numbers. I Crunched Them Again.

☐ I know that I need to keep it real. This is my money

I Visited the Market Before I Bought.

☐ My plane ticket is an investment in my real estate portfolio

Be the Master of Your Ship

As part of your due diligence, I encourage Canadian investors to look at their deals through the eyes of a skeptic. One of the best ways to do this is to ask the same tough questions you'd ask another investor. Here are some of the questions you might consider, and the answers a smart investor would give.

Q. *Are you going to allow someone to sell you a property just because it's a cheap price and has the potential for high rent returns?*

A. No! I'm going to look at what the overall market is like in that area. I'll find out what this neighborhood is like in particular. I will investigate the property's condition to make sure it's worth renovating.

Q. *Are you going to make an emotional decision because the house is new and pretty?*

A. Again, no. I want to know if there is rental demand, if there's cash flow and if the market has strong fundamentals.

Q. *Are you about to let the person who's selling you a fixer-upper quote on the property upgrade and tell you what work is needed?*

A. No way! I do my own research. (And I don't ask the barber if I need a haircut, either!)

Q. *Are you going to buy a house now and find property management later?*

A. No. I've done the opposite. Money follows management. I've got a property manager who knows my market and can meet my expectations.

Q. *Have you been crunching the numbers and building your team even before you've acquired a deal?*

A. Yes, because that's how smart investors work.

 KNOW HOW TO CRUNCH THE NUMBERS THAT COUNT

A good deal is only a good deal if the numbers work! Once you know your exit strategy, plug in the numbers to see if a prospective deal makes sense.

Buy and Hold

purchase price + closing costs + initial repairs = total investment

rents − debt service (mortgage, taxes, insurance) − 25% gross rents (contingency for repairs management & vacancy) = monthly cash flow

Fix and Flip

purchase price + closings + initial repairs = total investment

resale price − purchase price − repair costs − closing costs (both on purchase and resale) − holding costs (any interest, fees paid on money that funded the deal) − real estate commissions = profit

Renovations and Management

*"Success is not about just creating more
of the good days, but rather learning
how to handle the crap days."*

—Philip McKernan

The best real estate investment advice comes from the people who invest in real estate—that's why I went to Brian Scrone for help with Part 2. Brian is a public speaker, trainer and real estate investor whose expertise in the US buy-and-hold real estate market delivers the hands-on renovation experience that Canadian real estate investors can put to work as they aim to capitalize on this market.

Work Smartly With Contractors and Subcontractors.

Getting the Best in Terms of Time, Money and Quality Work

If you buy US residential real estate property that needs any kind of renovation or repair (often called a "rehab" in the US), you will need to work with contractors and subcontractors. If you are already doing this kind of investing in Canada, you probably already know a lot of the information we're going to cover here. Resist the temptation to skip this section! When it comes to making money from a residential real estate investment, this is one area where a significant amount of money can be made or lost very easily. Never presume you can't learn something new about the investor–contractor relationship or be reminded about something you could be doing better.

And that comment leads me right into a discussion about the value of a positive attitude. A good working relationship with your contractor will keep your renovation and repair projects on time and on budget. The right attitude is also an essential part of making sure you finish with a quality product. But this relationship is a two-way street. When time, money or quality is compromised by a won't-do attitude, your investment is at risk and a great deal can morph very quickly into a bad deal.

 SOLD

Your contractor needs to have a positive attitude, too! Where time, money or quality considerations aren't meeting your expectations, rethink your choice of contractor. When those three expectations are met, you probably have a contractor with the right attitude and by default you'll get a great job. If the relationship's working, let your contractor know. If the relationship's not working, cut your losses.

5 Common-Sense Rules

The five common-sense rules in dealing with contractors and subcontractors are designed to keep a project on time and on budget so that a quality job or product improves your investment. These five rules come from an investor who's dealt with literally dozens upon dozens of contractors on hundreds of jobs over more than a decade in the real estate investment business. Read them. Think about them and always remember: in the business world, as in life, common sense isn't all that common. But the people who try to circumvent these five rules are asking for a lot of unnecessary headaches.

1. Assume the Role of the Pack Leader.

Recognize that being the pack leader does not mean showing up to the job site and screaming or being overly aggressive about what you want done (and when you want it done). It does mean that you need to deal with situations as soon as you can when you see, or even suspect, that any of your expectations are not met.

This must be done in a calm and assertive manner—and the items you discuss should be positive and negative. When things look great on the job, offer praise. When things are not being done correctly on the job, ask for a resolution.

Once you develop this kind of honest communication with your general contractors, they will understand that any questions you ask are fair in the context of your relationship with them. And what kind of relationship is it? It's business, all business.

The way you communicate with your general contractors will affect how those individuals manage and communicate with their subs and labor on the job. That is a definite bonus and it should be good news to your bottom line and to the bottom line of the general contractor as well. In the end, clear expectations of everyone involved in a property upgrade increases the likelihood that everyone will make money.

 SOLD

As pack leader, you must also take responsibility for making sure the proper permits are pulled when necessary and on all jobs. City or county inspectors may fine you and the general contractor if you're caught doing unpermitted work. As the property owner, you could also find yourself having to pay to "undo" unpermitted work. In a competitive renovation and rehab market, you must consider as well that the contractors you didn't hire may think they have a vested interest in sinking your investment ship.

When work is permitted, a city or county inspector will come out and give a final inspection. They will pass or fail the work that's been done, thus providing you with a valuable guarantee that the work has been done correctly.

In the legal section of this book, you'll get a better look at why real estate investors working in the United States must consider how every aspect of their operation reinforces or weakens their comprehensive asset protection plan. From this perspective, a city or county work permit is one more investment fundamental—one more way to show a potential litigant that you did your due diligence.

---

2. Communicate. Communicate. Communicate. And Then Get It in Writing!

Bad things happen when people do not take the time to make sure that everyone involved with a renovation or repair project knows what's expected. Communication is key. Make it a point to be redundant. Your end goal is to make sure your contractor knows exactly what you expect on each and every job.

You also want to make sure you have one point of contact, one go-to person, for each job. This is usually the general contractor, since he's the one you're paying. A single point of contact helps avoid any breakdowns in communication.

Always get what you want in writing, too. This is important even if you have worked with the same contractor for many years. Skip the guesswork and ensure details are written down. Begin each project with a formal proposal or bid and make sure the scope of the work that you expect to be done is recorded and can be reviewed.

Never leave the details to a contractor's discretion. No two sets of eyes see a job the same way and you do not want to be disappointed when someone guesses what you wanted and gets it wrong.

 SOLD

Avoid the complications and potential costs of a he said/she said situation. A written scope of work is essential. It can be used to track work done and, where necessary, job amendments.

3. Pay What the Job Is Worth.

Investors who try to nickel-and-dime their contractors will live to pay the piper, as this is a save-now-and-pay-later strategy that will bite you in the bank account! Worse yet, this approach works both ways: if you try to cut corners on your contractors and their bids, it is guaranteed they will also cut corners that affect the quality of your job.

When it comes to budgets and estimates, be proactive and realistic. If you have done your cost estimates and you know it's a $25,000 job, don't expect to get it done for $18,000. Real estate investors who think they've gotten away with a lowball contract should be especially wary of what's really going on. Are you prepared to pay a stingy price today in return for having to pay to fix the problem later? Because that's what will happen after a tenant moves in and finds the problem. It's also a problem on resale. You may have to improve the property, or cut your asking price, before you can sell it.

If you are in the business of fixing up properties to operate as investments, you need to find quality contractors you can work with. But they need to be able to work with you, too. It is more efficient, economical and effective to get a job done right the first time.

 SOLD

Smart real estate investors build sustainable relationships with general contractors and subcontractors who do quality work. If you treat them the way you want to be treated, they will reward you by helping you make money. Always remember that, just like you, your contractors have bills and families to feed. The more turnover you have with contractors and the more contractors you have to hire and fire, the less time you spend marketing your real estate properties. That's going to cost you.

4. Know What Volume Can Buy You.

The property upgrade market in the United States offers some good opportunities for price discounts based on volume. The more volume you do with a vendor or associate, the better pricing you can and should expect on your jobs.

The industry standard is 25% margins of profit for general contractors in the single-family home renovation or rehab niche. Once you get to a point where you are doing more than five rehabs at a time, you should start to negotiate pricing discounts with the general contractors you are working with on those jobs.

Your goal is not to take advantage of a contractor, but to give both of you an opportunity to realize discounts for volume buys in materials, for example. Always shop for deals and ask your general contractor to do the same. In reality, no one cares about your money the way you do. But talking about the discounts you've come across is a good way to remind your contractor that you're watching the market and you expect him to do the same. In the end, a couple hundred dollars saved on each job adds up very quickly when you start to do volume.

One savvy investor says he keeps a close eye on the industry and is confident that a 12% to 15% profit margin is fair in the context of how much work he gives his general contractors and their subs. In fact, he talks about this openly with all of his general contractors and they agree with his position. What does this look like in the context of a job? If the contractor is looking at $10,000 in materials, labor and permits, the investor figures the bid should come in at around $11,500 for the total job, including materials, permits and labor.

He says his contractor would rather make a little less on each job but know he is guaranteed more work in the future as long as the investor's expectations are met on the current job. Again, it always goes back to relationships.

This kind of open communication acknowledges that the investor knows he's not the only one negotiating costs. He negotiates costs with the general contractors who do volume work for his business, but he knows they are also negotiating with their suppliers. In the end, it's the trickle-down theory at work and all parties need to seek win-win relationships.

5. Without Options, You Have NO Power. Always Get 3 Bids on Every Job!

This fundamental cannot be stressed enough! One of my contributors tells me that he learned this from one of his mentors many years ago and he's been reaping the benefits ever since. The basic premise is simple: With options, you can bargain from a position of power. Without options, you have nothing to negotiate with!

Apply this concept to the bid process and you can see why it is imperative to always get three bids on any major rehab you plan to undertake. Always use common sense here. When you need something like a $30 light replaced on a rental property, the process of seeking three bids is not efficient or effective. Keep in mind that your time is valuable and the work you have to do to save $5 on a $30 light is not worth it.

As a general rule of thumb, seek three bids on any job over $300. The property managers that work with one of my contributors get two or three bids on any work over $250. In fact, that strategy is stipulated in writing in the management agreement.

The key point here is that any significant property repair or upgrade should be shopped around for pricing. This also helps you maintain a healthy spirit of competition among your general contractors.

In the end, three bids are always better than two but remember to schedule your contractor bid meetings so that you don't have three general contractors pull up at your front door at the same time.

Don't Confuse Apples With Oranges

When you are comparing bids, check the quality of materials each general contractor plans to use. A lowball price is no good to you if it is based on substandard materials. This is a particular concern if you are getting bids on one of the Big 4 renovation items I'll address in Fundamental #17.

The nuance-filled bid process is one area where your relationship with quality contractors can make or break your investment deal, so ask lots of questions. For example, if one contractor recommends a 2.5-ton air conditioning system with no warranty and another bid features a 3-ton system with a warranty, you can expect a bid price difference. If there isn't one, find out why.

 SOLD

The cheapest bid is not always the way to go! Always check the references of prior jobs and take the time to inspect the previous work of a general contractor who's bidding on your job if he's never worked for you before.

You can also check county records or visit the Better Business Bureau website (www.bbb.org) to see if the general contractor has any complaints against him or her from previous clients.

15

Weigh Reno Needs Versus Nice-to-Haves.

Kitchens and Bathrooms Are a Reno Priority

You can move walls, paint, upgrade the flooring, enhance curb appeal and make sure the HVAC (heating and air conditioning), roof, plumbing and electrical systems are in dependable working order, but that might not seal the deal. Industry research shows that when it comes to making a sale or signing a rental contract, buyers and renters are predisposed to take a special look at two of the places they plan on spending a great deal of time: the kitchen and the bathrooms.

Other than replacing or repairing the Big 4, which is the topic of Fundamental #17, the real estate investor will likely spend most of the money in her budget on the kitchen. And that strategy is a good one. You'll sell or rent a house quickly if you've properly rehabbed the kitchen.

The Kitchen: Put the 3 *E*'s to Work

Every renovation project must be efficient, effective and economical. The three *e*'s are even more important when you are renovating a house as a business investment, since every extra day a house spends on the market has the potential to cost you money.

But where do you begin with a kitchen remodel? My US foreclosure market experts tell me new and updated flooring (tile or hardwood), paint and lights or chandeliers are a must for every kitchen remodel. In terms of efficiency and knowing where to start, these are your top picks. Zeroing in on these items also makes your project more effective, since these are among the first things a potential buyer or renter will notice.

Once you have a plan to improve those items, you have to decide whether you are going to demolish the cabinets and countertops or refurbish the existing materials. If you're not careful, cabinets and countertops can wreak serious havoc on your rehab budget.

Your Exit Strategy Defines Your Actions

Approach this part of the project with care—and good advice. Many older cabinets can be salvaged and refurbished to look new, but a cabinet and counter rehab is one area where your knowledge of your potential buyer must come into play.

Experienced investors in the US foreclosure market tell me that if their exit strategy is to buy and hold the property for long-term appreciation and current cash flow, and they don't need to gut and replace the whole kitchen, they always make sure the property goes onto the rental market with the cabinets freshly repainted and all hardware and handles replaced with new product. They will also lay new granite tile over the existing dated counter-tops and have a new backsplash installed.

 SOLD

Granite tile and new backsplashes are an investment in fewer future maintenance hassles.

Where they plan to flip a property, usually to a first-time homebuyer as a retail sale of a foreclosed-and-rehabbed property, they will spend considerably more time and money. Here, they will demo and replace the existing cabinets and counters with new cabinets and new solid-surface granite countertops and a stone backsplash.

They will also install new stainless steel appliances, including a stove with a hood vent/exhaust fan, a fridge and a dishwasher. If the property is to be rented out, they will still replace old appliances (unless they are clean and relatively new), but this time they will opt for a brand-new white stove and fridge (white appliances look great but are more cost effective than the stainless steel options). In a rental property, they'll look at whether the niche market and price point demand a dishwasher.

 SOLD

Pay keen attention to what is considered a "standard product" in the market you're entering. You will need to match or slightly upgrade your product to be competitive, but there may be nothing to gain from top-end additions. In many rental markets, a dishwasher is an extra, not a must-have.

What About the Floor Plan?

In addition to considering the cabinets, countertops and appliances, investors must look at whether they can improve a kitchen floor plan. An open floor plan kitchen is very desirable in contemporary markets and my US real estate insiders say they will remove an existing wall to open a kitchen up and make it appear bigger.

This can be a significant budget item if the wall you want to move is weight bearing (structural). In that case, you cannot remove the entire wall because it is supporting the weight and integrity of the roof. But you can partially open this wall with a pass-through arch or by creating a custom bar top. These can increase the kitchen's functionality and improve the space's aesthetics, often by adding the illusion of more space.

On projects where you do add a bar or an extra sitting area, always match the granite countertops to the bar top that you add. That might seem like a minor detail, but when these two counters do not match, it detracts from the overall impact of the changes you've made.

Let the Light Shine In

Also look for ways to add natural light to a kitchen. Where there is a double sliding glass door or an exterior door in or near the kitchen, my experts tell me it's a good idea to replace the sliders with new French doors or replace the exterior door with a glass door.

Always consider replacing outdated kitchen windows with new windows. Where possible, it also makes sense to add an extra window to an existing wall.

 SOLD

Anytime you add more natural light to an interior space, you make the space brighter and you make it appear larger. Since kitchens are a flash point for a renovation's success or failure, look for ways to augment the space's attractiveness with natural light.

Bathrooms

When it comes to must-have renovations, bathrooms are right behind kitchens in terms of their priority. Once again, investors should expect a good portion of their renovation budget to be spent on the bathrooms and they will need to make their choices based on what is efficient, effective and economical in terms of their exit strategy.

As your main goal with a foreclosure or renovation project will be rental or resale, investors must take a serious look at bathroom enhancements because buyers and renters will check out a home's bathrooms right after they've assessed its newly remodeled kitchen. Therefore, one of the first things you must consider when buying a foreclosure or reno project is the number of bathrooms. Experienced US investors tell me they will not buy a foreclosure or rehab project unless it has at least one full bath and one half-bath they can easily convert for marketability into a full second bathroom.

While market demographics must be considered, I urge you to think of the number of bathrooms as a key selling and renting feature in every market. A three-bedroom, two-bathroom home is always more desirable than a three-bedroom home with a one-and-a-half-bath or a three-bedroom home with one bath.

A lot of the foreclosures one of my investor colleagues buys in the US have three bedrooms with one bath or three bedrooms with one-and-a-half baths. In both cases, during the rehab he converts the properties to two full baths.

Finding the space to add a bathroom is easier than you might think. Many floor plans already have a half-bath, usually in the common space or a hallway. He simply adds a shower/tub unit to the half-bath, which is a relatively easy conversion because the plumbing is already there.

PROCEED WITH CAUTION!

The lack of a second bathroom in a property can stop a real estate investment deal in its tracks. If there is no space to add an extra bathroom, the property had better have some other great features before you jump in and buy. Always think functionality. Will the people who live there need a second bathroom? If it's a three-bedroom home, the answer is pretty obvious.

When it comes to adding a bathroom, a little creativity goes a long way. For example, if the existing floor plan is a three-bedroom, one-and-a-half bath arrangement and the half-bath is in the master suite, think about moving a wall to make the master bath into a full bath. You might lose some closet space—but your buyer or renter may never notice because they'll be so darn happy to have the extra bathroom!

Your goal as an investor is to think about what will quickly sell the home. There is no magic formula, but your buyers and renters will be looking at functionality. And when it comes to adding an extra bathroom, that functionality is a common-sense proposition.

SOLD

To reiterate, every remodeling project should be efficient, effective and economical. When you're deciding which budget items to keep or toss, think about your market and what will really sell a home to a buyer or renter. Kitchen and bathroom makeovers are essential.

16

Dial Up the Intellect (Dial Down the Emotions).

This House Was Made for Renting

There is a little saying in the real estate investment business that goes something like this: check your emotions at the door. One of the cardinal mistakes my contributors and I see real estate investors making time and again is unconsciously bringing emotion into the decision-making process when they are deciding what they need to do to buy or sell a property. We can guarantee you that those who bring emotions into investment decisions will make poor choices. They also will pay dearly for that mistake.

To be clear, we are not talking about restraining your enthusiasm for your work! Enthusiasm is great and I think people should be enthusiastic about investing in US residential real estate. When I recommend investors be "consciously emotional," I am referring to the need to be crystal clear that the decisions you make regarding improvements to an investment property should never be confused with the decisions you might make about upgrading a personal residence. (This is a great place to review the previous real estate investing fundamental—about recognizing the differences between a renovation need and a renovation nice-to-have.)

 SOLD

Some real estate investors struggle with what I call the "working difference" between emotion and passion.

Being *genuinely enthusiastic* about real estate investing means you leave a deal talking about the next one. You take a healthy pride in a job well done, a deal well executed. When things go well, you celebrate the fundamentals of your investment system and move on. When things go astray, you step up to the plate, deal with the problems and move on.

When *emotions* get in the way of a sound investment decision, an investor will find himself sentimentally caught up in the details of a deal. You will have very strong feelings about why certain aspects of the deal will work and those feelings will make you second-guess the need to check your fundamentals. When problems arise after your emotional investment decision, you will be disappointed and will want to look for someone else to blame. Here are some examples of what emotional investing might look like in action:

- A naïve investor is so star-struck by a master bathroom and powder room retrofit that she misses asking important questions about the overall plumbing. She mistakenly credits the upgrade in her offering price and, after the deal is complete, finds herself financially responsible for a major retrofit of the property's copper pipes.

- An investor who's also renting falls in love with a foreclosure property he tours. (This can be an especially costly mistake for foreign investors who let their appreciation for sun and palm trees get in the way of their investment fundamentals.) Because he *thinks* he can picture himself living in a particular neighborhood and on a particular street, he ignores the reality of that neighborhood's rental pool demographic. He pays more than he should and can't find a renter for a monthly rate that will make his bad deal work.

- An investor gets so excited about a discounted price that he throws caution to the wind and makes a cash deal. It turns out that the property needs major work. The neighborhood is rife with crime and the only people who want to rent a home there are the people who won't pay the rent! In return for ignoring his real estate foreclosure investment fundamentals, this investor is impaled on a very sharp financial hook. He feels as though he was lied to. In reality, he forgot to look for the truth.

How Much to Spend

One of the first things you need to remember is that financial decisions about how to upgrade a property range from inexpensive to over-the-top. I sometimes watch the Home & Garden Television network (HGTV) to get ideas for my renos. These shows also remind me that many of the decisions to be made are highly subjective, especially when you're improving a single-family home.

I've seen episodes, for example, where a general contractor spends $25,000 to landscape a front yard. These yards look great, but I am remodeling entire homes, including the landscape, for the same amount of money or less. Similarly, Italian marble countertops, imported French doors, limited-edition Swiss cabinets and Sub-Zero stainless appliances would look fabulous in a $100,000 rental home. But my choices should be driven by the financial reality of what I am trying to do. While I could easily spend $25,000 upgrading just a kitchen, I can also complete a functional kitchen and get an entire home ready for quality tenants to move in for the same $25,000 budget. Which option will help me make money? That is what I need to be enthusiastic about!

Exit Strategy

To keep emotions out of the equation, always keep in mind your exit strategy (sale or rental) and what price point in the market you are competing with. This will help you keep your upgrades in line. You also need to know the type of materials that are standard for that product or neighborhood. Again, this will help you keep your project's finances under control.

If you're still not sure about the differences between emotional decision-making and investing with passion, consider this: As a real estate investor, your goal should be to take one of the worst homes on the block and make it the best on that block every time. You want a functional, newly remodeled home with great curb appeal that someone in your target market will be thrilled to move into and take care of. Always remember that your investments are not homes you would necessarily move into.

 SOLD

Nothing increases enthusiasm for investing like staying on budget for a renovation or repair. Sure, you can install a high-end chic kitchen and sell a property more quickly, but if you don't make money on the deal you haven't met your investment goal. (Assuming you have one, of course.)

Look Around. Ask Around.

Experienced investors know it's okay to talk to general contractors and real estate professionals about what they should and should not do with a property upgrade. New investors should adopt the same strategy. Remember when we talked in the fundamental (#14) that dealt with contractors about the win-win scenario because everyone involved with a property rehab should be making money? Rest assured that experienced contractors and real estate agents put the same principle to work in their businesses. In other words, they know that a good real estate investor can help them make money, too.

Do the Big 4 Renos on a Rental Property—Now.

Pay Now or You'll Pay Later

Now that we've gone over the differences between needs versus nice-to-haves and the importance of checking our emotions, let's zero in on what I like to call the Big 4: heating and cooling systems, roofs, plumbing and electrical. As far as I'm concerned, you can either do the Big 4 right away or pay a lot more to have them done later.

Before we get into the specifics of the Big 4 I want to quickly reiterate the pay now/pay later rule of thumb, because it has obvious implications for virtually every aspect of the renovation process. What I want you to think about here is the idea that more than money is at stake. As Warren Buffett likes to say:

> *"It takes twenty years to build a reputation and five minutes to ruin it. If you think about that, you will do things differently."*

This applies to the point I am trying to make with this real estate fundamental: the renovation decisions you make will have long-term effects on your investment. Those who go for the quick fix when doing a property rehab are playing with fire. The quick fix may lead to a quick buck early in your investment career, but the investors, brokers, contractors, lenders and property buyers you need to make your real estate investment ventures a success over the long term will not stick with your team if you've got a reputation for sacrificing quality for speed. Good news travels fast. Bad news travels faster.

Make Sustainability a Fundamental Priority

One of my US investor colleagues insists that "sustainability should always be the underlying fundamental when making decisions about how to handle a renovation. Whether your exit strategy is selling retail or a long-term buy-and-hold rental property, always—I repeat, always—do what needs to be done up front to get the job done right on a reno."

And never forget what's really at stake. If you cut corners on the initial property upgrade, you will either have an upset buyer or renter, a property that sits unsold or unrented, a devastated reputation, or a wickedly unhealthy combination of all of the above.

PROCEED WITH CAUTION!

Be Honest About What a Property Needs

If you are buying bank foreclosures at deep discounts, you can expect that property will need a complete reno nearly 100% of the time. Factor that knowledge into your business strategy.

The Big 4

After doing hundreds of renos that were resold or held in rental portfolios, my real estate renovation insiders have convinced me that investors in the US foreclosure market have got to zero in on the Big 4. This means replacing or repairing the property's heating and cooling systems, roof, plumbing and electrical systems virtually every time you add a new foreclosure property to your portfolio.

If you have ever owned or rented a home, you probably already know that these four items are usually the source of most of the problem calls from or to your property manager, landlord or tenant. This happens because a lot of investors will try to deal with the Big 4 by doing only minimal repairs. They take a band-aid approach because their initial renovation and repair budget did not make these four areas a priority, or they spent too much on the property itself and are now trying to squeeze a profit from a bad deal.

Always remember what's really at stake: your reputation and potentially your relationships with members of your investment team. (Not only is the US foreclosure market not nearly as big as some foreign investors think, it's also a market niche within specific geographic areas. In other words, your reputation will haunt you.)

SOLD

Avoid being shocked by Big 4 repairs and replacements by factoring these costs into your investment plan up front. Then learn to take quick responsibility for your mistakes. If you've missed something in your initial renovation budget, deal with the mistake and accept that it will cost you. Savvy investors know they make their money when they buy, so as long as you buy at the right price (with the right reno budget figures included), a renovation surprise should not consume your entire profit because it will probably be a cosmetic item versus something from the Big 4 list.

Heating and Cooling Systems

In many parts of Canada, residents can enjoy summer temperatures without ever feeling the need for an air conditioner. In Nevada, Arizona, Florida and California, states with some of the highest foreclosure rates in the US, residential air conditioning is a fact of life!

In America, heating and cooling systems have an average life span of 10 to 12 years. Be realistic. If you are buying a property that's a bank foreclosure, it's likely the system was not properly taken care of or maintained by the property's previous owner or resident. One of the biggest problems is also painfully simple to solve: research shows tenants and property owners do not change out air filters every 90 to 120 days, the time span typically recommended, depending on the system. These filters literally cost $2 to $5. But because the air handler is in a closet (out of sight, out of mind), these filters are rarely changed out and often are not replaced for years. This basic lack of maintenance will destroy a system very quickly and can lead to a situation where the system must be replaced far earlier than the expected end of its life span.

Given the potential for this expense to cut into his profit margins, one of my American real estate investor friends follows a specific rule in his approach to the heating and cooling systems. When he buys a property that needs to be rehabbed and the heating and cooling system doesn't have at least five years of life left to it (the manufacture date is usually on the handler and condenser), he will plan to replace the entire system and include that cost in his budget. If the system has five years of life to it, he will, at minimum, plan to have the air handler and the condenser cleaned and serviced. He wants to make sure the system is working properly before he markets the home.

TIP

If you are going to buy and hold rental property, have your general contractor place six new filters in the house and let your tenant know it is their responsibility to change the filter every three months. Write that into your rental agreement with the tenants.

Roofs

North and south of the Canadian border, roofs are generally the most expensive item to replace on a typical investment property rehab. Apply the same five-year life-span rule used with the heating and cooling system to the roof. If the existing roof doesn't have at least five years of life left and shows signs of water damage on the interior ceilings, replace the entire roof.

If your roofer tells you there is five years of life left to the existing roof, have him inspect and seal or patch as necessary. In this scenario, always get a two-year roof certification, which will either guarantee his work or guarantee that the roof will not leak for two years.

TIP

A typical roof cert., which certifies the usual 25-year shingle roof, will cost you approximately $250. Manufacturers generally warrantee the material for the life of the shingle and the roofer will warrantee his labor for two years.

Plumbing

Many foreclosed homes, especially if they are 30 years old or older, will have the original copper plumbing throughout the house. Given the degradation that happens with these pipes, these homes will require a complete re-plumb of the hot and cold lines. Ignore this issue and you will pay later: ongoing plumbing issues are probably the No. 1 expense in rental property.

To alleviate a lot of this expense, experienced real estate investors in the US foreclosure market tell me they always factor in a complete house re-plumb during the initial renovation. This entails removing all of the original copper lines in the kitchen, baths and utility rooms, and replacing them with CPVC. This is a plastic plumbing material that is non-porous and does not corrode or rust like copper. This material is used in all new construction homes in the States.

TIP

If you plan to invest in the US foreclosure market, make plumbing retrofits a priority. If that doesn't work with the deal you're trying to make, you've got the wrong deal!

Electrical Systems

Again, this fundamental often applies to investment properties on both sides of the border, so Canadians shouldn't act like this is something new. Generally speaking, in any home 30 years old or older that's been purchased as a bank foreclosure, you can expect to have electrical issues as the system may not be up to code.

In some states, a 100-amp service was normal in homes built 30 years ago when the typical home did not consume nearly as much energy as a contemporary household (there may not have been dishwashers and washer/dryers, let alone microwaves and large heating and cooling systems). To be able to meet the electrical needs of the contemporary home in the United States, you will need to provide a minimum 150-amp panel service. Make sure your investment team includes an electrician who can help you with budgets.

If the US homes you are looking to buy were built before the 1930s, knob and tube wiring may also be a significant rehab issue. Comprised of insulated copper conductors, protective porcelain insulating tubes and nailed-down porcelain knob insulators, these systems have been replaced by power cables. Because of the threat of fire, knob and tube wiring is considered an insurance issue. It is permitted under the National Electrical Code in only a few very specific situations.

TIP

Knowledgeable industry insiders tell me that if you buy and flip or rent a renovated home in the United States, you should upgrade the panel to a 200-amp service if the home is 1,200 square feet or larger. This is a safety issue. You also need to make sure that all outlets within three feet of a water source (e.g., kitchen and bathroom sinks) are grounded with GFI (ground fault interrupter) outlets. Any inspector will require this to pass code requirements.

Remember, pay now or pay later. It's your choice.

18

Get Everything in Writing.

The Need for Written Contracts

The idea that you should always work with written contracts is nothing more than old-fashioned common sense. And that's why I am amazed at how many property renovations are completed (and property sales performed!) without a clear and legal written contract signed by both parties. Neglecting a proper contract is a bad idea when you are doing all of your real estate business in your home city and your home country. It's a *very* bad idea when you decide, as a Canadian, to start investing in US property. As far as I'm concerned, if you're doing renovation business in the US without a signed contract, you're putting your whole real estate portfolio at risk.

 PROCEED WITH CAUTION!

In addition to having a written contract for the scope of work you want performed, you must carry proper insurance. If you own a property where people have been hired to do repairs and renovations, you are responsible for what happens to them when they are on your property. You need property, disability and liability insurance as soon as you own that property. Now working in the land of the litigious, you also need an umbrella policy to cover all of the what-ifs involved with the business of renting property to others.

Learn to see the link between insurance and asset protection as an essential part of your business. Remember: 95% of lawsuits worldwide are filed in the US.

This tendency to skip the written contract seems to happen more often when the same homeowners/investors continually hire the same contractors to renovate their properties. The only way this scenario can have a happy ending is if both parties verbally agree on all the details of a project, after which every one of those details is realized. That means complete agreement on the scope of work, the type of materials to be used, the timelines from start to finish and the price. Without a written contract, you can only hope the project comes in on time, is on budget and ends with the quality finished product you were expecting. At this point, there's not much you can do about project deficiencies!

If you're reading this and you've had a project with no written contract go well, you are very lucky. If you think this is a good way to continue to do business, you are delusional.

The 6 Golden Rules of the Written Contract

Rather than focus on the many ways a handshake deal can go bad, I want to talk about what the smart real estate investor does when embarking on a repair or renovation project. The following six golden rules of the written contract come from one of my US investor colleagues who is especially knowledgeable about the property rehab market for buy-and-hold investors and the quick-flip entrepreneur.

His ideas are valuable to real estate investors in Canada and the US. Make them part of your business mantra.

1. Make Sure the Contract Is Signed and Dated and Both Parties Have Copies.

What's the fastest way to add value to a written contract in the United States of America? Make sure it is signed and dated by both parties and that both parties have a copy for their records. In the US, if both parties do not have a signed and dated written contract, the contract is null and void.

2. Include a Detailed Scope of Work.

The contract must detail the scope of work, the legal address of where the work is to be performed and the list of required permits.

Steer clear of contractors who tell you to save money by skipping the permit process. As the owner of the property, you can be fined by city or county inspectors for doing unpermitted work. If you follow the permit process, a city inspector will inspect the finished work and give you a pass or fail on the project. This is an excellent way for you to get a guarantee that work was done correctly. From an asset protection perspective, a permit (and that final inspection report) is also an indication of your due diligence.

3. Be Specific About the Payment Schedule and Detail Prices Line by Line.

How much money does the contractor require up front? When are subsequent payments due? The written contract must cover questions like that. If changes to the project scope force changes to the project price (e.g., higher labor costs) you and the general contractor can use the written contract to negotiate how those issues will be handled.

4. Always Detail the Materials to Be Used.

Your goal here is to be as specific as possible, so always include the manufacturer, size and type of the product you want as well as a price list. A detailed list of materials and products provides an important check-and-balance against a contractor who might try to substitute cheaper products. Since a lot of manufacturers market products at a wide variety of price points, you want to be specific about the materials and products you are expecting to be used or installed.

If prices or materials change, you and the general contractor can refer to this part of the contract to guide a conversation about how this will be managed.

5. Stipulate Project Timelines and Penalties.

The completion date of a property rehab will have a significant impact on your business plan. It can dictate when a property can go on the market for resale or rental, thus affecting how and when you cover loans. If a project completion deadline is missed, the contract should stipulate a clear penalty schedule. This keeps your contractor honest. He may have another project that needs his attention, but a penalty clause ensures that it is in his best interest to complete your job on time.

6. Keep Copies of Your General Contractor's Business Documents.

Fly-by-night contractors and tradespeople are a dime a dozen in up-and-down real estate markets on both sides of the border. If there's money to be made, there are crooks out to make it! For this reason, and the fact it offers some guarantee of quality workmanship, Canadians entering the US real estate investment market should always hire reputable contractors with current state licenses, proof of disability and liability insurance, and valid workman's compensation coverage.

The more you work in the US business environment, the more you will appreciate how best practices like this can keep your business on track while simultaneously reducing your exposure to lawsuits.

My American investor friends tell me that you need to see and keep copies of all of the contractor documents I noted above. If a general contractor bidding on your project balks at this request, don't consider his bid one of the three bids you need to get. Move on to a company that is prepared to demonstrate a higher level of professionalism. Keeping copies of the contractor's state license, proof of disability and liability insurance, and workman's compensation documents will help protect you or your company from liability.

How to Handle Contract Changes

If "get it in writing" is rule No. 1 about the rehab contract, rule No. 2 is "expect contract edits."

When questions about a contract arise or you need to clarify the language used, discuss the issue with your general contractor. When you agree on changes, make notes to the original contract and initial the changes. If there are issues or questions you can't agree on, do not hesitate to employ a real estate attorney to review the contract to ensure you are getting in writing exactly what you expect.

 SOLD

If this written contract process is new to you, seek legal advice before you sign a contract. This is also a good thing to do before you sign a particularly complicated contract.

From a business perspective, it makes no sense to avoid seeing an attorney so that you can save a few hundred dollars in legal fees if it leaves you and your company exposed to a legal dispute that could cost tens of thousands of dollars on a major property renovation that wasn't completed to your liking.

Keep It Simple

Some people who are new to the real estate investment industry may be tempted to view a written contract as an unnecessary complication. They are confused. In the end, any property rehab on a single-family home, which is the key market we're talking about in this book, really comes down to a structure that's four walls and a roof. We don't want to complicate that. But it will complicate itself very quickly if you, as the investor, are not willing and able to clarify exactly what you want done. That's right. The simplest way to make sure you get what you want—and what you pay for— is to decide what you want and then put it in writing!

Make Curb Appeal Count.

You've Got 7 Seconds to Impress Me

Research shows that it takes people just seven seconds to make up their minds about the people they date and the folks they plan to hire. Real estate investors should expect their resale and rental properties to elicit the same gut reactions from prospective buyers and renters pulling up to the front sidewalk. They will tend to like or loathe a place almost immediately (and they may not be able to articulate why they feel the way they do).

The raw potency of that initial reaction aside, we know that the key features of a home, from price to location, the number of bedrooms and bathrooms, and the layout of a kitchen, can and will make a difference to motivated buyers and renters. My warning here is to never assume that the wisdom of the sober second-thought experience is a license to ignore the significant dollar value connected to that age-old notion of curb appeal.

And let's be brutally honest for a minute. I've met real estate investors who believe curb appeal is so subjective it can't possibly matter. I'm here to tell you that it does matter. And it matters in every neighborhood and at every price point in the real estate market.

Indeed, if kitchens and bathrooms are requirements of a successful property rehab project, then boosting a home's curb appeal is the icing on the renovation cake. That's why successful real estate investors, including those working in the US foreclosure market, recognize that it's their job to take the worst-looking house on the block and make it the best. (It's also why there are so many real estate TV shows dedicated to curb appeal and landscaping.)

SOLD

> Not every investor "gets" curb appeal. If you can't look at the yard and the exterior of a home and see how you can improve it to encourage a buyer or renter, get help. This is a business decision, especially in markets where several homes on the same street may be for sale or rent. So keep your eye on the prize. Your goal as an investor is to move property as quickly as you can. Every time a buyer or renter chooses a neighboring property, it costs you money.

An Exterior Makeover

Think beauty is skin deep? Get over it. When it comes to curb appeal, you've got to acknowledge the value of the first impression. In the first section of this book, I talked about what it's like to find yourself in a "bad" neighborhood in the US. Well, I also know that some really good American neighborhoods have been plagued by foreclosures. Make sure your investment property's exterior view leaves buyers and renters curious to see inside your property.

Always remember that the need to upgrade an investment property's curb appeal holds true regardless of whether you intend to flip or rent the newly renovated home. Here are five specific areas to keep in mind with a curb appeal upgrade.

1. Make Sure the Property Looks Well Maintained.

Fundamental #16 talked about the risk of making a business decision based on emotions versus intellect. If you're an investor, you want to make smart decisions, not emotional ones. The inverse is true with your approach to using curb appeal to attract buyers and renters. Here, the investor wants prospective buyers and renters to have an emotional reaction to their first impression of a property. They are looking at your investment because they want a home. Your curb appeal goal is to make them want to live there.

At its most fundamental level, this means making sure the property looks like it's well maintained. Fix or remove broken fences. Trim the lawn and hedges, and remove weeds from flower gardens and planters. Repair broken steps and clear away all refuse.

2. Give It Some Fresh Paint.

It's tempting to think you need to spend all of your renovation money on the interior because that's where your buyers or renters will be spending their time. But if you want a home to rent or sell fast, you've got to look at fresh paint for the exterior.

A fresh coat of paint is the best bang for your buck after cleaning up the yard. A neutral palette is a good investment for the main part of the house. (Think contemporary, but classic.) Trim, fascia, shutters and the front door may be treated to a contrasting color that "pops" for visual effect.

If the house is a red brick house, simply pressure wash the exterior and only paint the trim, fascia, shutters and any exterior doors.

3. Improve the Landscape.

Nothing says "improved curb appeal" in a competitive market like improving the landscape. Unfortunately, this is the one area most frequently ignored by investors. That's a shame, since unless there is a whole lot of tree trimming to be done, you can probably improve the landscape for less than $1,000.

If you're not sure where to start, review what's there. Are there trees, shrubs or overgrown plants to trim or prune? Are there old plantings to remove and replace with newer and healthier varieties? Can you use a red mulch to control garden weeds and create a natural contrast with the greenery?

My industry insiders tell me it's a good idea to use mature plants that are at least two to three feet high if you're planting shrubs or bushes. Anything smaller tends to look cheap and anything much bigger will hide other improvements like fresh paint or newly cleaned-up flower gardens.

 SOLD

Some real estate investors appear to abandon the exterior upkeep of a rental property's landscape once the new plants are in place. That's a mistake. Protect your investment in landscaping by arranging to have a gardener or landscaper visit the property on a weekly or biweekly basis until the property sells or rents. Without regular attention while the property is vacant, the money you spent on landscaping may be wasted if the landscaping is not kept up.

4. Replace Windows and Doors.

New windows across the front of a home offer another quick fix with instant curb appeal. If the existing windows are outdated, consider replacing them. At approximately $30 a pair for new window shutters from a home improvement store, you may also want to think about adding them to dress up the front of the house.

Always (and that means always) replace the front door if it is outdated. At the very least, apply a fresh coat of paint to the front door and install new gold or silver hardware, a kick plate and a new door knocker. That will set you back less than $100.

If the home you bought features a beautiful old front door, consider refurbishing it rather than replacing it.

5. Install a New Mailbox.

The mail delivered to this property will be addressed to the people who live there. Making sure the mailbox matches the exterior color of their new home is another nice touch for improved curb appeal.

How do you know how much to spend on curb appeal improvements? My basic rule of thumb is to ask yourself if you're adding value or cutting corners.

If all the front door needs to look great is two coats of paint, go for it. If the painted door looks awesome but the door knob is loose or the knocker is missing, those are corners you should not cut.

Remember: Your buyer or renter will be motivated at some level by emotion and you want to heighten the positive experience of touring this property. Will a new front door make a deal? Probably not. Could a bad front door break a deal? Yes. Be honest about the business impacts of your choices.

Run If You Spot Any of the Top 3 Reno Red Flags.

It's Not Just About Doing the Right Things Right

While there are a lot of single-family homes on the US distressed property market, some of these properties need a lot of work, while others are located in neighborhoods with few buyers and renters. You want to be buying a deeply discounted property that just needs some work, not a structural do-over. As you move through the renovation stage, you must keep your eyes open and make good decisions.

Fundamental #15 talked about why kitchen and bathroom renovations have to be on the reno "need" versus "want" side of the budget ledger but still be efficient, effective and economical. Regardless of whether you want to renovate a home for the rental market or renovate it to flip it, every investor has to be able to rehab that home efficiently, effectively and economically. If you can't, the deal is not for you. Before I zero in on the top three things you need to avoid during a property renovation, I want to make sure you understand how to apply the three *e*'s to every reno decision you make. Asking yourself, "is what I am about to do efficient, effective and economical?" will keep you from making unnecessary mistakes and help you streamline a property renovation.

If you can't answer the three *e*'s affirmatively, identify the problem and deal with it. A little proactive action up front will save you cash and lessen the headaches down the road.

 SOLD

When you make yourself answer tough questions about what "has" to be done during a property renovation, you emphasize the "thinking" part of the process. Doing so reduces the chance that decisions will be made based on emotions. This approach helps you look ahead. When you know how you want a project to end, it's easier to put in place all of the steps you need to meet that goal.

Make Sure Your Project Is Efficient

This question is really about *how* you plan to proceed versus the specifics of *what* you plan to do. Answering this query honestly is critical to your success at renovating for the buy-and-hold or buy-and-flip markets. Since time is your most precious commodity, be conscious of how you spend your time on any renovation project. Novice investors sometimes "feel better" when they micro-manage details, but this is not a good use of your time or resources.

It takes practice, but you must always play your strengths and delegate your weaknesses. This allows your team members to focus on their skill set while you work on yours. For example, once your budget and scope of work are determined, let your contractors do their jobs. This gives you time to focus on an exit strategy for the property and shop for the next deal. It also frees you up to communicate with the contractors and stay on top of the project details that warrant your attention.

Keep the Project Focused on What's Effective

Here, the focus is on the final product or *what* you plan to do. Is the project going to produce the intended result? Can project timelines be met? Will your exit strategy timelines work? If you plan to rent the property, your decisions will be different than if you plan a retail flip. Everyone can spend more money—you must ensure your spending supports your strategy.

As the old saying goes, make sure your ladder is leaning against the right house before you start your work.

 SOLD

When you renovate a home to sell it, the speed of that sale factors into the effectiveness of your business strategies, so include the cost of a professional cleaning in your original bid. The general contractor will most likely subcontract the job, but this is one of the best ways to make sure your rehabbed house isn't full of dust when it's time to put the house on the market.

While someone else is busy cleaning, you can be shopping for your next deal.

Stick to Economical Options

Renovation budgets are notoriously subjective. Your goal is to make renovation choices that make sense for your strategic plan. While you can skin the rehabbed cat a thousand ways, you must focus on your buyer or renter and make sure your project sticks to a realistic price point. Figure out how much money it will take to fill or sell this property at that price point, and then make renovation decisions that fit the budget.

PROCEED WITH CAUTION!

Numbers Don't Lie!

My goal on every project, whether rental or resale, is to take one of the worst homes on the block and make it one of the best. That enables me to target homes at deep discounts. But that strategy only works if I can make the home something my target customer wants to rent or buy. This is why I am adamant about getting several bids for a reno project—I never want to be stuck with one number! It's also why I pay such close attention to my renovation budget. I know what I need to do when I buy a home and I don't want to have to leave items out to "save" me money.

The Top 3 Reno Red Flags

Sticking to the three *e*'s will help you avoid making expensive mistakes on a distressed property renovation, but knowing what to do is only part of the equation. It's also helpful to zero in on what we should not do.

The three biggest mistakes investors make involve the following:

1. Buying the wrong house (as in paying too much or buying a property qualified tenants and buyers will shun because of location)

2. Not planning for change orders or renovation surprises, and failing to budget for contingencies

3. Giving your general contractor more than 25% to start

The good news about these three mistakes is that each one generally comes onto the renovation scene waving a giant red flag. That's right. Investors who tell you they didn't see these problems coming simply weren't paying attention to the warning signs. The foreclosure market is booming with investment opportunity, but when opportunity knocks, the smart investor takes responsibility for what's going to happen when he opens the door. Due diligence is about making sure a deal works long before you are financially responsible for a property.

As part of that due diligence, be on the lookout for the following three red flags.

Red Flag No. 1: A Deeply Discounted Sales Price

Let's be realistic. You are taking an educated risk on every property renovation and you should be prepared for at least some surprises even on a cosmetic rehab. But finding out you need to upgrade light fixtures for a couple hundred dollars is very different from discovering you have structural issues with the foundation of a house. The latter could entail hiring structural engineers or architects and having to jack up and re-pour pilings or beams—actions that could break every window in the house and cause more structural issues with the roof.

My point here is that you need to find out what's behind a deeply discounted sales price because this is one red flag you never want to discover waving over a property *after* you've already bought it! The US foreclosures market is an extreme buyer's market, but not every home on the market is an investment deal and there is absolutely no reason to invest in a project with major structural issues. These "deals" may be significantly discounted, but your profit margins will be consumed by the structural remedy and few investors are able to make a deal like this work.

Buying the wrong house to renovate can also be a matter of location. See Fundamental #6: Recognize That a Bad Area in the US Is Very Different From a Bad Area Elsewhere.

PROCEED WITH ENTHUSIASM!

Make Your Money on the Low-Hanging Fruit
Smart real estate investors are attracted to discounted housing prices. But they stick to the low-hanging fruit. They will paint, they will update carpet, kitchens and baths and they will revamp the landscape to improve curb appeal, but they will steer clear of houses with structural or foundation issues because too many things can wrong.

My own renovation projects take a cookie-cutter approach. My general contractors know exactly what I want so there are few surprises for them, too. And that familiarity has a positive impact on bids; contractors who know they can deliver what I expect want to earn my business because they can make money with fewer hassles.

That doesn't mean I won't consider deals with some rather pricey property upgrades. I have bought foreclosures that need roof repairs and sometimes need entirely new roofs. I can manage these projects because I know what that kind of upgrade will cost me based on the reliable information I get from my contractors.

The moral of this story is all about good business. Hit singles and doubles again and again and you won't have to worry about the grand slam. It's less stressful—and you'll still win the game!

Red Flag No. 2: No Time for Proper Planning

Never let a "lack of time" interfere with your due diligence. You need to accept the fact that there will be change orders or surprises on every deal you do, because no project will ever come in at the exact penny your budget predicted. You can have projects that will come in under budget—and those are a nice surprise—but realistically, it's more likely you will go slightly over your budget. That's only a problem if you didn't plan for that possibility, or you paid too much for the deal to begin with. The latter is the toughest, because you're stuck with the deal and will need to find creative ways to make it work (or cost you less).

This is one red flag that investors should be waving for themselves, especially if they're swimming in the foreclosed properties pool! In this market niche, your deals must be based on the best information you can find. Rush that process and you'll pay.

On the plus side, once you accept that change orders are a fact of life, you can deal with them relatively easily by building a 20% contingency into your budget. This 20% contingency is probably even more important for investors buying single-family homes that are in foreclosure. Foreclosed homes usually have not been taken care of properly by the previous owner or tenant. Some of the things you may need to fix may not be identified up front, especially if you buy a property "as is" without conditions or a formal inspection.

Your team is very important when it comes to planning. Surround yourself with trustworthy professionals who know what to look for. Are the market fundamentals in place to make this property work? Do you have reliable cost estimates to plug into your budget? (If it turns out you don't need to replace a roof or HVAC system, great! But you'll want to be prepared for what you find when you assume ownership.)

As always, the more due diligence, the better, especially as a foreigner or newbie investor.

 SOLD

A 20% budget contingency is a standard used in the construction industry. On a $10,000 budget, that means adding a cushion of $2,000. If that money's not needed, it goes right to profit. Not bad!

As noted in Fundamental #17: Do the Big 4 Renos on a Rental Property—Now, I always plan on doing the Big 4 and work that into my budget unless I happen to know with certainty that something's not needed. (For example, I may know the deal has a two-year-old roof because I've bought the same type of product in the same type of neighborhood, so I won't have to budget for work to the roof.) Also, I keep budget numbers real by working with contractors I trust. Even with the 20% contingency you may still go over budget, but if the deal is good you should still come out of it with a decent profit. Remember, it's all about the singles and doubles, not the grand slams.

Red Flag No. 3: Your Contractor Wants More Than 25% Down

This red flag is easy to spot and easy to deal with. Never—ever—pay a contractor more than 25% of the total budget to start a project. If they need more than that to work with you, find a new contractor. Make no exceptions to this rule. Contractors will give you every excuse in the book for why they need this much money to start, but don't listen. If they need more than 25%, they are either using your funds to cover overhead from their last project that didn't go as planned, or they don't have the appropriate lines of credit or cash reserves to run their company. Either way, if you see this red flag, search for a new contractor.

Canadian investors who ignore this risk a hefty financial lesson. In a worst-case scenario, the 25% you give a contractor to start a property renovation could disappear into thin air before any work is done. A 20% contingency will cover some of your loss and you may still be able to get your rehab finished and make a profit. Without that contingency, though, you've got nothing.

 SOLD

Use common sense when scheduling and releasing payments to your general contractor. I suggest doing 25% draws equal to the scope of work that is completed to your satisfaction. Release each draw only after a thorough walk-through.

The final draw is always the most important payment you make to a contractor. Unless you are 110% satisfied with the finished product, do not release the final payment. You want to make sure the contractor has an economic incentive to complete the project to specifications.

Hire the Right Property Manager.

7 Questions That Can Help You Hire the Best Person for the Job

Canadian real estate investors who want to buy and hold rental property in the United States must make quality property management a top priority. This management must be effective, efficient and economical, and it must be in place at all times. If you believe, as I certainly do, that money follows management, then you will see this as an area that demands constant investor vigilance, because property management can make or break your buy-and-hold investment.

To help Canadian investors increase the odds of finding the right property manager for their US properties, I will share seven golden questions that an American colleague of mine asks when he's hiring property managers for distressed properties he's purchased and renovated for the buy-and-hold rental market.

 SOLD

When you're investigating contractors, you should get quotes from three people or companies. When you're looking to hire a property manager, you need to double that and interview at least six potential property managers.

Always let prospective hires know you are interviewing five others and that this additional attention to quality comes from your commitment to getting the right people for the job. Your goal is to build a long-term relationship with a property manager who sees the benefits of that quality-first approach.

Zero In on Excellence: 7 Questions to Ask

1. *Does the prospective property manager already manage property in the area where your house is located and do they manage the type of home you own?*

If the management company already has rentals under management in your specific area, meaning the same neighborhood or relatively close by, they are much more likely to be able to meet your needs. If their other properties are farther away, move on. Proximity to the properties they manage is critical.

Also make sure they manage the type of home in your portfolio. If your homes are 1,200 sq. ft. in a working class "regular Joe" neighborhood, you don't need a property manager who typically works with tenants of higher-end homes. Ditto for the property manager whose experience is with multi-family properties.

2. *Do they own their own investment property?*

Always ask about their personal real estate investing experience. Property managers who have "skin in the game" have better knowledge about what the role entails and almost always do a better job. Period. The broker/owner of the property management company one of my American investor colleagues works with owns several rental properties—and my colleague says it shows in the company's performance. You want your property manager to have a "landlord mentality." That can be learned, but it's easier to perfect if they own rental property themselves.

3. *How many houses does the company have under management?*

Volume is also an asset. If a property management company manages fewer than 100 properties in a market with a population of more than one million people, market-savvy US investors would consider them a very under-developed management company. You want experience.

Also find out how many different owners they manage for. If they have 200 units under management, but 198 of them are with one owner, be wary. If that owner pulls his portfolio from them, they could go out of business that day. For stability, you want a property management company whose portfolio includes various owners.

SOLD

If you want to grow your real estate portfolio in a particular part of a city, aim to be your property management company's biggest client. You may be rewarded with discounts for your high volume.

---

4. What are their rent collection and eviction policies and procedures?

If a prospective property manager can't give you a direct response on this part of their job, move on. This is an essential part of property management and you need someone who knows how to do this— and do it well.

A good management company will have a very clear system and a no-nonsense strategy for rent collection and evictions. This is a fundamental business priority: your mortgage payment is due every month, no matter what. Poorly conceived rent collection and eviction processes put your investment at risk.

PROCEED WITH CAUTION!

It's not uncommon for rental collection and eviction issues to wreak major financial havoc in the early days of real estate investing. Don't let poor management of your US properties make your business a statistic! Charity is a great thing, but it's not a good fit with a rental portfolio. Keep the two completely separate by making sure your heart never gets bigger than your head.

---

5. What is the property management company's vacancy ratio? What are their days-on-the-market stats for their current portfolio? How do these compare to the overall single-family market for that area? What will they do to make sure your property is rented?

Vacancy rates and days-on-the-market are as important as rent collection and eviction policies and procedures. Make sure they are a priority for the management company you hire.

This can be especially critical for Canadian investors as it's easy to lose sight of your basic cash-flow priorities when you're facing a spectacular deal. Let me be frank. It doesn't matter how great your deal is. If you can't keep that discount-priced home filled and performing, that great deal can put your entire investment portfolio at risk.

Drill potential property managers about their strategies to get and keep tenants.

- What type of marketing do they use to fill vacancies?

- Why is their approach successful?

- What type of signage, websites, ads, etc. do they currently use?

- Can they show you what they're doing for other owners?

- Do they have any ideas about how your properties should be marketed to give them an edge?

- Do they charge extra fees for marketing? (If they do, that's bad! This should be included in the service they are offering you.)

6. *What are their manager's fees?*

This question is very important. How do these people earn their money? A good management company usually gets a one-time fee for filling the property (a placement fee) and then a percentage of collected rents. If they are not collecting rents they shouldn't be getting paid!

In one US market in Florida, a key state for distressed US properties, standard property management fees are 10% to 12%. But they can be as low as 8% and as high as 14%. These fees will vary across the country and within states. Do your research and make sure you know what is reasonable before you start interviewing property managers. Be mindful of what's behind different rates. In property management, as with most service industries, you get what you pay for.

If you have no plans to buy multiple properties in the US, then you may consider offering a management company a higher rate to ensure they manage your smaller portfolio. An extra few percent will reduce your income and make sure you can sleep at night in Canada.

Do avoid a management company that uses maintenance or repairs as a profit center. You want a company that takes care of this part of the job at par pricing without add-on fees. You also should establish a procedure for repairs over a certain dollar amount. Some of my US insiders tell me they don't let a management company undertake a repair over $250 without their permission.

7. How will I get my money and statements from them?

This is another area over which you should have full control. A good management company should have auto-deposit available for you into whatever bank account you choose to receive your rental profits. They should have a specific date for depositing the rental profits and you should also receive a management statement every month. That statement will review the performance of the property by showing rents collected, expenses and fees, and the balance to be dispersed to the owner.

Make sure the statements you're getting are simple. If you can't understand their statements, then you can't manage your investments. My US real estate market insiders tell me that for efficiency, they prefer soft copies (e-mail) of these reports. They reconcile every statement and have a staff bookkeeper or accountant do the same. The extra set of eyes is an important way to ensure accuracy.

PROCEED WITH ENTHUSIASM!

When a real estate investor takes the time to do a thorough job of finding the right property manager, she satisfies a primary requirement of any solid due diligence strategy: always do your homework. The key to a buy-and-hold investment is the quality of ongoing management, so take your time, choose wisely and never be afraid to fire your property manager and redo the whole process if your expectations are not met.

22

Make Money by Delegating to Your Property Manager.

This Business Is About Relationships

Experienced real estate investors often say they make their money when they buy a property. That's true. Investors in the US distressed real estate market know that they can make more money on houses they buy at significantly discounted prices. The painfully simple secret to understanding the numbers side of this business is encapsulated in an age-old slogan: buy low and sell high. While that's tough to do in the stock market, real estate investing is a different story. You may not ever sell at the absolute peak of a market or buy at the market's lowest point, but as long as you stick to investment fundamentals and invest in properties with positive cash flow, your business will profit.

 SOLD

Make cash flow an investment fundamental. As long as a property is in a cash-flow position, you've got time to tweak your exit strategy.

But there is more to real estate investment success than the wisdom of positive cash flow and a buy-low-sell-high strategy. If you're going to make money in this market niche, you've also got to understand that this is a numbers game where your relationships with people will help you score the points you need to tally a profit. From this perspective, management is about more than sound business strategies, it's about building relationships with the folks who can help you put those strategies in place.

Put Your Money to Work

Fundamental #21 walked you through the seven best questions to ask prospective property managers. Here, I want to emphasize why property management is so important, especially on buy-and-hold rentals.

I know the work it takes to find a good property manager leaves some of my readers scratching their heads and asking why they need a property manager when it's going to cost 8% to 14% of their rental fees. As a Canadian investing in the US distressed property market, you must be honest about what you can and cannot do in terms of managing a property from hundreds or thousands of kilometers away. This is one area where an investor can micromanage her investment all the way to the red-ink side of the business ledger!

As an investor, you do not need to do everything yourself. That one-man show is required if you're day-trading stocks. In real estate, the lesson is simple: the more you leverage other people's time and expertise, the more successful you will be in real estate. Letting someone else manage your properties gives you more time to find deals and to develop relationships with other people who would be good additions to your investment team.

One of the biggest mistakes investors make is thinking that property management is all about regular property checks and minor repairs or hiring a qualified tradesperson when additional work is needed. If that's where your knowledge of property management is stuck, here are some things I want you to think about.

A property manager has consistent access to your property because he lives in the area. A property manager is

- in the right place at the right time to make sure your property maintains its value. If you've taken the worst house on the street and made it the best, you have a vested interest in making sure that property maintains its value. But if you spend all of your own time doing that, there's no time left for investing!

- the first person to know if rent is or isn't paid.

- ideally situated to develop and put in place a proven system to deal with rent issues as soon as they arise. (No flying in to meet tenants, no long-distance excuses.)

- in the right place to keep you up to date on your investment's performance. A property manager submits regular statements that show rents collected, expenses and fees and the balance dispersed to the owner.

- the right person for the right job. They have a good working knowledge of the market where your property is located. They know where to find local tradespeople when needed and they can be trusted to get minor repairs done without bothering the investor.

(I recommend allowing them to make decisions on repairs under $250.) All of this market knowledge is essential to keeping your units rented and cash flowing.

I can honestly tell you that I spend remarkably little time worrying about whether I "know enough" or am "smart enough" to invest in real estate. My success is focusing on what I do well, which is relationship building and relationship management. I can delegate everything else!

Property management is one of those areas where delegation is critical to an investor's success. These people can help you make money. It's that simple.

Professional Property Management Pays for Itself

In sum, the real estate investment business is a good example of an enterprise where money follows management. It is imperative that you manage your systems and team, but you need to understand that growth and control enjoy an inverse relationship. If you micromanage in an area like property management, you compromise your ability to make money by buying property!

You need to manage people and strategies, but it's okay to let others do the hands-on work.

 SOLD

I believe that success comes from an attitude that celebrates cooperation over competition. I do not try to compete with the people I meet in the real estate investment community. Instead, every person I meet is a potential expert at something that will enhance my life and business. My goal is to add reciprocal value to these relationships by helping others.

Communicate With Your Property Manager.

Set the Rules Up Front

I've gone over the important questions you need to ask to help you hire the right property manager for your US rental properties and I've emphasized why good property management will make you money. Do I really need to talk about the value of good communications with your property manager? Yes. And that's because this fundamental is one that far too many investors are willing to address with lip service instead of action.

So let me be clear. If you plan to take your Canadian dollars and use them to buy distressed properties in the US, you need to be honest about how that investment might be affected by the distance between you and your property manager. Real estate investing is a great way to put your money to work for your long-term wealth. That does not mean you get to park it in an investment property and leave the country.

As with most relationships, the key to good communication typically boils down to making sure that all parties know and understand the rules. That means you set the rules up front, not as you go.

Get Your Communications Plan in Place

This is one relationship where a real estate investor can expect to reap what she sows. As soon as you hire a property manager, set the foundation of your communications plan and be thorough and consistent. (If you've stuck to the ideas laid out in Fundamental #21: Hire the Right Property Manager, this individual has already had a good look at how you work and what you expect them to know and do.)

A full-time US investor I know is in daily contact with his property management company, which manages more than 100 of the properties he owns outright or with investors. As these are all rental properties, a portfolio of that size has a great deal of moving parts. While daily contact may not be appropriate on a smaller portfolio, every real estate investor must be clear about what they need to keep their investment on track.

Monthly Reports

Monthly reports are standard fare. Information about rents, expenses and cash flow is essential to your portfolio's sustainability. Do not compromise on this point. Every investor needs a monthly report.

Weekly Contact

Some investors will physically meet with their property managers once a week. While weekly face-to-face meetings are only necessary when you own a significant number of properties, you must never let a property manager think your absence equates to disinterest. If face-to-face meetings are not pragmatic given distance and portfolio size, then monthly reports should be supported by regular phone conversations and communication updates delivered via e-mail and phone texts.

Weekly phone or face-to-face meetings may run 30 to 60 minutes. Use the time to address maintenance issues, collections, vacancies, move outs, evictions and Keys for Cash candidates (see Fundamental #24).

 SOLD

Money follows management. Regular communication with your property manager is the best way to keep abreast of management decisions and issues. No matter how good a manager is, the property's success hinges on your money. If the ball gets dropped, it's your money that's at risk.

Stick to Business

Make sure your regular meetings are informative and efficient. I know investors whose property managers prepare a detailed report every week and they use that to guide their face-to-face or phone meetings. This boosts productivity by keeping the conversation on track. Meetings detract from the time you spend finding deals (or enjoying a life where your money's working even when you're not.) Remember that your property manager probably feels the same way; these meetings must be productive because they cut into his hands-on management time.

Use Technology Wisely

E-mails and texts can save you and your property manager a lot of time. If you have a good rapport with your property manager and trust his recommendations, you can develop a communications plan using e-mail or texts to review and approve bids, authorize expenditures or address other issues the manager can't handle without your consent.

 SOLD

You can run your business, or let it run you. As a foreign investor living a long way from your investments, you must stay on top of property management decisions and be prepared to step in if a property manager needs direction. But the more you can delegate to your manager, the better. After all, that's what you pay them to do!

As you set your communications plan in motion, make sure your property manager knows there are four key expectations you want him to be able to discuss—and meet.

1. You Want to Keep Your Properties Full.

A good property manager will fill your properties quickly with qualified tenants. These are tenants who can pay the rent! Make sure your property manager understands that you know what happens when a property manager slams unqualified tenants into your vacancies. Tell him this causes a high turnover rate and often leads to property damage. As such, it runs counter to a sustainable business strategy that will protect your investment and keep your property manager employed.

Let him know that you want your property to be product and price competitive with other homes on the market in your area. If he has issues with what constitutes product or price competitiveness, or that changes over time, he needs to address those concerns with you.

2. You Want a 3E Approach to Maintenance and Repairs.

Talk to your property manager about expenses. Tell him you want maintenance and repairs to be effective, efficient and economical, and that you will need some assurances that's what is happening. (You may want to see some evidence of bids, for example.)

Quality renovations generally cut maintenance and repair costs, which keeps tenants, property managers and your bank accounts happy. But things do require maintenance and repair. Work with your property manager to satisfy reasonable tenant requests even when they aren't expected or they seem unwarranted. You do not have to meet every request, but if it's reasonable, you and your property manager may want to address it. Again, you want your property manager to talk to you about situations like this. Together, you can find a three *e* solution that keeps a long-term tenant happy.

3. You Want Your Property Manager to Manage.

Let your property manager know you want him to handle the day-to-day issues that arise. That's what a good property manager does. A good investor supports a good property manager. This approach lets you both do what you're good at!

4. You Want Resolutions, Not Confrontations.

Communication is a two-way street. If you or your property manager feel like your expectations aren't being met, you need to be able to point out why you're not satisfied and be prepared to quickly resolve the issue.

When resolution is not possible, skip the confrontation and hire a new property manager. This is a business decision, so keep emotions out of it and act swiftly. The longer you take to make the right decision, the sooner you'll pay for it. Procrastination is your enemy.

Be Smart About Rent Collection.

Activate the Keys for Cash Program

I can't stress enough the importance of making sure you have quality property management in place with a solid plan for collecting the rent. This fundamental is critical regardless of whether your revenue properties are in Canada or the US.

One of the best rental collection policies I have ever seen comes from a US investor who specializes in the distressed property market. He buys his properties at significant discounts, renovates them to make them market ready and then works with his property managers to put in place what he calls the Keys for Cash program.

It is, bar none, the best passive approach to handling non-performing (delinquent) tenants that I've ever come across. If you want to be smart about rent collection and save yourself a lot of headaches and cash, you need to adopt the Keys for Cash program.

Warning: What I'm going to tell you about—the Keys for Cash program—might shock novice investors and those still "thinking about" real estate investing, because you're still prone to making an emotional response to a business decision. If you read what follows and don't think the Keys for Cash program is necessary, take heed. You'll find that the Keys for Cash program is simple and effective and veterans of the industry love it because it protects their investments and integrity.

From Delinquent to Delivered

If your tenant can't pay the rent, he is already in a financially stressful situation. Understand intellectually what that means. You can feel badly for him, but if you really want to help, make sure your choices do not compound his pecuniary issues and exacerbate your own. Know that when you allow tenants to take advantage of your emotional response to their plight, you will pay the piper because you will make the problem more difficult and expensive to solve.

The Keys for Cash program works like this. Let's say the rent is due in full on the first of every month, with no exceptions. If a tenant is late, your property manager will send out a three-day pay-or-quit letter. It notifies the tenant that he has three days to pay the rent or quit the property. That letter should include an option for Keys for Cash to the delinquent tenant. This option stipulates that:

> . . . to avoid eviction, you, the tenant, have an option to move out of the house completely, including all of your belongings, within 7 days of receiving this letter. The home is returned broom swept, cleaned, and in the same or better condition to when you moved in. In return, the owner will not pursue the eviction or you for the delinquent funds and will not report you to the credit bureaus for eviction, which will affect you finding another home to move to. In return, you, the tenant, will receive $XXX* cash in 7 days after a satisfactory inspection is completed by the property manager, at which time you will turn over the keys to the property manager and receive your money.
>
> By signing this agreement, you, the tenant, agree to forfeit any security deposit and will not pursue the owner for any further losses or liabilities of any kind in the future pertaining to this lease.

* Sum to range from $100 to $500, depending on the rent or situation.

This letter must be signed and dated by the tenant and you or your property manager. This shows that all of the terms of the Keys for Cash program were accepted and that you have the acceptance in writing, regardless of whether the tenant does or does not meet all the requirements.

 SOLD

If your property manager will not adopt the Keys for Cash program, find a new property manager. Rent collection is essential to your cash-flow business strategy. Do not let your deal be compromised by delinquent tenants.

What you're doing is very smart. The sooner you can get your non-performing asset back with as little damage as possible, the more money you make or avoid losing, period. The eviction process is a long and very expensive procedure. It includes eviction costs, loss of rents, and damages to the property left by an unhappy tenant. Why not allow the tenant to leave with some dignity and get your asset back in great shape so you can get it filled again as soon as possible?

It's All About the Business

Some new investors balk at the idea they should give a tenant's security deposit back when the tenant defaults on rent. I look at this differently. From a purely business perspective, this is money you would return to a renter if their lease was up or they were planning to move out and had not damaged the property.

I know it rubs some investors the wrong way, but I will even give the delinquent tenant a good recommendation to their next landlord if they were good tenants up to this point. I will, of course, take steps to make sure their situation is legitimate. (Perhaps they just need to downsize to a cheaper rental because of job loss, health issues, etc.) Out of respect to the next landlord, I will explain the tenant was delinquent. But I will also tell them the tenant agreed to the provisions of the Keys for Cash program and met all its requirements. To me, this is about doing business in good faith. I believe in karma, that law of moral causation, and always try to treat people the way I want to be treated, even if they are non-performing tenants and other landlords. (You never know where a relationship will lead you!)

Rest assured I am not naïve about the situation, either. I do recommend that your property manager meets the delinquent tenant at the property with a locksmith on the move-out date. As soon as the property inspection is complete, the locksmith should change the locks. This is one more way to make sure the tenant understands that this is a business decision and you take your business seriously.

 SOLD

If you are going into the buy-and-hold rental real estate market, you need to accept and respect that tenants who pay, consistently and on time, are essential to whether your business succeeds or fails. Their rental payments are your income and without it, your business doesn't work.

Paying the rent on time is non-negotiable, but you can be flexible and exercise integrity to keep your assets performing. The Keys for Cash program is a great example of how you put to work an outside-of-the-box solution.

The
Real
World

Mitigating Your Risks and Going Behind the "Foreclosed" Sign

An Investor Finds Gold in the Property Reno Niche

Brian Scrone likes to tell people that he makes his living by identifying the buy-and-hold potential of deeply discounted homes that other investors dismiss, often because they don't recognize the easy-to-rent potential of a particular property in a particular neighborhood. The "cash now" side of that business buys, fixes up and flips properties back onto the retail sale market. The "cash later" side builds a rental portfolio. He'll also tell you that his business model can be replicated, especially with the current US housing market still reeling from a major recession. But saying it *can* be done doesn't mean it will be easy, says Brian, who's bought more than three hundred US properties since 1999. "There are opportunities for people with liquidity and access to funds, but you still have to pay attention to investment fundamentals."

And those looking for fundamentals that only apply in an extreme buyer's market will be disappointed. While there are currently more discounted houses on the US market than ever before, the investment rules are "really global fundamentals. I follow the same rules now that I did when I was starting out. That's really important," continues Brian.

Opportunity Abounds

Today's US market holds special investment opportunities for anyone with liquidity or access to funds, including foreign investors, he adds. "If I was being completely unemotional about it, I would say it's the perfect storm." Noting the boom, bust and recovery real estate cycle, "we've obviously just come out of the bust and are headed into the recovery and that's where you want to be in acquisition mode as a real estate investor."

With American banks highly motivated to sell the unprecedented numbers of foreclosed properties in their portfolios, access to 30-year fixed-rate mortgage products, and a Canadian dollar hovering near par with its US counterpart, "we probably won't see something like this again in our lifetime," predicts Brian.

Based on his own experience with the bust-and-recovery continuum of the real estate cycle, Brian says it's especially important that Canadians entering the market stick to proven investment fundamentals. These aren't difficult to learn or apply, but they do require discipline. To help Canadian buyers understand why they need to stick to the tried and true, Brian offers the following insights.

Stick to Properties That are Easy to Renovate and Rent

Brian likes deeply discounted properties, but he always finds out what's behind the foreclosed sign. These days there are a lot of distressed properties on the market that do not need much more than cosmetic upgrades. They are located in low-vacancy neighborhoods where people have jobs and want to live. These comprise what Brian calls "the low-hanging fruit." They're easy to pick—and easy to profit from.

In contrast, a dirt-cheap property requires closer study to find out what's behind that foreclosure sign. These properties generally require significant renovations, including structural work. If they are located in a bad neighborhood (high vacancies, high unemployment and problems getting property managers), they're too much risk for Brian. "Why would you go into that market when there is so much low-hanging fruit to pick?"

Avoid Those Who Promote a Get-Rich-Quick Approach

The experienced investor warns Canadians who think they can come into this market and get rich quick. The market is good. Opportunities are real. But those looking for overnight success are in the wrong business and those promoting overnight-success schemes probably make their money by ripping off naïve investors versus securing sound real estate investments.

Canadian eh?

If you're doing business in the US, expect Americans to recognize your accent as foreign. And recognize how that knowledge could leave you vulnerable to scams. "As soon as a Canadian opens his or her mouth I know where they're from. If I were you, I would be extra wary of being taken advantage of because Canadian investors may represent low-hanging fruit to some people in the business," warns Brian.

He recommends that market newcomers apply extra due diligence to everything people in the real estate business tell you about—from the desirability of a particular neighborhood to why a property is priced so low and what contractor bids should be. An extreme buyer's market coupled with a poor employment situation brings out fly-by-night operators who are looking to score easy cash from market newbies.

Be On Your Guard With Contractors

Brian's worked really hard to establish good working relationships with the contractors he hires to renovate his properties. But he would "never take a bid or proposal from a new contractor and go with it." When you're getting into the market, shop around for referrals and always get three bids.

Brian says Canadian investors must do their due diligence on a contractor's work, too. Ask to see previous work and talk to previous clients. Also make sure the scope of work (including materials and budget figures) is in writing and ask for documentation. You want copies of insurance, business licenses and work permits for your files.

As for payment, link checks to project milestones and make sure the first payment is the first draw on the project. If you ignore this advice, your contractor could use your money to pay other bills. Brian's seen this happen and he figures it's entirely preventable. If a contractor balked at this requirement, Brian would go elsewhere because he'd start to question the integrity of the contractor.

Focus On an Area

There are real estate opportunities in every state and every state will have marketers making their pitches. Brian suggests market newcomers look at focusing on an area. He and his business partner have invested in their backyard and other markets—both nationally and internationally—and insist management is the key to success. "Finding and sticking to your niche, while remaining flexible and having the right teams and resources in place in those respective markets, will bring sustainability and success."

He routinely hears stories about foreign investors buying properties they've never seen and thinks that approach is ridiculous. When he and his business partner shifted their portfolio's focus from the west to east coast, they dispersed properties and moved.

"If you're coming in and buying a $100,000 rental property, I think it's insane if you're not getting on a plane to go and see it."

Take Legal Liability Issues Seriously

Making sure your business is appropriately structured and insured to protect your assets from lawsuits is a basic part of doing business in Canada and the US. But reducing your exposure to potential liabilities is especially important when you invest in the US—the world's most litigious culture. "It's not negotiable. You need to do certain things in this game and it doesn't matter what business you're in here, you can't let your guard down. Business is business and this is a serious part of the enterprise," admits Brian.

Build an Investment Team

Property acquisitions are the one thing Brian never delegates "because no one cares about my money the way I do." But he admits he's no expert on many of the other things he has to deal with. To counter that, he surrounds himself with the right people, and then uses their knowledge to make decisions about how his money is spent and made. "I play my strengths and delegate my weaknesses."

That translates into specific decisions; Brian doesn't swing a hammer on a renovation job, but he knows how to compare project estimates and how to read statements. "At the end of the day you either deposit the check or you write the check. I think the underlying theme is the sustainability of the business. Whether it's relationships or deal flow, finance or construction, I don't care what niche in the real estate industry we're talking about, it all goes back to sustainability. Everyone wants to get rich yesterday and is trying to get to the finish line as soon as possible. But that will not work in this business. I'm here for the long haul and I've got nothing to gain from rushing relationships and decisions or trying to force numbers. If you do that, you're going to be dead in the water pretty quick."

Recognize the Value of Patience

The current market is attracting a lot of investor wannabes and stories abound about how quickly foreign and domestic buyers are pulling the investment trigger. Brian encourages a different approach. He says Canadians serious about investing in US property should understand that the time they spend finding the right real estate agent to work with, the right property to buy and the right contractor to rehab the place isn't lost time, but an investment in future wealth.

Remembering his own mistakes from his early days in investing, Brian advocates a slow-and-steady approach. "The goal is not how much money you make, it's how much money you keep, and that goes back to how you treat people and build sustainable relationships. If the deal's not right, don't force it."

With brokers telling him the current recovery period will last three to five years, foreign investors should recognize that time is on their side. "Remember, speed kills. If you've got capital, you've got time," adds Brian.

Understand That Money Follows Management

Brian's last bit of advice focuses on his approach to management and underscores an ongoing theme of his business strategy. It takes a team to make money in real estate and Brian likes to manage that team based on proven practices or fundamentals. Taking a "slow to hire and quick to fire approach" to his business, he takes special care with property management, but applies the same philosophy to all of the people he works with.

That focus on making sure people meet your expectations can be especially important to foreigners who aren't living near their investment properties, warns Brian. He's got firsthand knowledge of times when his own "great deals" were ruined by contractor overruns, repair and maintenance costs and tenant issues. Putting that experience to work in his current business, he looks ahead, not back, and recommends other investors benefit from his trials. "I have held onto people that I shouldn't have because of the emotion and it cost me money and unnecessary stress. I will not make the same mistake twice."

Tax Planning

"It's generally the things we don't do that haunt us forever."

Philip McKernan

PART

3

Tom Wheelwright is a Certified Public Accountant with 30 years of experience and a reputation as the go-to guy for tax questions relating to the US real estate investment property market. Tom is an acclaimed speaker and educator, and has recently written a book on important tax strategies for the smart real estate investor. I am thrilled to be able to base Part 3 of this book on Tom's experience and research in an effort to draw attention to these strategies.

Understand How US Tax Laws Can Work to Your Benefit.

The Rules Can Lower Your Taxes

Experienced Canadian real estate investors know their businesses must be in compliance with Canadian tax law. They also know that quality tax and accounting advice can save them money, not because they are "avoiding" tax, but because tax and accounting professionals can help investors make sure they are not paying any more tax than they are legally required to pay.

Guess what? The rules for Canadian investors doing business in the US real estate market are pretty much the same. You will be required to pay tax on the money you earn in the US. With good advice, you should never pay more than you are legally required to pay.

An Overview of the US System

In the United States, as in Canada, the primary purpose of federal tax law is to raise revenues for the government to operate. Believe it or not, in the US that's accomplished by a single line in federal tax law. That line says all income is taxable unless the law says otherwise. That line is backed up by about 30 pages of tax tables and related information.

The Internal Revenue Code of the United States, however, is more than 5,800 pages long. If a mere 30 pages are about raising taxes, what are the rest of the pages for? Very simply, they're devoted to providing incentives to taxpayers for carrying on certain types of business and investment endeavors.

That's right, US tax laws are really a series of stimulus packages for entrepreneurs and investors. This is important to real estate investors, and my US tax expert encourages Canadians entering this market to approach

US tax law knowing these laws are made for you. That doesn't mean you can ask for special treatment. It does mean that if you take the time to understand the fundamentals of how the rules work, you can use those laws to vastly lower the American income taxes you will pay on your real estate investment income.

 SOLD

> Real estate investors often talk about building an "investment team." These are the people, from real estate agents to general contractors, home inspectors, lawyers and accountants, who help you operate your business and stick to your investing fundamentals. When you make a significant shift in your investment structure, you may also need to significantly change the members of your team.
>
> I urge you to recognize that investing in US real estate is a significant shift in your system! Make sure that your tax and legal professionals are familiar with US tax law.

The Role of Stimulus

The first thing you need to understand about a tax system based on economic stimulus is how Congress uses this approach to encourage certain behavior. First, it wants to encourage business. Businesses add value to the economy by building the economic base so there is even more income to tax. Businesses also add social value to the economy by providing jobs. That's why tax law includes so many incentives to add employees.

Next, Congress wants to make sure there are adequate commodities like oil, gas, timber and food, so the people can comfortably work and play. This is why the tax laws provide incentives to oil and gas developers, timber producers, farmers and ranchers.

Congress also wants to make sure there is a strong supply of housing to shelter its citizens. This goal is advanced by giving tax incentives to people who own their own homes and to those who provide homes for others. Real estate developers and real estate investors, including foreign nationals, fall into this latter group of taxpayers who qualify for tax incentives.

Tax incentives for those who develop and invest in commercial properties also are available, since Congress recognizes the need for commercial and industrial buildings to house businesses.

General Guidelines

Later fundamentals will take a more detailed look at a variety of tax benefits available to those who invest in US real estate and what you have to do to take advantage of them. Before that, I want to share what my Part 3 tax specialist says are the five key concepts that guide tax planning in the US. They are:

1. Deductions

2. Preferred income

3. Shifting tax brackets

4. Income elimination

5. Entity structure

Deductions

As in Canada, the US only taxes net income or income reduced by certain deductions, so the first way to reduce your taxes on US investment income is to increase your deductions. We'll get into specific deductions in a later fundamental. Here, we'll look at the general requirements for making an expense deductible.

There are two primary requirements for making an expense deductible. First, the expense cannot increase the value of the property and, second, the expense has to be ordinary and necessary to the real estate business. An expense increases the value of the property when it adds longevity to the property or adds a durable feature to the property (minimally one year).

Suppose you plan to rent out a single-family home you purchased in the US through foreclosure. The house cannot be tenanted until renovations are completed, so you set about hiring contractors to go in and complete the upgrades. Some of the work they do is going to extend the life of the property. They may put on a new roof or replace the HVAC (heating and air conditioning) systems. These expenses are going to make the property last longer. They may also do some renovations, such as adding a bedroom or converting a carport to a garage. These renovations add long-term value to the property.

Expenses that cause the property to last longer or that add a feature that increases the value of the property cannot be deducted immediately. Instead, they are added to the cost of the property and are depreciated over several years. (See Fundamental #28 for ways to increase your depreciation deductions.)

If the contractors complete a lot of maintenance, cleaning and minor repair of the property, these expenses are treated differently. While they are certainly important in terms of making the property available for lease, they don't extend the life of the property and don't really add value. They simply make the house livable and provide curb appeal. These expenses don't have to be added to the cost of the property and depreciated. Instead, they can be deducted. Similarly, utilities, property taxes, advertising and insurance also can be deducted.

You must take care to ensure that deducted expenses are ordinary and necessary for the real estate business. An ordinary expense is one that is common in the industry. Cleaning, yard care, taxes and insurance all qualify. Some expenses may not qualify. As in Canada, the most challenging are those related to travel, meals and entertainment.

In the meantime, you must realize that expenses must be considered "necessary" to qualify for deduction. This means that the purpose of the expenses is to increase the income from the property. As long as you are spending the money with the intention of increasing your income or preventing a loss of income, then the expenses are necessary.

Preferred Income

The second way to reduce your income taxes in the US is by changing the character of income from "bad" income to "good" income. There are three basic types of income in the US: ordinary income, investment income and passive income. For real estate investors, "good" income is the kind of revenue you earn from passive income, while ordinary income is "bad." As you'll read below, those definitions are based on US tax law.

Ordinary income includes income that is earned from a job, income you earn a business that you run and income from a pension plan or an Individual Retirement Account (IRA). The latter is the US equivalent of a Registered Retirement Savings Plan (RRSP) in Canada. Ordinary income is taxed at the regular tax rates. Ordinary losses (typically losses from a business that you run) can offset any other type of income. That makes them the best, most preferred types of losses. Sometimes, ordinary income is subject to an additional tax, the self-employment tax. In the US, the self-employment tax is on top of the regular tax and in 2010 is 15.3% of the first $106,900 of self-employment income and 2.9% (going up to 3.8% in 2012) of everything over this base amount.

Investment income is income from investments, such as stocks and bonds. Capital gains are included in this category. Some investment income is taxed at a preferred rate. Currently, long-term capital gains (gains from the sale of investments you own for more than a year) are taxed at a maximum rate of 15%, likely going up to 20% in 2011. Dividends are taxed at the same rate. Interest income, however, is taxed at ordinary income rates.

Still, interest income has some tax benefits. For one thing, expenses related to investment income can only offset investment income. So, the interest expense you pay that relates to your investments can only be deducted if you have at least as much investment income as you have investment expenses. Examples of investment expenses are as follows:

- Fees paid to a fund manager or investment advisor

- Interest expense on a stock margin account used to purchase stock

The final category of income is passive income. Passive income is income from a business that you own but you don't run yourself. For example, suppose you invest in a limited partnership that is developing a new medical device. You are a limited partner and your only participation is as an investor, meaning you don't do any of the work. The income and losses that you report on your tax return from this investment will be treated as passive income or loss.

The significance of passive income and loss is that, like investment expenses, passive losses can only offset passive income. This is important because, in the early years of an investment, you will likely have losses from the business. If you don't have other passive income to offset in these years, the passive losses from the business will be carried over until you have passive income from this or some other passive investment.

The passive loss rules are particularly important when it comes to real estate investing. That's because real estate rental income and losses are passive even if you participate in the activity. There are two exceptions to this rule: the active real estate investor rule and the real estate professional rule. We will talk about both of these later. For now, what you really need to understand is that you must pay close attention to the passive loss rules and their exceptions to make sure you maximize your tax benefits from real estate.

 PROCEED WITH CAUTION!

The real estate passive loss rules only apply to losses from the rental of real estate. If you are invested in a business that wholesales properties, fixes and flips properties, or otherwise develops or deals in real estate, you are invested in a business. You are subject to the regular passive loss rules, not the special rules that apply to rental real estate.

The bottom line is that passive income is always a preferred type of income as it can be offset by passive losses from real estate and other passive investment activities. Investment income is also a preferred type of income, since much of this is taxed at a lower rate and you can offset this income with investment expenses. The worst type of income is ordinary income, especially self-employment income.

Shifting Tax Brackets

Like Canada, the US uses a progressive income tax bracket system, which means the last dollar you earn is taxed higher than the first dollar you earn. The income tax brackets are different for single individuals versus married couples and for corporations versus individuals.

If you are a single individual, your tax brackets in the US would look like this for 2010:

Net Income	Taxed at
$8,375	10%
$8,375–$34,000	15%
$34,000–$82,400	25%
$82,400–$171,850	28%
$171,850–$373,650	33%
Over $373,650	35%

This means that the first $8,375 is taxed at only 10%. If you earn $373,650, then everything over that is taxed at 35%. Obviously, one of the keys to reducing taxes in the US is to use as many tax brackets as possible.

Let's say you have a married couple with two married children and four unmarried children. My tax insider says that by dividing ownership of the business between the husband and his family, the husband stands to save a lot of money. Provided the business was structured correctly and given the fact his children did not have much taxable income of their own, the business could earn $340,000 and still have every dollar taxed at only 15% or less.

Without proper tax planning, the situation is remarkably different. If the couple were the sole owners of the business and had to pay tax on the entire $340,000, they would've paid more than $90,000 of federal income tax on the business income in addition to any employment taxes they owed.

Instead, they paid less than $47,000 in taxes—a tax savings of more than $43,000. What's more, they received this benefit and more each year as the income grew. Even when the children started earning more of their own income, this couple would still save thousands of dollars of tax every year because they were using their children's lower tax brackets.

Canadians investing in the US can also take advantage of multiple tax brackets by using corporations. In the US, there are two types of corporations: S corporations and C corporations. Only full-time residents of the US can own S corporations, so I won't discuss them in this book. The good news about C corporations is that they have their own tax brackets. I'll talk more about that later, but for now the take-home message is that you want to structure your business with as many taxpayers as possible because you can use those taxpayers to lower tax brackets!

Income Elimination

The fourth way to reduce your US tax liability is to eliminate income. The US tax law allows you to eliminate or in some cases permanently postpone tax on certain types of income.

The best way for a real estate investor to do this is to use the like-kind or 1031 exchange rules. These rules allow you to sell one parcel of real estate and pay no tax so long as the proceeds from the sale are reinvested into another parcel of real estate. (See Fundamental #29: Use the Like-Kind Exchange to Boost Your Tax Strategy.)

Entity Structure

The fifth and perhaps most important way for Canadians to reduce the tax on their US real estate investments is to use the right entity structure. Again, there are strong parallels to the Canadian system and the way a business structure affects tax planning. In both countries, an "entity" is merely a way to own and manage your real estate. A limited partnership is an entity, as is a corporation. The US also has limited liability companies and trusts. The role of entities is the topic of the next fundamental. Read it carefully, as it talks about how you can set up your entity structure so you pay the least amount of tax on your US real estate investments.

PROCEED WITH ENTHUSIASM!

The right entity structure is essential if you want to avoid double taxation. It can even get you a Canadian tax credit. Pay attention!

The most important aspect of your entity structure is that you don't pay tax in both the US and in Canada. In fact, if you set up your entity structure the right way, there is a credit that you can take on your Canadian tax return for taxes paid in the US. If you fail to structure your entity properly, you can easily pay tax twice—once in the US and again in Canada.

The other critical reason to be careful with your US entity structure will become more apparent as you work through the Legal Planning section of this book. It will highlight the fact that every tenant is a potential plaintiff, as is anyone else who visits your property, including contractors, property managers and, believe it or not, trespassers! Indeed, the fact that more than 95% of the lawsuits filed worldwide are filed in the US is an issue for anyone who does business there. You will want to make sure that you are protected from potential lawsuits—and tax planning is an essential part of that asset protection plan!

SOLD

So let's get on with it and go into how to set up the right entity structure for you before you ever invest in the US. The sooner you do, the sooner you will be protected from lawsuits and the sooner you can reduce your US and Canadian income taxes.

Choose the Right Entity to Structure Your US Business.

Seek Advice From a Cross-Border Tax Specialist

If you ask a US investor about the best way to structure your US real estate investments, the most common answer you'll get is "put it in a limited liability company (LLC) that is taxed as a sole proprietorship or a partnership." The LLC would hold title to the property, providing good asset protection (with its "limited liability" rules) and some tax benefits.

That's good advice, but Tom Wheelwright warns Canadians doing real estate business in the US should be careful. First, even for Americans, this answer is only true for investment real estate, and second, it may not be the best entity for a Canadian purchasing buy-and-hold rental properties in the US. For us northerners, a different limited liability entity may create fewer problems with double taxation.

Using LLCs for Investment Real Estate

According to the IRS, if your business involves buying real estate to fix it up and then selling an upgraded product, this is not an investment, it's a business. Your business can still be held in an LLC, but you need to elect to have it taxed differently.

An American who is flipping real estate as his primary operating business would typically want to elect S corporation status to reduce their taxes. As you'll learn in the next fundamental, however, Canadians cannot own property in an S corporation. This does not mean Canadians cannot participate in the fix-and-flip sector, but you will need help structuring that enterprise.

While an LLC is not a tax entity, it can be taxed as a C or S corporation. If it does not make an election, it will be taxed as a sole proprietorship if there is only one owner, or be taxed as a partnership if there is more than one owner.

Ideally, you will set up that LLC and work with your tax advisor to decide how you want it to be taxed. If you run your own business as a sole proprietorship or partnership, all of the net income is subject to self-employment taxes. With self-employment taxes as high as 15.3%, your taxes can certainly add up.

Income in a C corporation is not subject to self-employment taxes. However, if you work in your corporation's business, then your corporation must pay you a salary and that salary is subject to payroll taxes. Half the payroll taxes are paid by the employer and half by the employee, whereas self-employment taxes are paid entirely by the sole proprietor. (Minimizing payroll taxes and other tax issues associated with C corporations are discussed in the next fundamental.)

Rental income from real estate is normally not subject to self-employment tax. So an LLC taxed as a sole proprietorship or a partnership is typically the preferred structure for investment real estate. However, some states have specific taxes on LLCs. In these states, consider setting up an actual corporation or partnership rather than an LLC taxed as a corporation or partnership. This can reduce or avoid these additional state taxes.

More importantly, research the states you're considering before you decide where you're going to set up your LLC, corporation or partnership, and remember that the company does not have to be formed in the state where you are going to do business. Let's say you plan to purchase buy-and-hold investment real estate in Arizona. This is an LLC-friendly state, with no extra taxes or filing requirements for an LLC compared to other entity types. In California, all entities have an $800 minimum tax. If you plan to do business in Arizona, you wouldn't want to set up your company in California.

 SOLD

Check out state websites and talk to a knowledgeable cross-border tax advisor before you register your company in the US. Most states provide detailed information on their websites about how each entity is taxed and that information can help you decide if you want to register in one state and do business in another. A tax advisor can help you decide what works best for your business.

The Canadian Connection

Tax advisors tell me Canadians face some interesting challenges with an LLC when they elect to tax it as a sole proprietorship or partnership. While the "limited liability" provisions are critical from an asset protection perspective, LLCs are taxed as corporations in Canada. In other words, you can "elect" to be taxed as a sole proprietor in the US, but the Canada Revenue Agency will levy corporate taxes. This could result in taxation in both Canada and the US on the same income.

One option to reduce taxes may be to set up a Canadian company that holds the US sole proprietorship in an LLC. You would pay US tax on income earned, but hold it in the Canadian corporation. You could argue that without a distribution, you would not have income in Canada. And even if you have income in Canada, you should receive a tax credit for taxes paid in the US on that same income.

A Different Limited Liability Entity

Canadian real estate investors should look at the family limited partnership (FLP) as well, because it does not seem to present any problems with double taxation in Canada.

Ideally, you would use a US C corporation as a 1% general partnership in your FLP. A foreign trust, or even a Canadian corporation, could be the limited partner and hold up to 99% of the limited partnership interests. This meets the US/Canada tax concern and provides critical asset protection for a Canadian doing business in the US.

 SOLD

A serious real estate investor should never pay tax in the US. Read Fundamental #29 to learn how you can use the US like-kind exchange to shelter your income while channeling your buy-and-hold profits into more investment property.

Use Your C Corp to Win the War on Double Tax.

Conquer Your Fears of Double Taxation

The Canada/US Income Tax Treaty ensures that a resident of one country is not taxed by each of the two countries on the same income in the same year. Known as "double taxation," that would seriously undermine the potential profits a Canadian real estate investor could make in the United States.

There are two types of US corporations: the C corporation and the S corporation. Under US law, the C corporation is a standard business corporation with the potential to double tax because the corporation pays tax on business profits and shareholders pay income tax on any money they draw out of the company as dividends. That concerns a lot of novice Canadian real estate investors when they learn that Canadians are not entitled to set up the other type of corporation—a US S corporation—which, by its nature, precludes double taxation. (Defined under Subchapter S of US tax law, a corporation with S corporation status elects a special tax status with the IRS. An S corporation itself pays no tax. Instead, income is "passed through" to shareholders, who then report the income or loss on their individual tax returns.)

Fear not! My American tax expert says the C corporation's tax rules can be used as an opportunity to save you money by allowing you to use a lower tax rate. Also, the C corporation allows you to borrow money from it, deduct up to $250,000 of depreciable personal property in the year the property is placed in service (for your business), pay you an automobile allowance and minimize your payroll taxes. I'll look at each of those rules here.

The C Corporation and Tax Rates

The C corporation has its own tax rates. When a C corporation pays tax, the tax is calculated using the C corporation tax rates, which are as follows when net taxable income is:

Less than $50,000	15%
Between $50,001 and $75,000	25%
Between $75,001 and $100,000	34%
More than $100,000	34%–39%

The highest individual tax rate is 35% and the C corporation's lower tax rates are 15% and 25%. This provides an opportunity to attack high taxes using the C corporation's separate tax rates. Because the first $50,000 of net income in a C corporation is taxed at 15%, if you are in the highest individual rate of 35%, you can use the tax rate differential to save $10,000 in taxes.

In addition to the immediate advantage of lowering your taxes, these are permanent tax savings because you paid tax at a lower rate.

Fund Your Next Investment

Not only can you use the C corporation's tax rules to reduce your taxes, you can also let your C corporation act as a kind of bank to finance your next investment. This gives you tax-free access to the money and the ability to set the loan terms.

Let's say your C corporation generates $50,000 to $75,000 of net taxable income each year. You have three options with the profits, each with pros and cons. You can:

1. Pay dividends.

Paying a modest dividend is good but a corporation doesn't usually distribute all of its money as dividends, because these are subject to double tax.

2. Pay your salary and benefits.

Your C corporation can pay you a reasonable salary and provide employee benefits. The salary portion is taxable to you and the benefits may or may not be taxable to you. Again, these amounts must be "reasonable," i.e., not likely to use up all of your C corporation's money.

3. Invest the money.

It is not generally a good tax strategy to hold appreciating assets like stocks or real estate in a C corporation. This is because appreciating assets typically generate capital gains, and a C corporation does not have a preferential capital gains tax rate like individuals do. Investments that generate interest income do not usually appreciate, so these types of investments can work well in a C corporation that continues to operate its normal business and wants to invest its cash.

Individuals often fund their personal investments with loans and in Fundamental #9 (Know Your Financing Options) I talked about how difficult it can be for Canadian investors to borrow money for US investment properties from traditional American lenders. This situation prompts many Canadian investors to fund their first US acquisitions with money from their own Canadian equity. Once your C corporation owns investment property and has made some money, it offers an alternative: you can borrow money from the C corporation for your next investment. This has the added bonus of being tax free.

To make this strategy work, be sure to document the terms of the loan, including the loan amount, interest rate, payment amounts and the due date. Then be sure to follow those terms. You will need to pay the loan interest, but it goes directly to your C corporation.

 SOLD

If you plan to borrow money from your C corporation, make sure the transaction follows what the IRS requires and that you can document the veracity of the deal. Investors must always aim for audit-proof records.

Deduct Those Depreciable Assets

Under Section 179 of the C corporation tax rules, a taxpayer can elect to deduct up to $250,000 of depreciable personal property in the year the property is placed in service (i.e., when you take possession, for example). All taxpayers are allowed a Section 179 deduction, but when a partnership and S corporation take it, it flows through to the individual shareholder, which can limit the amount of the Section 179 deduction.

If you add a C corporation to your business structure and buy more than $250,000 of tangible new equipment in a year, such as office equipment you purchase for use in your trade or business, you can use the

Section 179 deduction. (You cannot use the section in lieu of depreciation for a rental property.)

PROCEED WITH ENTHUSIASM!

Make sure your tax advisor knows what you've been buying for all aspects of your real estate investment business. He may be able to find a way to have your C corporation buy a portion of certain equipment to access the C corporation's Section 179 deduction.

Get an Automobile Allowance

Common business practices include visiting customers and clients, picking up supplies, meeting with vendors and attending seminars. In the US tax system, this may all be considered business use of your personal vehicle. Your C corporation can reimburse you for that use and the reimbursement is fully deductible to your C corporation and not taxable to you.

To make this work, my CPA tax specialist says the reimbursement you receive must reflect expenses you incur to maintain your vehicle. You can submit a reimbursement request to your C corporation each week, month or quarter. If your C corporation's use of your personal vehicle is routine, you can use the same weekly, monthly or quarterly amounts as a normal reimbursement. The reimbursed amount can be calculated on your actual expenses or the standard mileage rate can be used. Be sure to update it at least annually so your reimbursement stays tax free.

Minimize Your Payroll Taxes

You must draw a salary from your C corporation. If you keep that salary as low as possible, the payroll taxes are minimized; however, your salary must be reasonable for what you do in your role as an employee.

To calculate a reasonable salary, you must consider your total compensation package. Since your employee benefits can include items like a medical expense reimbursement plan, that compensation is likely to exceed market averages. That means it is reasonable for your salary to be smaller. For example, if reasonable compensation for your work is $30,000 a year and you receive $10,000 a year in medical expense reimbursements, your salary can be $20,000.

PROCEED WITH CAUTION!

Medical Expense Deductions Can Crush Tax Savings

Individuals can only deduct medical expenses that exceed 2% of adjusted gross income. C corporations are allowed to provide employee benefits to their employees. One type of employee benefit is a Medical Expense Reimbursement Plan (MERP). A MERP reimbursement from the C corporation is a non-taxable benefit to the employee and the medical benefit is fully deductible to the C corporation.

This must be done inside your C corporation! If a MERP is done in any other entity, the benefit becomes a taxable benefit to the recipient. Inside the C corporation, a MERP can cover family members, too.

Increase the Depreciation Deduction and Benefit From Depreciation Recapture.

Then Use Your Tax Savings to Buy More Real Estate

"Depreciation" is an accounting term that applies to the way you can spread the cost of an asset over a period of several years, in effect accounting for how the asset depreciates or drops in value over its lifespan. In real estate, depreciation enables investors to recover capital costs on items that depreciate over time. A relatively new fence on a property I just purchased may be worth $1,000 today, but it certainly won't be worth $1,000 when I sell the property five years from now. If I handle that issue properly, I can use the depreciated value of the fence to reduce my taxes every year that I own that property.

I want to be very honest here. Real estate investors can put depreciation to work for their businesses on both sides of the Canada/US border, but some tax advisors may question the wisdom of speeding up your depreciation timetable since taking the depreciation now means a tax bill later (when you post a gain on the property upon disposal).

Tax advisors familiar with the real estate investment market would disagree. They say you should take your tax savings up front and use them to invest in more assets that produce more depreciation. With this strategy in play, your tax liability vanishes—and you increase your earning power.

How Does the US System Work?

What do you see when you look past the building and land involved with your business or rental property? Landscaping, appliances and fixtures all add value to your rental property. They also represent the key to reducing your tax bill.

Say you buy a rental property and then depreciate 80% of it as building and 20% of it as land. This strategy is relatively common. It's also a big mistake because it devalues your real estate investment in two ways.

First, when you buy a property, you buy so much more than the building and the land. This is especially apparent to investors working in the US buy-and-hold market when they're purchasing properties they need to renovate to put onto the rental market. The base purchase price includes landscaping, fixtures and often pools, fences, appliances and electrical and plumbing systems. The IRS requires these items be depreciated as what they are. That's right, even though tax preparers find it easier, the IRS does not want these various assets lumped into the building and land category.

Second, when you take the 80/20 split, it depreciates your property over the longest possible period of time. This represents a huge cost to you in immediate tax savings. It also costs you in terms of the opportunities you miss to do something with those tax savings!

The Cost Segregation Study

To take advantage of those immediate savings and give yourself a chance to benefit from the opportunities those savings propose, you need to undertake a cost segregation study, also known as a chattel appraisal. Tom Wheelwright recommends you have this study done when you buy the rental property, because it will identify the many other things you've bought in addition to a building and land.

Let's say an investor buys a property for $400,000 and it's equipped with an extensive commercial kitchen because he plans to lease the property to his catering business. This is a little more complicated than the typical rental property purchase, but it helps illustrate my point. In this case, a cost segregation study reveals that his $400,000 purchase breaks down into the following components:

Land	$80,000
Building	$210,000
Fixtures and appliances	$85,000
Special wiring for the kitchen	$10,000
Landscaping and parking lot	$15,000

Using an 80% building and 20% land allocation, this investor's depreciation over the first seven years will be $58,000, but if the cost segregation analysis is applied, his depreciation over that time span will be a far better $140,000! This means he will save more than $25,000 in tax thanks to the cost segregation allocation. It also means he will have more money to invest in the early stages of his business. Smart.

Put this strategy to work and invest the tax savings in more properties that produce more depreciation deductions!

File a Change in Accounting Method

Taking all of the allowable depreciation claims we can is a strategy that makes a lot of sense to real estate investors in the buy-and-hold market. But Tom Wheelwright tells me this is a business practice that's routinely overlooked!

If you've missed out on this strategy because you've been sticking to the 80/20 allocation on your tax advisor's advice, it's not too late to reap the rewards. Under US tax law, you can maximize your depreciation this year by filing a "change in accounting method" with your next tax return and deducting all of the depreciation you missed in prior years. The IRS wants you to depreciate items based on their true nature, so the change in accounting method is actually a move towards the preferred method versus an incorrect method. This makes it an automatic change, meaning the IRS does not have to approve your request before you put it into action.

What happens if an investor missed this strategy for three years and then realized his error? He would file a change of accounting method with his current tax return. Based on the numbers from the CPA cited previously, the year he switches to a cost segregation study allocation he would receive an extra depreciation deduction of $62,000. That saves him more than $20,000.

If there is a "trick" associated with using a cost segregation study, it's the fact that you must be careful if you plan to supply your own numbers. On larger properties, like office buildings or multi-family complexes, you must hire a professional to do the study. (Costs will vary with property size.) A professional study will include photographs, engineering studies, research on comparisons and much more, all of which will document the allocations. On large properties, anything less risks the IRS deciding that your numbers won't stand during an audit.

Single-Family Home Rental Properties

On single-family home rental properties, you yourself can do a cost segregation study and appraise all of the chattels associated with the property. That's extremely time-consuming. My US colleagues say you also can use an online service offered by Marshall & Swift, a company that bills itself as "the building cost people." The online service walks you through the information you need to gather about your property. You simply enter the information into their website to get your cost segregation allocation.

This strategy does not meet the strict definition of a third-party study. But since it uses third-party pricing and is a thorough review of the property, it typically passes IRS muster. You can strengthen the foundation of your cost segregation study numbers by documenting how you got the numbers you entered into the online service.

 SOLD

Real estate investors should always take care to make sure they are running an "audit-proof" business. It won't prevent you from being audited by the US Internal Revenue Service (IRS) or the Canadian Revenue Agency (CRA), but it will prepare you to answer questions and to justify decisions.

 PROCEED WITH ENTHUSIASM!

Ask Your Tax Advisor the Right Questions

Real estate investors do not need an in-depth knowledge of US tax law but do need a working understanding of how that tax law works. This understanding will help you ask your tax advisor the "Should I? Would I? Could I?" questions that will trigger her to gather information for your return and help you fine-tune current and future tax strategies.

Do talk to your tax advisor about how a cost segregation analysis enables you to cut your tax bill by adjusting the timing of allowable depreciation deductions associated with your rental properties.

When a depreciation expense is accelerated during the early stages of a property's life, the tax payments decrease. Find out what you need to do to

1. Create a quality audit trail and make sure your asset classifications meet IRS standards

2. Capitalize on retroactive savings

3. Identify other tax benefits with the information gleaned from your cost segregation study; the data can pinpoint opportunities to reduce other real estate tax liabilities and highlight future tax-saving opportunities

Depreciation Recapture

While US taxpayers can use depreciation to offset their ordinary income, and real estate investors can use what's been called the "magic of depreciation" to cut their tax bills and free up more money for investment, they do that knowing that the offset will be "recaptured" by the IRS. That is to say, when the taxpayer sells the asset that was used to offset the ordinary income through depreciation, he will be taxed on the gain as if it were ordinary income, not capital gains.

When depreciation recapture is triggered after you sell a property that has been depreciated, two different calculations are used. The first is for real property and the second is for all other depreciated property, meaning everything from fences and light fixtures to drapery. Both calculations are based on you having a gain when you sell the property. If you do not have a gain, then you will not have depreciation recapture.

Let's say an investor sells his business computer for $500. The man bought the computer for $1,500 and has taken $1,200 in depreciation. The computer's adjusted basis is $300 ($1,500 cost − $1,200 depreciation) and the gain on the sale is $200 ($500 sales price − $300 adjusted basis). Because there is a gain, depreciation capture is triggered.

For personal property, depreciation recapture is the lesser of the total depreciation taken or the actual gain. In this example, the gain of $200 is less than the $1,200 taken in depreciation, so the depreciation recapture is $200. That depreciation recapture is triggered at the investor's ordinary tax rates.

If he sold his computer for $200, there would have been a loss of $100 ($200 sales price − $300 adjusted basis). With a loss, depreciation recapture is not triggered, arguably because there's nothing to recapture.

Tax regulations are highly interconnected and one action typically triggers another. When a taxpayer takes a loss on the sale of an asset, for example, there is no depreciation recapture, but the taxpayer may qualify for ordinary loss treatment under other tax rules.

Recapture on Real Estate Property

If an investor sells a building for $200,000 and land improvements for $20,000, the situation is different. Here, the building would be depreciated using the required straight-line method and that exempts it from depreciation recapture. The straight-line method computes depreciation (or amortization) by dividing the difference between an asset's cost and its expected salvage value by the number of years it is expected to be used. This is the simplest way to calculate depreciation, as it spreads out the cost of an asset equally over its lifetime.

The land improvements were depreciated over 15 years. As that employed an accelerated method of depreciation, there will be depreciation recapture if there is a gain on the land improvements. Depreciation recapture on real property is calculated on the amount of depreciation taken over what would have been allowed using the straight-line method of depreciation.

Turn Recapture Into a Tax Benefit

In sum, my American tax specialist tells me the depreciation deduction provides a legal way to fast-track depreciation prior to disposal and can reduce your taxes, even if you don't spend any actual cash. The IRS will seek to recapture that depreciation when you dispose of the property, but you can turn that to your advantage, too. When you deduct the depreciation of your real property, you are deducting it at your ordinary tax rate, with the highest rate being 35%. Since depreciation recapture is taxed at a maximum rate of 25%, you will reap a permanent tax savings of up to 10%.

You can also make that depreciation recapture disappear completely. To do that you must sell your rental property in a like-kind exchange and be strategic about the property you are acquiring. (See the next fundamental!)

MYTH OR FACT

Myth: Taxes are out of our control.

Fact: Taxpayers have a great deal of control over how much tax they pay. Tax avoidance or mitigation is the legal utilization of tax laws to your advantage. (It has nothing to do with tax evasion, which is illegal.)

Use the Like-Kind Exchange to Boost Your Tax Strategy.

Like-Kind Exchanges Can Nullify Depreciation Recapture

If you like knowing that you can gain up to a 10% tax rate discount on depreciation recapture when you sell your real estate rental properties (Fundamental #28), you'll love the like-kind exchange, which can make the depreciation recapture disappear!

A like-kind exchange occurs under Section 1031 of the Internal Revenue Code. It allows real estate investors to exchange like-kind property for other like-kind property without triggering any gain. This is a valuable investing tool but there are specific rules about what constitutes like-kind—and they aren't rules investors can circumvent.

You should also be aware that if you are selling a property that has been depreciated based on a cost segregation study allocation, then the like-kind property requirement applies to all the various parts of the property. In other words, you are not just selling a property. You are selling the building, land, land improvements, appliances, fixtures and all of the items allocated in the cost segregation study. Because you only have depreciation recapture on the pieces you would sell for a gain, make sure these pieces are covered in the like-kind exchange.

 SOLD

Use the cost segregation study as a strategic tax-planning document to fast-track depreciation, recapture depreciation and get the most from your 1031 exchange.

Audit-Proof Your Like-Kind Exchange

To make your like-kind exchange audit-proof, my CPA tax specialist tells me the property and the deal must do the following five things:

1. Pass the qualified use test

2. Be verifiable like-kind properties

3. Adhere to the time limits of the statute

4. Satisfy title issues

5. Follow the equal-or-up rule

1. Pass the Qualified Use Test

The first step in a like-kind exchange is to make sure the property you are selling and the property you are buying both pass the qualified use test. To pass the test, a property must be considered a "qualifying property," which is tangible property that is held for investment or held for production of income in a trade or business. Property not held for investment or used in your trade or business is not considered qualified use property and will not qualify for tax-deferred exchange treatment. This non-qualifying property includes intangibles, such as paper assets (e.g., stocks and bonds), and interests in a partnership. Inventory doesn't qualify, nor does your personal use property, such as your personal residence, your vacation home and your personal car. Dealer property does not qualify either; this includes properties purchased for fix-and-flip purposes.

To make this strategy work, you need to ensure your property qualifies before you sell it, by which I mean you must hold it for investment or for production of income in your trade or business.

Apply the qualified use test to the property you want to buy. If it doesn't pass, it can't be used for a like-kind exchange.

Let's say an investor has two separate real estate activities, one active in rental real estate and the other upgrading real estate for the quick-flip market. For legal and accounting purposes, she keeps these businesses separate. After meeting with her accountant, she understands the properties related to her rental real estate business may meet the qualified use test because they are used in her business for the production of income. She also understands that the properties held in her fix-and-flip business do not meet the qualified use test because of her dealer status. This knowledge helps her plan strategic sales of her qualifying properties.

2. Ensure Your Property's Like-Kind Status Is Verifiable

The property you sell must be like-kind with the property you buy in order for your exchange to qualify under Section 1031. The term "like-kind" is defined by the IRS and refers to the nature of the property, not its grade or quality.

For real estate, the rules for like-kind exchange are very broad. For example, raw land is like-kind with a commercial property, an apartment complex, an industrial building or a single-family rental home.

Personal property, which is tangible property that is not real estate, is treated much differently. To qualify for the tax advantages of a like-kind exchange with personal property, you must follow very narrow rules. For example, a car is like-kind with another car, but not with a truck. (Livestock of different sexes do not qualify for the like-kind exchange, either. It's a cow for a cow or a bull for a bull.)

Again, the trick to making the like-kind exchange work rests with knowing that what you plan to sell is like-kind with what you plan to buy. For example, if an investor owns several single-family rental homes and wants to sell some and benefit from Section 1031, he should identify the type of property that will replace the one he is selling *before* he puts that product on the market. If he plans to sell a single-family home and buy a multi-unit residential property, his replacement property is like-kind with what he's selling.

This information helps the investor strategically plan his like-kind exchange and provides strong audit protection.

 SOLD

Note to Canadian investors: The rules for like-kind exchanges with real estate are very broad—unless the exchange involves foreign property. You cannot exchange US personal property with a property outside of the United States, or vice versa, and avoid paying tax on the gain. Ditto for rental properties.

3. Adhere to the Time Limits of the Statute

Strict time limits apply to like-kind exchanges. Section 1031 requires you to identify the replacement property within 45 days of closing on the sale of your property. You can identify a maximum of three properties, or as many properties as you like provided the combined purchase price of the properties does not exceed 200% of the sale price of your property.

SOLD

Given the time restriction, it is always a good idea to identify more than one potential purchase. If one deal falls through, you will have another one lined up.

You must provide your qualified intermediary with your list of potential properties by midnight on the 45th day following the sale of your property. Generally speaking, a qualified intermediary should be a corporation in the full-time business of facilitating like-kind exchanges. Also known as an accommodator, the intermediary cannot be related to the taxpayer or have had a financial relationship with the taxpayer in the last two years. (This rules out the taxpayer's current certified public accountant, attorney or real estate agent.) You can change or revoke your identification as often as you wish during those 45 days but the identification cannot be changed or altered after that deadline has passed.

The 180-Day Rule

The 180-Day Rule requires you to buy your replacement property within 180 days of closing on the sale of your property. The property you purchase must be one or more of the properties on your 45-day identification list. And be careful! Filing your tax return can shorten the 180-day limit. You have to complete your purchase earlier than the 180-day limit if the tax return that will report your like-kind exchange is due before the 180th day. This can be a good reason to extend your tax return, as it ensures you will get the full 180 days.

 PROCEED WITH CAUTION!

That 180-day period is not negotiable and applies regardless of whether the deadline falls on a Saturday, Sunday or legal holiday.

Suppose the investor we talked about above decides to sell one of his rental properties for $250,000 and use a like-kind exchange to save tax. To make sure the 1031 exchange works, he looks for his replacement property before the first rental property is sold. This helps him meet the closing date on the sale of his property.

As soon as that property sells, he gives his qualified intermediary a list of five potential replacement properties. The combined purchase price of the properties is $495,000, which is less than 200% of the sales price of the property he sold. This investor has used strategic planning to make sure he meets all of the 1031 provisions. Investors who fail to meet the various requirements may sacrifice the tax benefits when a gain is triggered.

4. Satisfy Title Issues

Under Section 1031, the title must be in the same taxpayer's name before and after the exchange. This means the property being sold must be titled to the same taxpayer buying the replacement property. There are three exceptions to the general title requirements. How you hold title to the property you sell can be different from how you hold title to the property you buy if one of the following applies:

1. The property is titled to a disregarded single member limited liability corporation (LLC) and you are the owner of that single member LLC.

2. The property is titled to a disregarded LLC owned by you and your spouse.

3. The property is titled to a revocable trust (such as a family trust) and you are the trustee of that trust.

To illustrate, let's say an investor decides to sell one of his rental properties for $250,000 in a like-kind exchange. He reviews the title and sees it is titled to him individually. He now wants the property in the 1031 exchange to be titled to his LLC—a disregarded LLC owned by him and his wife. This type of LLC meets the exception to the general title requirements, meaning the transaction qualifies as a like-kind exchange even though there are differences in how the exchanged property will be titled.

5. Follow the Equal-or-Up Rule

The numbers in a like-kind exchange can be confusing. A general guideline to follow is that the exchange must be made into a property that is equal or up. This means the property you are buying has a purchase price that is equal to or greater than the selling price of your property. It also means that the cash plus debt you put into the property you are buying is equal to or greater than the cash (equity) plus debt in the property you are selling.

Under this rule, in order to defer all of the tax gain of the property you are selling, you must do the following three things:

1. Buy a property (or properties) with a price equal to or greater than the property you sold.

2. Reinvest all of the net proceeds, including cash proceeds, from the sale of your property.

3. Have debt on the property you purchase that is equal to or greater than the debt on the property you sold.

Avoid the Boot

If you do not meet the equal-or-up requirements, the difference (which could be a cash distribution or reduced debt) is treated as what's commonly known as "boot" and is subject to tax in the year of the sale. Again, you can avoid this issue by partaking in some strategic planning.

If you decide to sell a $250,000 rental property with a mortgage of $200,000 and benefit from the 1031 exchange, you need to look at new properties with a purchase price of at least $250,000. You must also be able to obtain financing of at least $200,000 and put down at least $50,000 cash on the property. Anything less and you invite an unwelcome surprise when the like-kind exchange is denied and you have to pay tax on the gain realized from the sale of that rental property!

Boost Your Cash Flow by Using Your Tax Losses.

More Ways to Legally Shelter Your Income and Keep More Cash

I've covered a few of the more innovative tax strategies you can put to work in your US real estate investment business. You will, of course, need to discuss what's best for your business with a tax advisor who is familiar with how decisions in the US might affect your Canadian tax position.

This fundamental draws on the advice and expertise of my US tax expert to focus on a variety of other strategies you should consider, all of which provide ideas for how you can use tax losses from your real estate ventures to increase your cash flow—and build your investment pool. These tax losses may be from actual cash-flow losses, but you can also create tax losses through deductions for payments to related parties or related companies you own.

Be Active in Your Real Estate

Rental real estate is typically considered a passive activity and rental real estate losses are "per se" passive. The general rule for passive losses is that they can only be used against passive income. If your passive losses exceed your passive income, you do not get to use your excess passive losses in the current year. These excess passive losses carry over to your next tax year.

Up to $25,000 of rental real estate losses can be taken against any other income every year if the taxpayer "actively" participates in their real estate activity, meaning they are participating in management decisions. You need to exercise independent judgment and not simply ratify decisions made by a manager, but no specific hour requirement must be met.

This rule phases out when income exceeds $100,000 and is completely phased out when income is more than $150,000.

Be *Very* Active in Your Real Estate

To avoid not being able to take all of your rental real estate losses and shelter an unlimited amount of income, you need to be what the IRS defines as "very active" in your rental real estate. If you qualify as a "real estate professional" and materially participate in the real estate activity or activities that generate the loss, you can use all of your rental real estate losses against any other income.

To determine if this holds true for you, consider the following three questions:

1. Do you spend more than half of your personal service time in real estate activities?

Your total personal service time includes time spent at your job, business and real estate business. Real estate activities include development, redevelopment, construction or reconstruction, acquisition or conversion, rental, management, leasing and brokerage. Services you perform as an employee do not count unless you are at least a 5% owner.

2. Do you spend more than 750 hours a year in your real estate activities?

If you can't answer yes to questions 1 and 2, you are not a real estate professional. If you can answer yes to both, you must determine whether you "materially participate."

3. Is all of your real estate activity time spent on one real estate property? One rental property is considered one activity.

If you can say yes here, then you materially participate and all of your rental losses can be taken. If not, consider making an election to group your real estate activities into a single activity in order to take your rental real estate losses. Without doing this, the material participation test must be met for each real estate activity.

 SOLD

If you're not able to take your rental real estate losses because you don't own at least 5% of the company for which you perform real estate activities, form your own company, hire yourself as an employee and have your current employer hire your company.

A little restructuring could enable you to keep doing the same thing but save a whole lot more in taxes! The time you spend as an employee of your own company qualifies for the 750-hour test and you may even qualify for additional tax savings by having your own company.

Shift Income to Your Children

If your income is in the phase-out range of the $25,000 deduction because it's above $100,000, or you no longer qualify for the deduction because your income is more than $150,000, you can shift income to your children by hiring them to do specific tasks. This lowers your personal income and takes advantage of the tax rules only offered to those at a lower income level. Also, the children's income may be taxed at a lower rate than that of the parents.

There are rules relative to where the work is done, so this provision can be more complicated for a Canadian investing in the US. Make decisions based on sound advice.

Shift Income to High and Low Tax Years

You can structure your work so you earn bonuses every other year. For example, instead of taking a $50,000 bonus every year, you could take a $100,000 bonus every other year, potentially lowering your income below the $150,000 threshold in certain years.

In the years when the total income equals $100,000, you can use the entire $25,000 real estate loss limit. That produces $6,000 in tax savings in those low-income years.

PROCEED WITH CAUTION!

Tax Plan With Prudence
The best tax-planning strategies are put in place alongside a business plan that looks at what you plan to do this year and for several years in the future, so make purchase and sale decisions with a tax strategy already in place.

Take Unused Passive Loss Carryovers

When you sell a rental property that has a passive loss carryover, you can take all of the losses in the year you sell the property. You do not have to have passive income to take these losses.

To do this, you must completely dispose of the rental property in a taxable transaction with no like-kind exchange and to an unrelated party. (If you elect to aggregate your activities to meet the real estate professional rules, you have to sell all your property to qualify for this rule.)

As noted in Fundamental #31, you can use this rule to sell your worst-performing property, use your passive losses against the sale income and then use the money you save to invest in more real estate.

Shelter Income With Deductions

In addition to the depreciation deductions discussed in Fundamental #28, you can increase your passive losses by spending more money on your rental properties by completing repairs. To keep your tax strategies audit-proof, always retain receipts for work done.

Obtain Tax Benefits From Your Worst-Performing Property.

There's Value in Your Passive Losses

My focus is on cash-flowing properties that put money in your bank account while producing long-term appreciation, but you must also know how to deal with losses, especially in terms of how they affect your tax situation.

As discussed in the last fundamental, real estate losses are "per se" passive. According to my US tax specialist, another way to deal with unused passive losses from your US rental real estate properties is to sell your worst-performing rental and use your passive losses against your passive income. Even better, the gain is taxed at the preferred capital gains rate and your losses are deducted at the ordinary tax rate. This is a direct play on the tax rate spread—and it results in cash in your pocket.

 SOLD

Real estate insiders call this tax rule a double win. You get rid of your worst-performing property and you get to use that property's unused losses against your other income.

Applying the General Rule to a Single Property

The general rule is that rental real estate losses are "per se" passive, and passive losses can be applied only against passive income. If your passive losses exceed your passive income, you do not get to use your excess passive losses in the current year. These excess passive losses do carry over to your next tax year but, again, they can only be used against passive losses.

Let's say an investor works for a property management company and his salary is $200,000. He has one rental property with the following history:

Current-year loss = $10,000

Prior-year loss carryover = $30,000

Under the general rule, the investor cannot take $10,000 of current real estate losses against his salary income because the losses are *passive* and his salary is *active*. The $10,000 of current-year losses are added to his loss carryover.

If he completely disposes of the rental property in a taxable transaction (meaning no like-kind exchange as discussed in Fundamental #29) and to an unrelated party, then any passive losses from the activity in the current year and any that have carried over from prior years can be used to offset his income. Once his property is sold, he does not need to have passive income to take these losses.

 SOLD

When you sell a US property that has a passive loss carryover, you can take all of the losses in the year you sell the property.

So if the investor sells his rental property, he can take the entire $10,000 of current losses plus the entire $30,000 of prior-year losses. This effectively shelters $40,000 of his income. At current US federal income tax rates, that results in a tax savings of more than $11,000.

Applying the General Rule to Multiple Properties

Investors with multiple US properties or other passive activities (see Invest in PIGs and Modify Your Investment Strategy, below) can reap even more benefits from the same tax rule. My US tax advisor provides a scenario where we have an investor who works for a property management company. Her salary is $350,000. She also has 10 rental properties with the following loss history:

Property 1, current-year loss	=	$10,000
Property 1, prior-year loss carryover	=	$30,000
Properties 2–10, combined losses	=	$90,000
Properties 2–10, loss carryover	=	$270,000

As with the situation where an investor owns a single property, when she disposes of a rental property in a taxable transaction (meaning there is no like-kind exchange) and the sale is to an unrelated party, then any passive losses from the activity in the current year, plus losses that have carried over from prior years, can be used to offset any other income she has.

If she sells Property 1, she can use the $10,000 of current-year loss plus the entire $30,000 of prior-year losses. This effectively shelters $40,000 of her income.

Because the net gain on the sale of the rental property is passive income, it can free up her passive losses. The net gain on the sale of a rental property is determined by taking the gain on the property and subtracting current- and prior-year losses that are freed up on the sale of the property.

If this investor's Property 1 sells for $400,000 for a net gain of $175,000, the current- and prior-year losses, which total $40,000, are freed as a result of the sale. The net gain is $135,000 ($175,000 gain less $40,000 loss). This $135,000 is passive income, so she can use it to take additional passive losses in the current year. This means that $90,000 of the current-year losses from Properties 2 to 10 and $45,000 of the prior-year loss carryover from Properties 2 to 10 can be used in the current year.

The Capital Gain Benefit

The end result is a $175,000 gain and $175,000 ($40,000 plus $135,000) loss. On the surface, it looks like there is no tax difference since the gain equals the losses. However, the tax rates are different. The gain is a capital gain, taxed at 15%, and the losses are ordinary, taxed at 35%. The 20% difference in tax rates produces a significant tax savings of $35,000.

Invest in PIGs

Passive income generators (PIGs) are another form of US investments that yield passive income that can be sheltered by your passive losses from real estate, creating the opportunity to save thousands in taxes.

Any of the following can be PIGs:

- **Commercial rental property.** While residential rental property commonly produces passive losses, it is not uncommon for commercial properties to produce passive income, even after depreciation.

- **A limited partnership.** A limited partnership interest in a limited partnership that operates a business can also be a source of passive income. The type of business can vary because what makes this PIG work is the fact that you are a limited partner. A limited partner cannot materially participate, making the income to that partner passive.

- **Membership interest in an LLC.** This is also taxed as a partnership. Make sure that your membership interest does not have management authority attached to it. If you want the income to be passive, your role must be passive as well.

Modify Your Investment Strategy

Some real estate investments have what the tax industry calls "built-in" tax savings. These investments do not require you to do anything extra to write off the losses against any other income you have. Oil and gas is one example of these real estate investments, where up to 90% of the investment can be written off in the first two years.

To take advantage of these built-in savings, your oil and gas investment must be a "working interest." It must be operated as a general partnership and you must be a general partner. Oil and gas operations are allowed to write off intangible drilling costs, which is very similar to writing off depreciation in rental properties (see Fundamental #27). These intangible drilling costs often result in taxable losses that you can take against your other income.

Consider an investor who invests $100,000 as a general partner in a general partnership that has a working interest in an oil and gas operation. In the first two years, he will be allocated losses from the partnership totaling $90,000. He can offset his other income by the amount of losses allocated.

 MYTH OR FACT

Myth: Making more money always results in more taxes.

Fact: There are legitimate ways to shelter your income. Do not wait until you are making money from US real estate before you talk to a US tax advisor.

Limiting Your US Taxation If You're
a Canadian Snowbird

Jim Yager, CA, Talks About Residency and Estate Issues

It is no surprise that many Canadians deal with the Canadian winter by steering clear of it. Colloquially known as Canadian snowbirds, they migrate to sunny US states for several months a year. The weather is enticing, but the Internal Revenue Service (IRS) may have a few unpleasant surprises for the uninformed.

Now that you've been introduced to some of the US tax rules that are especially important to real estate investors, Canadian CA Jim Yager wants to delve into some of the potential tax pitfalls that await Canadians who "visit" the US for several months of the year, especially if they sometimes rent out their homes-away-from-home. Since these properties are typically held personally, the tax issues differ from those held as investment properties. Selling that personal property may also trigger nasty US tax implications that you may be able to avoid with a little pre-planning.

Here is an updated version of a report Jim first prepared for the American Chamber of Commerce.

Residence Rules

Canadian snowbirds who never spend more than 121 days in the US in any tax year are not considered US residents for income tax purposes under the IRS's substantial presence test. You may be considered a US resident if you are present in the US for 183 days under the following formula: days of US presence in the current year, plus ⅓ of days of US presence in the prior year. However, even if this adds up to 183 days or more, you would not be considered a US resident if you have a closer connection to another country and you file Form 8840 in a timely fashion. You cannot claim a closer connection if you have applied for permanent residence status or if you are present in the US for 183 days or more in the current year. If you fail all these tests, you can still seek relief under the Income Tax Treaty between Canada and the US. It determines residency based on the location of your permanent home, center of vital interest, habitual abode and citizenship. To claim the benefits of the treaty you must file a treaty-based return. If you still fail all of the tests, you are considered a US resident for income tax purposes and you are required to file a US income tax return and report income from all sources, including income from Canada.

Renting Your Property

Snowbirds who rent out their American condo or other real estate properties should be aware that a withholding tax of 30% normally applies to the gross amount of any rent paid to a resident of Canada on real estate located in the US. Unlike withholding taxes on interest and dividends, this tax is not reduced by the Canada/US tax treaty.

Canadians can avoid the 30% gross withholding tax by filing a US tax return and electing to pay tax on net rental income. Then, they can receive a refund for any taxes withheld to the extent the withholding amount exceeds the tax payable. This is most likely to be advantageous where one incurs significant expenses such as mortgage interest, maintenance, insurance, property management and property taxes, since tax at the graduated rates will likely be substantially lower than the 30% withholding tax.

The election of the net rental income method applies for all future years and may be revoked only in limited circumstances. The election applies to all of an individual's rental real estate in the US but a state tax (and possibly a city tax) may also be payable on the rental income if the election is made on the federal return.

Once the election is made, the taxpayer should provide IRS Form W-8ECI to the tenant, and the 30% withholding will not be required. Avoid any confusion by making sure your tax preparer understands cross-border issues.

Selling Your Property

If a Canadian sells real estate located in the US, a withholding tax of 10% of the gross sales price is normally payable under the *Foreign Investment in Real Property Tax Act* (FIRPTA). The tax withheld can be offset against the US income tax payable on any gain realized on the sale and refunded if it exceeds the tax liability. The 10% withholding requirement on the gross sale price applies regardless of the seller's adjusted basis (the net cost of an asset after adjusting for tax-related items) in the property.

There are two exceptions to FIRPTA's 10% withholding requirement that may reduce or eliminate the requirement. Exception No. 1 kicks in if the sale price is less than US$300,000 and the purchaser intends to use it as a residence. The buyer need not be a US resident.

For this exception to apply, the purchaser must have definite plans to live at the property for at least half of the time that the property is in use during each of the two years following the sale. The gain on the sale will still be taxable in the US and therefore a US tax return must be filed.

Exception No. 2 involves a "withholding certificate." Withholding tax may be reduced or eliminated should a Canadian obtain a withholding certificate from the IRS on the basis that the expected US tax liability will be less than 10% of the sales price. The certificate will indicate what amount of tax should be withheld by the purchaser rather than the full 10%.

If an application for a withholding certificate with respect to a transfer of a US real property interest is submitted to the IRS, but has not been received by the IRS at the time of the transfer, the buyer must withhold 10% of the amount realized. However, the amount withheld, or a lesser amount as determined by the IRS, need not be reported and paid over to the IRS until the 20th day following the IRS's final determination with respect to the application for a withholding certificate.

The buyer's legal representative will generally hold the 10% withholding in an escrow account until the withholding certificate is received and then refund to the seller the amount permitted pursuant to the withholding certificate. If the seller does not apply for the withholding certificate, he must wait until after year-end to file a tax return to claim a refund for the excess of the withholding amount over the ultimate tax liability.

Gain: Filing Requirements

For income tax purposes, a Canadian investor must file a US federal tax return and report the gain on the sale of US real estate. The resulting tax will be offset by the FIRPTA tax withheld. An individual may also be subject to state income tax withholding and filing requirements. Some states, including Florida, Texas, Washington, South Dakota and Alaska, do not have a state income tax on individuals.

If an individual owned US property and has been resident in Canada since before September 27, 1980, he can likely take advantage of the Canada/US tax treaty to reduce the gain. In such a case, only the gain accruing since January 1, 1985, will be taxed. This transitional rule does not apply to business properties that are part of a permanent establishment in the US.

To claim the benefit under the treaty, a Canadian will need to make the claim on a US tax return and include a statement containing certain specific information about the transaction.

Foreign Tax Credit

US tax on the sale of US property will generate a foreign tax credit that may be used to reduce the Canadian tax on the sale; however, if the amount of the gain taxed in Canada is reduced because of the principal residence exemption, the foreign tax credit available may be limited. Additionally, a strengthening Canadian dollar in relation to the US dollar may result in a larger taxable gain in the US than in Canada. The opposite would be true if the Canadian dollar declines in value from the date of acquisition.

Although the US estate tax was repealed for the 2010 tax year, the law that repealed the tax sunsets after 2010 and the estate tax returns in 2011 and future years. The estate tax unified for a descendant who is neither a US citizen nor a US domiciliary is $13,000, which can offset an estate up to $60,000. However, the treaty between Canada and the US allows a Canadian resident to claim an enhanced unified credit. The enhanced unified credit is equal to the unified credit applicable to a US citizen, multiplied by a ratio of the descendant's US situs assets divided by global assets. The unified credit for a US citizen for tax years 2011 and after can offset an estate of up to $1 million. An additional credit can be claimed if the US situs assets are transferred to a Canadian citizen or a resident spouse.

Estate Taxes

US estate taxes can also impose a burden on the estates of Canadians who own US real estate at death. Talk to your tax preparer about ways to minimize these taxes. Ideas include holding the property through a Canadian corporation, splitting interest, obtaining non-recourse debt financing and partaking in a partnership structure.

Holding Property Through a Canadian Corporation

If you hold business real estate through a Canadian corporation rather than personally, no US estate tax will apply. This is because the shares of the Canadian corporation are not considered "property" within the US. Ordinarily, if US real estate is used personally by a Canadian shareholder, for Canadian tax purposes the Canadian would have to recognize a taxable benefit equal to the value of the rental usage of the property, unless the shareholder pays the rental value to the corporation.

The CRA used to have a liberal administrative policy of not assessing a taxable shareholder benefit for personal use of a corporate-owned US vacation property if it was owned by a "single-purpose corporation" that met certain requirements. The CRA recently revoked this policy for property acquired by or transferred to a single-purpose corporation after 2004. Prior to that ruling, a single-purpose corporation's sole objective was to hold property for the personal use or enjoyment of the shareholder. Although a single-purpose corporation may provide some shelter from US estate tax, it is not the most efficient structure for income tax purposes.

Today, single-purpose corporations properly structured to acquire US real estate prior to 2005 continue to be covered by CRA's initial policy. For US estate tax purposes, there may be an issue as to whether the IRS will respect the single-purpose corporation as the true owner of the property. If the single-purpose corporation is the nominal owner of the property on behalf of the Canadian shareholder or the corporation is deemed to be the owner on behalf of a shareholder, the IRS may ignore the corporation for estate tax purposes. Consequently, the shareholder of a single-purpose corporation may be exposed to the US estate tax, regardless of the corporate ownership of the property. This exposure is exacerbated for single-purpose corporations, because compliance with CRA guidelines (for property acquired prior to 2005) effectively causes the corporation to be viewed as a mere nominee of the shareholder.

Income Tax Issue

Owning US real estate through a corporation can significantly increase the income tax arising from the sale of US real estate. Current US federal tax law provides a maximum income tax rate of 15% on long-term capital gains (gains from the sale of capital assets held for at least 12 months). (The 15% rate will increase to 20% beginning in 2011.) There are no preferential rates for capital gains recognized by a corporation. The federal corporate tax rate on such gains can be as high as 35%. Furthermore, some states impose a higher tax rate on gains of a corporation. For example, although Florida has no individual income tax, it imposes tax at a rate of 5.5% on corporations realizing capital gains on Florida real estate. Therefore, the federal and Florida tax rate on the sale of a Florida vacation home could exceed 40% if sold by a corporation, but would generally be limited to 15% if sold by an individual.

Although these taxes may be less than the potential US estate tax, the ultimate cost of the Canadian corporate structure should be weighed against the potential benefits. The likelihood of selling the property prior to the investor's death is another element of this equation.

Splitting Interest

Another technique to reduce exposure to US estate tax is to split interest ownership of the property. Under such an arrangement, an individual would acquire a life interest in US property and her children would acquire the remainder interest in the property. Upon the death of the individual, there would be no estate tax on the life interest, since the life interest would have no value upon death. If the children die while holding a remainder interest, the estate tax would be assessed on the value of the remainder interest. Generally, the children can obtain term life insurance at low costs (because of their age) to protect them from estate tax exposure.

A split-interest arrangement usually involves a trust or partnership structure. The structure may result in significant complexities but the tax savings may be worthwhile for certain family situations.

Obtaining Non-Recourse Debt Financing

A non-recourse mortgage outstanding on US real estate reduces the value of the property included in an individual's taxable estate. A non-recourse mortgage is one that entitles the lender to have recourse only against the property mortgaged. If an individual defaults on payment, the mortgaged property can be seized, but there will be no further liability if the value of the property does not satisfy the debt.

Since most US lenders are reluctant to provide a mortgage on a non-recourse basis, it may be necessary to seek other sources. One possible source of non-recourse financing may be a spouse. Assume a wife has $100,000 to invest in a US vacation home. Instead of investing directly, she could loan her husband $100,000 on a non-recourse basis to acquire the property. Should he die, there will be no value in the estate, since the non-recourse debt from the value of the property situated in the US will be deducted. If she dies, there will be no value in the estate since the loan is not property situated in the US. In order to be respected as true debt, the debt should have commercial characteristics, such as a market rate of interest and repayment terms.

This may create a problem, because the wife would have interest income for Canadian tax purposes and the husband would have no interest expense deduction. Since the US rules do not specify that the funds received from the mortgage must be used to acquire the US property, it may be possible for the husband to acquire investment assets with the funds received. Acquiring additional assets may allow for a deductible carrying charge for Canadian tax purposes.

Another problem with non-recourse debt is that the debt does not change as the property appreciates. Consequently, should the property substantially appreciate in value and/or the principal of the debt be repaid, the debt will offset less of the value of the property.

Partaking in a Partnership Structure

Although this is what insiders like to call an "unsettled area of law," you could argue that a Canadian partnership holding personal use US real property is not property situated in the US and therefore the Canadian partner is sheltered from US estate tax.

Another strategy is for such a partnership to elect corporate status for US tax purposes. This makes the partnership a "foreign corporation" for US tax purposes and therefore exempt from US estate tax. To make this election, the partnership must have some business activities beyond just the holding of personal-use real estate. One of the attractive features of this strategy is that, since the partnership will continue to be recognized as a partnership for Canadian tax purposes, the Canadian partner will not have a "shareholder benefit" (as this only applies to shareholders of a corporation). Unfortunately, because the partnership will be considered a corporation for US tax purposes, the tax arising from the sale of the property will not be eligible for the lower individual tax rates.

Under certain circumstances it may be possible to elect corporate status for US tax purposes after the date of death of the partner. This will allow individual income tax rates on the sale of the property before death and provide insulation from the estate tax upon death. This is a complex strategy that requires extreme care in both planning and implementation.

Review US Estate Tax Plans

Although the Canada/US tax treaty reduces the US estate tax bite for many Canadians holding US property, it will not provide complete relief for larger estates. Other issues for snowbirds include insurance. While a Canadian's insurance proceeds are not subject to US estate tax, the insurance proceeds can substantially increase the value of a decedent's estate at death and that could trigger US estate tax.

Jim Yager's final word on the topic of snowbirds and the US tax system echoes what accountants and lawyers on both sides of the border say: assess the impact of the US estate tax on your estate and seek professional help to put tax-mitigating strategies to work in Canada and the US. While a properly drafted will is a minimum, estate planning should be considered well in advance of any purchases of US property. From this perspective, that makes estate planning (and US estate tax avoidance) part of a smart investor's early due diligence.

Legal Planning

PART 4

"What you don't know could kill you."

—Philip McKernan

James Burns is an in-demand asset protection and tax attorney who has designed his US practice around real estate investors. In addition to publishing several books on related topics, James channels his real-world experience into helping clients avoid multiple probates and learn to properly transfer their real estate holdings to the next generation—free of tax and lawsuits. I am grateful to offer my readers the benefit of James's legal expertise.

Cover Your Ass(ets).

The Pillars of Asset Protection for Real Estate:
What Asset Protection Is and Isn't

In all of the debate about the differences between US and Canadian culture, a US predilection for litigation is one subject that almost always generates a great deal of talk. Speaking from the vantage point of an Irishman, I don't think the two countries are all that far apart. At the very least, this appears to be one area where Canadians are on track to catch up with their American cousins. In fact, that's the No. 1 reason why property and liability insurance rates are climbing in both countries.

A case in point: In early 2010, an insurance company in Canada named a 14-year-old babysitter in a claim after a residential fire spread to a neighbor's property. The babysitter got the kids out of the dwelling, called the fire department and alerted the neighbors. Her name was later dropped from the suit, but the brief media frenzy over the story gave a lot of Canadians new reasons to think about the potential liabilities associated with allowing their children to make a few extra dollars by babysitting. Thanks to the mere potential for litigation, a seemingly innocuous activity has assumed far more ominous possibilities.

Even though situations like this are becoming more commonplace in Canada, Canadian real estate investors are probably unprepared for the litigious realities of doing business in the United States. The wealth of media headlines aside, my American colleagues tell me that even their own countrymen are taken aback when they find themselves in the US court system. My main message here is that Canadian investors can certainly expect to get a big lesson in what's considered "fair" if one of your business dealings ever ends up in a US court. And consider yourself forewarned: my US investment team tells me that the "fair" treatment doled out by American courts typically feels like anything but fair!

In fact, a report by the U.S. Chamber Institute for Legal Reform pointed to several states and counties where biased judges and juries are a known problem. That makes court decisions a real crapshoot in terms of the outcome you can expect.

A recent poll shows that three-quarters of all small business owners in America expressed concern that they would be the target of an unfair lawsuit. Six in 10 said the fear of lawsuits makes them feel more guarded about the business decisions they make. As well, 54% said lawsuits or the threat of lawsuits forced them to make decisions they ordinarily would not have made.

The 3 Pillars of Asset Protection

Canadian real estate investors cannot expect to change the US legal system. Nor can they expect special treatment. They can, however, expect to improve their asset protection by following three core pillars shared by my US investment team.

As you read through the following three pillars of asset protection, think about the areas where you may be vulnerable to problems:

1. Separate certain assets from yourself through title with entities.

2. Insulate yourself with proper insurance and estate planning.

3. Remove assets and equity from real property from harm's way by using global solutions or entities (e.g., trusts, limited liability companies, family limited partnerships).

 SOLD

Canadians investing in the US real estate market must accept that the legal system is not fair. There is no substitute for good legal advice.

Learn What Asset Protection Is and Isn't

There are a lot of misconceptions about US asset protection. Much of that comes from misinformation shared by legal charlatans with unethical websites that discuss all manner of benefits that are illegal and improbable.

Investors new to the US market need to know that asset protection in this country does not involve

- Evading tax

- Defrauding current creditors

- Hiding assets

- Rendering yourself insolvent

Asset protection in this market is about

- The strategic placement of assets

- Protecting your assets

What does this mean? The strategic placement of assets aims to reduce liabilities and vulnerabilities, but never aims to circumvent the law—it's all about proactive action. Using the three pillars, the asset-protection-wise investor will separate (and sometimes remove) certain assets from himself through title with entities or business structures (like the family limited partnership or trusts). Appropriate insurance and estate planning will also ensure the investor and his companies are insulated from asset claims. These practices, adopted with the help of a legal and tax professional familiar with the investor's business situation, provide some "distance" between his assets and his business liabilities.

The aim of protecting your assets is about leveling the litigation playing field. Since the US court system cannot be relied upon to always deliver fairness, real estate investors must take care to protect their assets from litigation.

Perform Due Diligence by Considering the 4 Layers of Asset Protection

I've said it plenty of times before and I'll say it plenty of times again: opportunity abounds in the current US real estate market and it makes sense for Canadian investors to be eyeing that market in an effort to capitalize on those opportunities.

But Canadians entering this market must recognize that these opportunities are driven by real estate market fundamentals like positive cash flow and market appreciation. This bears repeating because the media frenzy over nominal changes in interest rates and the Canadian dollar's relative strength against the US greenback are not real estate market fundamentals. While they may factor into some of your investment decisions, they are just as likely to lead you astray by adding a complicated emotional element to your decisions.

Market opportunities aside, there is no excuse for thinking you can check your due diligence strategies at the border! Indeed, when it comes to protecting their US property investments, Canadians must look at four key areas in terms of their asset protection plans:

1. Proper insurance

2. Limited liability entities

3. Stripping of equity from business or real estate

4. Global solutions, like banking in another country

While asset protection plans require the input of legal, tax and insurance professionals, I would like to draw your attention to some key points with respect to insurance and limited liability entities.

Proper Insurance

Decisions about the kind of insurance you need will depend on your budget and what the industry considers your "insurable needs," i.e., how much insurance you need to protect your assets and your estate. Life and property insurance are among the products real estate investors must investigate fully.

The amount of life insurance you need depends on two factors. One is the succession of capital to create a legacy, pay down taxes and pay expenses. The other is "lifestyle capital." This can be designed as a supplemental retirement income—taking advantage of the tax code. The lifestyle capital would consider over-funding the policy beyond the insurance cost to build a tax-free cash value that the insured could take out as loans in the future.

According to a US legal specialist familiar with the real estate investment market, a person does not have "enough" insurance if their current coverage or lack thereof would not replace their income for a number of years, or cover the expenses of a larger estate. Depending on how one views it, it is also a way to create a tax-free legacy to loved ones or a charity based on an inevitable event. The goal is to get the insurance when you are young and insurance is inexpensive, and lock in the pricing so that you can maximize the internal rate of return over the cost of the insurance.

Use of Limited Liability Entities

The exact kind of structure you need to set up to protect your assets is very difficult to stipulate except on a case-by-case basis. At the very least, a person who owns property should want a basic asset protection plan that includes a limited liability entity like a limited partnership or family limited partnership to separate and control the asset, create some estate-planning options and limit the remedy a creditor would have should they sue you based on the asset in the entity, which most of the time is real property.

PROCEED WITH CAUTION!

Limited liability entities are not created equal—Canadians need to seek advice from a cross-border legal and tax specialist when setting up limited liability entities. Canadians who set up a US limited liability company (LLC), for example, may leave themselves exposed to double taxation. A family limited partnership (FLP) offers some protection from liability and double taxation.

33

Develop an Asset Protection Plan and Be Prepared to Avoid Lawsuits.

Lawsuit Statistics and Crazy Cases That Threaten Your Real Estate Riches

The three pillars of asset protection provided you with a sense of what you must do to protect your real estate investment wealth. To reiterate, you must

1. Separate certain assets from yourself through title with entities.

2. Insulate yourself with proper insurance and estate planning.

3. Remove assets and equity from real property from harm's way by using global solutions or entities (e.g., trusts, limited liability companies, family limited partnerships).

As a Canadian investing in US real estate, you must ensure you use these pillars to protect your US investments. You must also go into this market keenly aware that you are now doing business in one of the world's most litigious societies. How litigious? Drawing on some of the latest statistics, my insiders tell me there were more than one million lawyers in the United States in 2006. Four years before that, 16 million civil cases were filed in state courts, according to the *State Court Guide to Statistical Reporting*. One year later, trial lawyers in the US earned an estimated $40 billion in lawsuit awards.

Even with a very proactive asset protection plan, Canadians must enter this market fully aware that anyone who does business in the US puts themselves at risk of legal action. In fairness, another statistic from the Bureau of Justice Statistics shows that in 1995, 97% of US legal cases were terminated before they went to trial. My US-based real estate insiders tell me that statistic holds relatively true in 2010; the vast majority of cases never make it to trial. But if you think that sounds like good news, think again. Not everyone who files a civil lawsuit intends to fight it through to its legal conclusion. Some litigants may be motivated by the opportunity to cost you money and to make you and your business "disappear" from a certain market. Never forget that it takes real money to fight a civil action—no matter how frivolous—and it can take almost as much money to *prepare* to fight a civil action that is eventually terminated.

The situation is not any better if you are the plaintiff in a legal action. While anyone can file a civil lawsuit in the United States for any reason, it is much harder to win a case. As mentioned in Fundamental #32, the US court system cannot always be relied upon to deliver fairness.

Here are four hair-raising examples of real US legal cases. I share them to help readers understand the kind of legal environment they will be working in. Rest assured that a lot of Canadian real estate investors will never encounter a lawsuit while doing business in the United States. I want that to be your experience, but you must always be prepared for what could happen in this litigious environment.

Case 1: The Vexatious Litigant

One Seattle woman made headlines because she had 45 lawsuits going on simultaneously. She is what's called a "vexatious litigant." That's a person who brings legal action to harass or subdue an opponent. Vexatious litigants typically launch frivolous lawsuits or file repetitive grievances not based on the merits of a situation. These individuals may be motivated by malice and the desire to annoy or embarrass an adversary.

Some states have a statute against this kind of activity and some do not. Regardless, you need to be aware of the people you encounter and prepared to question their motivations.

An ounce of prevention is worth a pound of cure.

Case 2: The Cyclist

A man was riding his bike at night. It was equipped with reflectors but not lights, and he was struck by a vehicle. The cyclist was awarded $6 million because he maintained he was not warned that reflectors might not be enough to prevent an accident. The take-away message is remarkably loud and clear: you are not protected from someone else's ignorance. (Indeed, you can't use ignorance as your defense, either!)

Review the 10 biggest threats to your wealth.
If something concerns you, prepare for it.

Case 3: The Toppling Toddler

An American woman was awarded $700,000 when she tripped over a toddler who was running around in a furniture store. The crux of this case did not rest on the extent of the woman's injuries, nor did it matter that the toddler she tripped over was her own child. Instead, the business responsible for the space where the accident occurred had to pay a significant settlement for a mishap that arguably resulted from the injured woman's own negligence.

You think this is ridiculous? It doesn't matter what you think!
What matters is that you know what could happen and
you take steps in advance to protect yourself.

Case 4: The Weekend Getaway

In another case that defies what some might view as a common-sense approach to legal jurisprudence, a man was awarded $500,000 after he was trapped in someone else's garage for a weekend. The successful litigant had broken into the home. He sued for emotional distress because there was only dog food to eat and Coca-Cola to drink. (In fairness, he was trapped for the whole weekend!)

Again, it's not about what you think.
It's about what you know might happen.

My advice here boils down to one salient point: lawsuits threaten your assets. Develop an asset protection plan and make sure you are as prepared as you can be to avoid a lawsuit. Pay particular attention to the 10 threats identified in the next fundamental and never forget that you are now doing business in a country whose legal system does not appear to value personal responsibility (or common sense) when weighing the claims of plaintiffs in civil lawsuits to the same level as Canada does.

 SOLD

These warnings, stories and statistics tell me that Canadian real estate investors should want to avoid getting caught up in the American legal system. Once you are in that court system, anything can happen.

Counter Threats to Your Wealth With Foresight.

The 10 Biggest Threats to Your Wealth

Even though Canadians are familiar with the horror stories generated by the US legal system, when they are asked what constitutes the biggest threat to their US real estate investment wealth, a lot of them talk about their fear of mistakenly buying properties that are not a good fit with their investment strategies. They worry, in other words, that they may make a poor investment choice based on misinformation from a relative stranger. As an extension of that worry, they may also fear that a US investment-turned-sour could put their Canadian assets at risk should some kind of legal liability occur. (And they are right—a US judgment can go after your Canadian wealth.)

I'm here to tell you that there's good news and bad news. The good news is that proper due diligence offers some real protection against buying the wrong properties. It will also help you identify those times when you need to revise an exit strategy. (An awareness of market changes may lead you to sell a property you had purchased to buy and hold, for example.)

In addition, due diligence on the asset protection front can help you set up the appropriate kinds of asset protection for your US enterprise, from arranging a particular corporate structure, to increasing your insurance coverage, putting an equity reduction plan in place and keeping a Canadian bank account.

The bad news is that some of the most significant threats to your real estate investment wealth come from problems you can't necessarily solve with that kind of due diligence. You can adopt and practice "the best" business strategies and "the best" asset protection plans, but those actions won't necessarily protect you from a legal blindside.

That's because, believe it or not, some of the most significant threats to your wealth will come (quite unexpectedly) from people you know—and sometimes from people you know really well!

This does not mean you should be too wary to invest. It does mean you must always be realistic about how your real estate investments could be affected by influences far beyond your portfolio. Remember the last fundamental and its recounting of some truly inane American legal decisions? My No. 1 motivation in sharing those stories was to help you, as a Canadian real estate investor, understand that when it comes to doing business in the US market, your first rule of thumb should always be *protect yourself*.

And exactly what are you protecting? My American investor colleagues tell me you should zero in on the following three areas:

1. Your business

2. Your personal life, including accidents and other unforeseeable events

3. Your investment properties

If this list makes it look like you have to be watchful in *all* aspects of your life, you're right!

Unfortunately, an all-inclusive list like this won't necessarily help you decrease your liability exposure because it's way too logical! I want you to start thinking about all of the what-if scenarios that could negatively affect the wealth associated with your business, your personal life or your investment properties should a lawsuit be filed. This kind of forward thinking can be a little scary. It's also essential.

To help get the what-if discussion started, I've asked one of my US lawyer colleagues to give me a list of what he sees as the top 10 threats to the wealth of a real estate investor. I think you'll find the list enlightening. I hope it will help you see how important it is to continually review your business, personal life and investment properties to look for potentially problematic areas where you need to update your approach to wealth protection.

Canadian investors will find themselves in a far more litigious business environment as soon as they start buying property in the US. Learn to make what-if questions a staple of your business decision-making process, then take action to decrease your exposure to legal action.

The Top 10 Threats to Your Wealth

According to one of my US-based legal experts, the 10 biggest threats to your wealth are the following:

1. **Your own physical or mental incapacity and the need for nursing care.**

   What happens to the business if you do not have disability insurance? Does your business plan include a way for other business partners/family members to step in and carry on?

2. **A divorce.**

   No one wants to think about how the dissolution of a marriage could affect a business, but you do need a plan that establishes shared assets and liabilities. If it's necessary to buy a domestic partner out, you may need to sell all of your assets.

3. **A business liability.**

   You don't have time to establish a workable plan that protects every aspect of your business from a potential liability. Talk to your lawyer, and establish a good rapport with an insurance professional. As your business changes, so will your liability exposure. Be prepared.

4. **Tenants.**

   Yes, you can be sued for injury to a tenant, even if their activity caused the safety issue, so keep your properties well maintained, carry property insurance and make sure your tenants know they are responsible for insuring their belongings. In many cases, all parties, including the company that insures the property, could be held liable for problems on a particular property. But the landlord is ultimately responsible, meaning that you need regular property insurance plus an umbrella policy that covers things beyond the normal policy.

5. **Accidents.**

   Realize that courts will often deem "accidents" to have been preventable. Keep your properties well maintained and make sure your liability insurance is adequate. What's adequate for someone else may not be adequate for you and your business, so seek specific advice.

6. **Trespass on your property.**

   You can be held liable for injuries to someone who is on your property illegally! Again, be prepared for the what-ifs. Quality property maintenance is key, but you still need liability insurance to protect your assets.

7. **Worker injury on your property.**

   Ditto the message of the last three points. You can be held responsible when bad things happen on your property.

8. **Illegal music downloading.**

   This is a good example of an area where Americans (and their Canadian counterparts) may not have been paying close enough attention to what industry experts were trying to tell us. There are legitimate sources of music and software online. But many Internet service providers are cooperating with the Recording Industry Association of America to pursue illegal downloads. Avoid becoming a statistic!

9. **Blogging or tweeting defamation.**

   In all honestly, defamation is defamation; the Internet has merely blurred the lines because some users mistakenly believe the Internet is a private forum. Always conduct yourself online as you would in person. Be wary of how an online conversation can be used to bait you. Never assume the information you blog, tweet or e-mail is private.

10. **Ownership of animals that might harm someone.**

    Again, plan for the what-ifs.

If some of these items gave you pause, that's good. You must always act as though some of the most significant economic perils to your business interests lurk where the naïve investor least expects. So don't be naïve. Do try to

- **Anticipate problems before they arise.** Conduct regular property inspections, keep maintenance and repairs up to date, and ensure your rental property is being taken care of.

- **Be prepared by planning for the what-ifs.** Talk to your insurer about changes to your business that could affect your coverage level.

Work with your lawyer and tax accountant to plan asset protection contingencies that cover changes to your personal and professional situation.

- **Get advice before you need it.** A proactive approach to asset protection means seeking quality advice often. Let your legal, tax and insurance professional know you take asset protection seriously and want their help.

- **Learn from your mistakes and from those made by other people.** Be a student of your industry. Follow up on good ideas you hear from other investors. Develop a best practice model for how your business operates.

Draw Up a Blueprint for Your Estate Plan.

A Long-Term View of Asset Protection

Nearly all of the real estate investors I've met over the years understand that they are in business to make money. Many of them have a basic understanding of the importance of asset protection and the fact that asset protection is an even greater concern if you're doing business in the United States, given the litigious disposition of that business environment. What an amazing number of these investors do not understand is the critical role that estate planning plays in terms of long-term asset protection.

Listen, no one likes to think about dying. But that fear doesn't make dying any less of a possibility. It does, however, get in the way of your ability to ensure your hard-earned assets make it into the hands of the people you have chosen to control those assets after you die.

One member of my US investment team describes estate planning as a kind of risk-management "blueprint" for your business. He hammers this point home in the seminars he delivers by asking investors if they would trust a builder to build a home without a blueprint. Most admit that's a ridiculous idea. He then asks them why they'd ever consider building their businesses without a risk-management plan that includes provisions to secure the money they've worked so hard to earn. There's no good answer to a question like that!

 SOLD

Real estate investors who seek help to design a solid estate plan are proving they know what long-term asset protection is all about.

Here's an overview of the basic information you need to know as you set up an estate plan. Here, and in the fundamentals to come, we'll also look at some of the additional risks you could face as a Canadian business or property owner with assets in the United States. Much of this information is applicable on both sides of the border.

Probate

Probate is the legal process that kicks into action after someone dies. It means that the court and legal system step in to interpret the terms of your will. If you have a well-written will that clearly lays out what is to happen, then the will is administered accordingly. If you depart *intestate* (without a will), the legal system will use a statutory scheme to distribute your belongings to the next of kin. This is an effective way to make sure your loved ones receive your property, but it's also expensive and often turns into a battlefield where families play tug-of-war for the assets. By not preparing a will, you give up any say as to who gets what upon your death.

The most important point to remember here is that estate planning is massively important to anyone with assets. Your passing will be hard enough for your relatives and business partners; don't make it even more difficult by exposing your estate to lawsuits, probate fees and other costs.

 SOLD

If you want to protect your loved ones and make sure your assets are distributed the way you want them to be distributed, you need an estate plan.

Estate Tax

Canada, unlike the United States, does not have an estate tax. Nevertheless, estate tax could affect Canadians who own US real estate (or other US assets). There is a prorated exemption and it has increased over the last number of years. To find out how it might affect their US assets, Canadians must talk to a cross-border tax specialist.

Probate Fees

In both countries, you want to avoid probate fees for the court process used to authenticate (or probate) a will. Probate fees cover the cost of filing and recording documents, but additional fees may apply if the process is contested or complicated. You may have to probate a will in any state where you have assets, and the actual fees can differ from jurisdiction to jurisdiction.

Adopt a Plan

One of my US legal experts uses the following planning quadrant to break the areas of estate planning into four key blocks. He uses this guide to show clients the advantages of a good estate plan. His arguments hold for any size of estate, from one worth a few hundred thousand dollars to one worth billions. The quadrant is also a good reflection of what Canadians should be doing when they plan their estates. Remember, the information here comes from an American point of view. As a Canadian investing in US real estate, you will need the advice of an attorney and a cross-border tax specialist who understands how your assets could be affected by the estate laws of both countries.

THE BURNS ESTATE PLANNING QUADRANT

BASE PLAN	ESTATE FREEZE
RISK MANAGEMENT AKA ASSET PROTECTION	ESTATE DRAIN

Your real estate investment portfolio can fall into any one of these quadrants. Ideally, you want to stay on the left-hand side of this diagram—a good base plan will improve your risk management and asset protection strategies. Without that base plan, you risk an estate freeze, a complicated probate process and the additional risk of having to liquidate non-protected assets, thereby draining your estate.

The Base Plan

Given the importance of the base plan, I want to look at that section of the diagram a little more closely. (The basics of asset protection are covered in Fundamental #32: Cover Your Ass(ets).) Remember: your goal with estate planning is to ensure your assets are distributed according to what you want done. With the base plan, there are three areas where action is warranted.

1. The Departure Documents

The top layer of a base plan focuses on what I will call "departure documents." These documents come into play upon your death and they are essential to the probate process. They include the revocable living trust, the pour-over will and the general assignment.

The Revocable Living Trust

A trust is really an agreement between you and someone you've assigned to manage your assets. Therefore, a revocable living trust is an agreement you can revoke or amend during your lifetime. In fact, you can even act as the trustee of your trust while you're first starting out, and then move the assets to a company that has more experience.

When you die, the terms of your trust become irrevocable and your assets will be allocated accordingly. Because the trust contains provisions for the distribution of your assets on and after your death, the trust acts as a substitute for your will. This eliminates the need for the probate of your will with respect to those assets that were held in your living trust at your death.

Trusts can be designed in many different ways, depending on the size of the estate's worth and what the estate tax credit is at the time the living trust is created. At the time of this printing, the individual estate tax credit in the United States is $2 million per person or $4 million for a married couple that preserves its credits with a trust.

The Pour-Over Will

A will simply names the people who will receive your assets upon your death. When crafting a will, you'll need to nominate an executor. This individual will manage and distribute your estate in addition to paying debts and settling accounts. In your will, you will also name the guardians for your children should they be underage upon your death. Remember, only assets in your name will be subject to your will.

In the United States, pour-over wills are used in some states as a catch-all to ensure that all of your assets will flow into that revocable living trust that becomes irrevocable upon your death. This is valuable because it covers assets that you may not have had time to re-title in the name of the trust prior to your death. A pour-over will acts as an addition to your existing will or trust. (Again, Canadians holding US assets will want specific legal advice about how to ensure their assets will be protected after they die.

Where possible, you want your base plan to lay out a specific course of action. When it comes to issues like title, it's best to structure the acquisitions properly from the outset, versus buy them and trust you will have time to stipulate title changes before you die.)

General Assignment

A general assignment of personal property takes care of property that doesn't have a title to it. This includes things like tools and sporting equipment. Make sure that you're specific about what goes to whom upon your death. If you have jewelry and other miscellaneous items of value, a general assignment will help your executor know who gets all of the untitled property you own.

2. Incapacity Issues

The second layer of the base plan is designed to deal with incapacity issues— when people are still alive but have been rendered incapable of making decisions on their own, because of traumatic injury, stroke or any other frailty that could arise. (These concepts may have different names in Canada and can even differ from province to province. Always get good legal advice.)

Durable Power of Attorney

Power of attorney (POA) authorizes one person to act on behalf of another. This should not be confused with an executor, who has been authorized to carry out the provisions of a will. Some people don't realize that a power of attorney is only good until you become incapacitated. A "durable POA" is one that remains in force even after you lose mental capacity. You need to make sure that your power of attorney is durable so that your family, or whomever you've granted this power to, doesn't have to go to court to secure it.

 PROCEED WITH CAUTION!

Get Your Durable POA in Place!

My legal experts (north and south of the Canada/US border) tell me that when domestic partners or others go in on real estate together, they always recommend the partners prepare a plan that goes into action should one of them be incapacitated.

In the US, a durable power of attorney can give non-family members the authority to act on behalf of the incapacitated partner. Imagine what would happen if your partner in US real estate property experienced a seizure one day and never recovered. Without having the durable power of attorney, you would have no authority to get things done with the property, including selling it without the person's signature. Transactions would literally be frozen (moving your business interests to the right-hand side of the diagram printed earlier in this fundamental).

Healthcare Directives

The existence or absence of a healthcare directive document has generated a lot of news in recent years as high-profile cases have seen families battle over the healthcare decisions of loved ones. Having a healthcare directive ensures that someone you've chosen will have the power to decide whether to accept or decline health measures on your behalf, should you become incapacitated.

The "agent" assigned by you (usually an attorney) must act according to your wishes. This document also provides you with some legal protections because the agent can be removed from the decision-making process should he or she act illegally or contrary to your written wishes.

Without one of these documents, lengthy legal battles can arise in the case of medical incapacitation. This is what happened in the well-known case of Terri Schiavo, who lingered for years in a vegetative state while her family fought it out in the courts, trying to decide what she would have wanted.

3. Other Considerations

The final layer of the base plan can include community property agreements, separate property agreements, deeds for re-titling real property, and more than 160 other strategies to accomplish the other corners of the quadrant. Strategies that keep your business on the left-hand side of the quadrant will focus on risk management and asset protection.

Over the last seven years, one of my American legal experts has focused on assisting real estate investors with both tax efficiency and risk management. He tells me that experience is a good teacher and real estate investors can learn a lot from the good and bad examples of others.

We are going to go over one of those examples in the next fundamental, #36. For now, the most important take-home lesson from this fundamental is that you can exercise control over your estate—but that control has got to kick into place when you are very much alive!

 SOLD

Do not allow ordinary events to undo your asset protection plan. Risk management always includes an estate plan.

Expect That Every State Will Want a Piece of Your Pie.

What All Investors Must Know if They Invest in Multiple States

It makes sense for some Canadian real estate investors to eye more than one American state for investment opportunities. If that's the route you take, the most important thing you need to know is that each state in which you own real estate has an interest in your estate when you perish—unless you disinherited them with a properly structured estate plan.

Never think your case will qualify for some kind of special treatment. If you have properties in multiple states, you could be subject to multiple probates in each state. This comes with a massive legal price tag. (If you are from the US, it gets even worse; without the proper protections in place before you die, your estate could be subject to multiple probates in each state, followed by a probate filed in your home state.)

To illustrate what can go wrong, let's look at a story shared with me by a US-based legal expert well versed in real estate investment. It's a good example of why you want to put this fundamental in place.

A Lawyer Talks: Investor Joe
(The names in this story have been changed to protect the uninformed.)

When Joe came into this lawyer's office, he was 62 years old, divorced, with adult children, and had just purchased 10 properties around the US. On some of the properties, Joe held titles with his daughter. On others, he held titles with his ex-spouse. According to him, neither his daughter nor ex-wife had stable personal finances. Joe himself had no estate plan, no incapacity plan, no life insurance and no umbrella insurance. There were, in other words, a lot of serious risk management issues in plain view.

Remember the facts:

- 62 years old
- On title with daughter
- On title with ex-spouse
- No living trust
- No durable power of attorney
- No limited liability entity

Identify Potential Issues

When you review the facts of an investment situation, including your own, look at what you know to be true and then look at what those facts could mean. Joe's lawyer accomplished this by asking the what-if questions.

Q: *At this age, is Joe vulnerable to death, incapacity or severe illness?*

A: Yes, of course he is.

Q: *Is the jointly held property with his daughter a gift, possibly exceeding his annual exclusion?*

A: This is an open question, but it appears to be a gift, absent a document to the contrary like some type of note.

Q: *Is the jointly held property with the ex-spouse a gift?*

A: Again, it's an open question, but it appears the same as above. This is his ex-spouse, so no special treatment applies in the absence of a document to the contrary.

Q: *If Joe has a stroke or other incapacitation, will his daughter have the authority to act on his behalf?*

A: No. She may need to go to court and get a court appointment. This may be required in each and every state where they own property together.

Q: *If Joe has a stroke or other incapacitation, will his ex-spouse have the authority to act on his behalf?*

A: Same as above.

Q: *If Joe dies and his ex-spouse can't qualify for the loan on a property, will she lose a step-up in basis creating capital gains when she sells it?*

A: Yes. The ex-spouse will lose this by being on title. It would have been better to transfer the asset through Joe's living trust, if he had one.

Q: *If Joe dies and his daughter can't qualify for a loan on the property, will she lose a step-up in basis creating capital gains when she sells it?*

A: Yes, same as above.

Q: *When any of the jointly held properties are sold, does Joe kill half of the step-up in basis creating capital gains tax?*

A: Yes. One-half of the property will not be subject to capital gains tax upon the sale, since the step-up in basis is lost. Also, if the other parties keep the properties, they will be required to submit a death certificate, and this could create reassessment.

Q: *If Joe is sued because of an event on one of the properties, for a sum that exceeds his ordinary hazard insurance, will his personal assets be at risk?*

A: Yes. If he doesn't have enough insurance, then the titleholder of the property will be responsible, which means that everything he owns is up for grabs.

Q: *Has Joe limited the remedy a complainant can get from him because of an injury on the property?*

A: No. He never set up a limited liability company (LLC) or family limited partnership (FLP), legal structures which can limit how much money a legal complainant can seek. Without this kind of structure, his personal assets are completely exposed.

Q: *If Joe dies, will his estate have nine probates to take care of in other states before his estate could be settled in California, where he was a resident?*

A: Yes, without a doubt. And this would be expensive.

Q: *Can Joe pass his properties, which have appreciated over the years, to his descendents at a discount?*

A: No. This can only be done by using either a limited liability company or family limited partnership.

Remember when the lawyer told us that Joe did not have any life insurance? This means that someone would have to find liquid dollars to pay Joe's portion of the loan, or the entire loan, owed on each property. Since a loan is based only upon the income of the individual who applied for it, it does not automatically transfer to the joint titleholder. This could mean a mass liquidation of Joe's properties and the joint titleholder would not have any control over market timing. If this forced liquidation occurs at a bad time in the market, this could create terrible losses.

Joe also didn't have any long-term care plans. Lawyers tell me long-term care plans are another form of asset protection planning. In the US, a long-term care plan can prevent the confiscation of assets by the government if you need state nursing home assistance.

As you can see, it was great that Joe set out to invest in real estate and become wealthy. Unfortunately, he didn't think like a savvy investor. Instead, he created 10 potentially catastrophic situations in one buying spree! Fortunately, he was able to connect with a capable attorney who helped him identify and resolve all of the areas of risk he'd left open like a gaping wound. Ideally, you do not want to be exposed at all—ever.

This situation is entirely avoidable. Before you buy anything, get your wealth vision plan in place. This plan must be on paper. It must be reviewed by a real estate-knowledgeable attorney. It must be supported by documentation that clearly establishes what you want done if you are incapacitated or die.

 SOLD

Successful real estate investors *think* like successful real estate investors! You need a blueprint to stay on course and that includes a solid estate plan for asset protection and risk management.

Steer Clear of Asset Protection Fakes, Scams and Planning Errors.

Nothing Is Foolproof

Canadians who are thinking about investing in US real estate are wise to take asset protection seriously. You need to be especially wary of anyone who tries to tell you there is such a thing as "complete" asset protection or a bulletproof asset protection plan. These do not exist.

Fundamental #5 in Part 1 of this book addressed the variety of scams that can put your assets at risk as soon as you try to enter the distressed property market. The essential message there was that there will always be individuals and groups of individuals trying to take your money under the guise of helping you make money. That doesn't change as your portfolio grows and you have more assets to protect. Well, maybe it changes a bit. At that point, scam artists may recognize your asset base and take a run at it simply because they can.

What's an investor to do? One of my US legal advisors tells me that investors new to the US market should take care to act with prudence and wisdom. It may be possible for you to pursue a failed asset protection strategy all the way through the American court system. Possible, but not necessarily wise. In fact, any approach that anticipates using a lengthy court battle to solve an issue of asset protection leaves you vulnerable precisely because decisions will be rendered by a 12-person jury. (Or, as my advisor likes to describe it, a 12-person lottery!)

So first and foremost, run from anything that purports to offer complete asset protection or bulletproof asset protection. It's likely a scam. If you do try to pursue a problem arising from this kind of scam through the US court system, you will likely never see the issue make it to trial. There, your real goal will be some sort of settlement. Ergo, at that point in the game the best course of action would be to make sure you have the legal advice you need to exert some input over what those settlement figures would be.

Here are some arrangements you should be extremely cautious about getting into.

Land Trusts

A land trust is a special trust ownership structure that enables the owner of real property to place the legal ownership of that property in the name of a trustee. This arrangement, which is not allowed in every US state, is a way to keep confidential the names of the "true owners" of the property. Once real property has been transferred to a land trust, the owner maintains only an "interest" in the trust, which is administered under personal property laws, not real estate laws.

The land trust is a legitimate way to place real property into a governance arrangement. In the real estate investment world, however, extra caution is warranted when dealing with a land trust. Whereas the arrangement is sometimes marketed as a de facto means to protect your assets, the only thing the land trust accomplishes is getting title out of your own name. It will not protect the asset from a committed attorney who is out to collect on behalf of his client for an injury connected with the property.

This takes some investors by surprise, because the land trust is frequently touted as the best thing since rolled tobacco. That's a problem. My US legal insider tells me that a land trust offers the same asset protection as rolled tobacco offers for cancer protection: that is, no protection at all.

In many states, including Arizona, you must disclose all trustees and beneficiaries of a land trust. If you are trying to use the land trust for asset protection, you will likely want to be on the list of beneficiaries so that you can have at least some input into the trust. As soon as you do that, however, you leave yourself exposed to a future liability related to that trust. Think of it as a win-win scenario—with a recognizable potential to morph quickly into a lose-lose situation.

Generally speaking, you would want to set up your US land trust as what is referred to as "self-settled," which is a special needs trust that's funded with property that belongs to the beneficiary. This is only allowed in a few states, so you must be mindful of what's possible in the state where you are doing business. Indeed, most states disallow such a transaction and will not provide any protection to the investor for a liability connected to their real estate. Again, know your options and get good advice specific to your situation.

Limited Liability Companies

Whereas a family limited partnership (FLP) may offer Canadians some asset protection via limited liability and avoid double taxation, a limited liability company (LLC) usually spells trouble. In an LLC, the owners and managers are given a "limited liability." That is, they receive some protection against being held personally responsible for the financial debts and obligations of a company should those debts and obligations not be met. Typically, their losses cannot exceed the amount they invested.

Like the land trust, LLCs are only authorized in some states. A bigger issue for real estate investors is that while some marketers may try to sell you a properly organized LLC that offers great asset protection, there are tax issues for Canadians and setting up a US LLC could lead to double taxation. Like all business transactions, this is an area that should be examined closely by an advisor with good cross-border experience. By default, you must be cautious when dealing with people who insist the LLC is always an option for your real estate holdings and a good vehicle for asset protection.

For US citizens, a US LLC works to

1. Get their name off title.

2. Access pass-through provisions for an appreciating asset.

3. Use a structure that limits liability like a charging order, which is a court-authorized right granted to a judgment creditor made from a business entity that includes an LLC (notwithstanding fraud or another compelling court interpretation, a charging order is the maximum remedy).

4. Provide a significant ability to have appraised at a discount the LLC membership interests or limited partnership interests in an FLP (this is generally a huge saving and allows you to transfer assets to the next generation free of gift and estate tax).

These can be compelling reasons for a US citizen to set up an LLC. But my point here is that they do not provide foolproof asset protection, especially when they are not properly set up and administered. There can also be issues with how the LLC is capitalized and with personal guarantees that leave you exposed to financial liabilities.

An LLC's liability may not be so limited, especially for foreign investors! Do not try to file the LLC papers on your own. This is one area where you need professional assistance.

Understand Your Strategy: Probate Versus Credit Protection

People must be clear about the type of protection they're getting when they opt for different structures. Is it protection from probate, which is the court process to decide distribution of a deceased's property, or is it protection against creditors? Many times the planning may be exclusive. That is, the provisions you put in place for probate protection (like a good will and estate plan) may have little effect on creditor protection, for which you will need completely different strategies. Again, this makes advice specific to your circumstances absolutely essential.

 SOLD

> If you're looking for asset protection advice, take a pass on the kind that comes to you via a series of CDs you have to buy and listen to. What you really need is advice based on your situation. "Thinking" you have asset protection is not the same as having it! Your business goal is to protect your assets from lawsuits. This is not an area where it makes sense to do it yourself.

Offshore Trusts and IBCs

Sometimes investors are sold on very expensive offshore trusts or international business companies (IBCs). When transferred into these entities improperly, you risk cataclysmic tax consequences regardless of whether you are a Canadian or American citizen. Here the issue is the perceived ownership of a foreign entity. In the US, this triggers a branch of international taxation that is costly to solve and report annually. It can also complicate the tax situation for Canadian investors.

But be forewarned: hucksters never tell people about the foreign entity tax considerations, nor do they share that information on their websites. It's buyer beware!

Homestead Exemption

The same goes for investment deals that try to talk up the homestead exemption. Homestead exemptions are found in state statutes and US constitutional provisions. They exist to protect the value of residents' homes from property taxes, creditors and circumstances that might arise from the death of a homeowner spouse. These generally do not apply to investment property and are meant for limited use with your own personal residence. Ignore that and it will cost you.

PROCEED WITH CAUTION!

It really doesn't matter whether you're buying investment real estate in Canada or the US. Your team must include good legal and tax advisors and you must be careful about acting on any advice that hasn't been vetted through a legal and tax specialist. Many of the people you meet in real estate investment do want to help you make money. Good advisors will help you keep it.

38

Be Extremely Wary of the "Best" Plans.

The Biggest Legal Strategies That Do Not Work

A few fundamentals back we briefly discussed the fact that Canadian investors eyeing the US real estate market are often intimidated by the chance that they will be talked into buying an investment property that does not work in their system. They worry that information may be "misrepresented" to them on purpose and that a lack of experience in the US market might leave them vulnerable to poor choices at best and to fraud at worst.

As always, there is no substitute for due diligence. If you don't know, ask. If you do know, ask anyway. Given the risk of litigation and the potentially heavy costs of defending yourself in a lawsuit, seek qualified information from legal experts who understand the American real estate sector.

Some of your best due diligence will come from having, at the very least, a "big picture" knowledge of what you should know when you are looking at real estate deals in the US. In this fundamental, I want to point out three legal strategies that *do not* work to protect you and your assets from litigation. I will revisit land trusts and limited liability companies as two of the legal strategies that don't work.

Land Trust

Investors who spend any time on the real estate seminar circuit will likely find themselves at a seminar that promotes the land trust as a kind of silver bullet protection against lawsuits. I'm here to tell you that it's not.

Under US law, there are two types of trusts: revocable and irrevocable. The irrevocable trust can give some protection against litigation. It also comes with significant handcuffs, since an irrevocable trust enables you to gift the asset into the trust, but once this is done you no longer have control over the asset. This would mean you cannot sell or liquidate the asset any longer and that an independent third-party trustee must oversee all trans-actions on behalf of the trust. Without those provisions, the irrevocability of the trust would be considered a sham.

The land trust is effectively the same as the living trust we talked about in Fundamental #35. In other words, it is a revocable trust, or an agreement you can revoke or amend during your lifetime. It becomes irre-vocable only upon death, when it sets out how your assets will be allocated. From that perspective, it has real value in an estate plan.

As an investment tool to protect your assets from lawsuits while you're still alive, the land trust's value is questionable. A land trust usu-ally involves an independent third-party trustee who does not carry your name. But in some states, including Arizona, for instance, you have to dis-close all beneficiaries and trustees on the documents filed. As such, even if you're not the trustee in control, you will at least want to be the beneficiary and have access to the asset. Real estate investors who do a good job of their due diligence likely will find this out. Depending on who your credi-tor is and how much they assert you owe them, rest assured they will do what it takes to discover all of your assets.

These concerns aside, the land trust can be effective in Illinois and Florida, where there are specific statutes regarding their use. Then again, do not expect more than what this revocable trust offers—and think about why you would want to show up to a gunfight with a pellet gun!

Instead, look for better and more reliable tools you can use that also offer significant estate planning benefits. This is the best way to ensure you can transfer an appreciated asset to your loved ones while reducing taxes.

Limited Liability Companies

There is a lot of confusion over the usefulness of US limited liability com-panies for Canadian real estate investors. One of the asset protection strategies that bears a close second look is the single member limited liabil-ity company, or LLC. For American citizens, an LLC is a great protection tool under most circumstances. It helps their estates avoid probate and offers tax benefits for an appreciating asset. For Canadians, the limited lia-bility protection is generally not enough to make a US LLC a good idea because the US LLC can leave you vulnerable to double taxation!

The bottom line for Canadian investors is that you need the advice of cross-border legal and tax specialists. Whereas a US Family Limited

Partnership (FLP), which centralizes a family business or investment accounts, may provide some limited liability protection and not compromise your Canadian tax situation, an LLC may leave you exposed to double taxation. Always seek advice specific to your circumstances. Most important, be wary of a "sales job" that includes an offer to protect your assets with an LLC.

Transferring Assets to Family Members

In Canada and the United States, individuals facing a pending lawsuit often look for ways to transfer their assets into the names of family members. It is a bad strategy on both sides of the border because a court will examine the substance over the form.

Courts in the US are adamant that you must be able to demonstrate an arm's-length transaction. Ergo, if you have sold an asset, there should be a transfer of funds. When it comes to the transfer of property, the courts will, in all likelihood, determine that it is not reasonable that a person would make such a substantial gift to another person. The court is especially likely to dismiss such a transaction if the transfer frustrates a creditor who has won a judgment. Indeed, the court may order that this kind of transfer be unwound or returned so that the asset or proceeds can be delivered to the creditor.

 SOLD

Courts will bring hindsight to bear on an investor's actions. This is why your asset protection plan needs to be in place before or as you buy real estate, not after a deal is done. As with everything in your investment life, steer clear of taking quick action on "foolproof" strategies. If a deal is being sold as "too good to last," make sure your due diligence also looks at whether it's "too good to be true."

Putting Someone Else's Legal Experience to Work

Legal Attorney James Burns of California Talks Real Estate Law

James Burns is a lawyer, author and educator who's been working with real estate investors for about 10 years. He's also an experienced real estate investor in his own right, and he sees great opportunity in the current US foreclosure market. All of this makes what he has to say about real estate investing and the US legal system especially compelling.

The Case for Good Legal Advice

If there's a single issue James likes to focus on when talking about the risks associated with the US real estate market, it's the need to make sure your real estate business assets are protected from liability.

While there's no such thing as foolproof asset protection, James's experience shows that too many investors simply don't take a due diligence approach to this part of their business. To help them understand the folly of that approach, James describes the real estate investment business as a winding road. Well-meaning investors often think they know where their business is headed, so they don't seek legal advice about what could happen. All too often, these investors are woefully unprepared when they come around a business bend and find themselves face-to-face with the liability issues they could have anticipated had they done a little planning.

This lawyer recommends a simple solution. He says Canadian and US real estate investors need to be more mindful of potential liabilities—and that means seeking sound legal advice every step of the way. A veteran of the American court system, James admits he's still surprised to see how a seemingly mundane event can garner the attention of a creative legal team that might then help a plaintiff "connect the dots to an investor's personal assets or to other business assets."

Ready or Not, Here They Come

Insurance and personal exposure are two areas where real estate investors are most frequently caught off guard, says James. He remembers talking to a real estate investor with a particularly sad story. The guy was in the property renovation business, buying physically distressed properties at a discount and putting them back on the market, often with relative speed.

It seems the investor hired a plumber to go to one of his properties and do what looked to be a fairly routine plumbing job. While there, the plumber slipped on some ice. The fall shook the guy up, but he thought he was okay. Later that day, the plumber ended up in a hospital emergency room and died.

The man seeking legal advice from James was distraught. According to him, lawyers acting on the deceased plumber's behalf said the fall exacerbated a preexisting health condition that contributed to his untimely death. As they saw it, the fall was part of a wrongful death suit.

James was dismayed to hear the real estate investor had failed to put insurance or workers' compensation coverage on the property he was rehabbing for market. Because the investor was expecting a quick turnaround on the deal, he had also failed to put the title of the property in the name of a business entity.

James isn't sure how the case turned out, but he is sure the investor's liability exposure could have been mitigated with some good legal planning. "Make that *business planning*," says James, "because that's what we're really talking about. In my view, you can never be too careful and doing it wrong is not a part of being in business."

Further to that, James is concerned when real estate investors talk as if they can naturally separate their "business" interests from their "real estate investing." From where he sits, that's more than naïve or unwise, it's ludicrous.

Get Advice Early and Often

And that's why James, with two law degrees and an Advanced Masters of Law in Tax, is so shocked when real estate investors tell him they don't seek legal advice because they are worried about the upfront cost.

"The thought process is, 'I would like to get this done cheap.'"

Just how cheap is it if they have to spend tens of thousands of dollars or more for protection after the fact—and much more to defend themselves if a lawsuit is filed?

Protecting yourself is about being able to negotiate a fair settlement on your terms and not putting yourself at risk of losing everything, insists James. On this point, the lawyer is crystal clear. "You can pay me a little now or you can pay a defense lawyer a lot later, often with unimaginable costs." If you do need to settle a lawsuit later, doing things properly from the beginning, with appropriate insurance and the right business structure, will make it much easier to hire a lawyer.

James dismisses the idea that businesspeople can always anticipate problem areas and ward them off at the proverbial pass. One of the "crazy cases" he cites involved a successful claim on behalf of a woman burned by hot coffee. In another, a psychic successfully argued a claim to have lost her powers after a CAT scan.

So how often should an investor review his business plan with his lawyer? As often as necessary, says James; this is case-by-case depending on how often a client changes what he's doing and how aggressively he's jumping on opportunities. Clients with sophisticated businesses who often change direction may need a legal team to ensure their assets are protected. Others will need a legal team and frequent meetings with a tax advisor to make sure their business is also tax compliant.

It really all comes down to vision, James finishes. And if you're in business to make money, that vision better be appropriately insured and properly structured, with asset protection as one of your primary business goals.

General Information about Investing in the United States

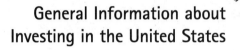

"The ultimate destination of fear is regret."

—Philip McKernan

Understand Cross-Border Issues.

Canadian Property Buyers Have the Same
Legal Rights as US Citizens

Forewarned is forearmed, so my goal with this section of the book is to provide you with a little more practical information about how issues like insurance, bugs and finding joint venture investment partners can affect your US residential real estate investment decisions. I even address the confusion over whether you're buying an investment property or a second home—because not being straight about your motivation can lead to real problems down the road.

Overcome Your Citizenship Issues

Before we get into what some Canadians would consider to be among the grittier topics associated with US real estate investment, I want to take a broader look at cross-border issues. Fundamentals #9 and #42 tackle the problems Canadians encounter when seeking to acquire financing from US lenders. Here, with the help of US immigration attorney Andy Semotiuk, I want to look at what's behind those problems and give you some ideas about how you might circumvent those issues by paying a little extra attention to your immigration status.

First, rest assured that when it comes to buying US property, Canadians have the same legal rights as American citizens, so there are no barriers to a Canadian who wants to buy a residential property in the States. But virtually every American lender will ask you about your immigration status, and your ability to get US financing will be impaired or eliminated if all you have is temporary status as a tourist or businessperson and you are not a US citizen or a permanent resident with a green card.

To be clear, the green card attests to the *permanent* resident status of an alien in the US. (This is completely different from the *temporary* status afforded by the basic business or tourist visa Canadians can get at a border crossing.) "Green card" also refers to the immigration process you follow to become a permanent US resident, and from the conventional US lender's perspective, this policy is in place to protect them from being burned by foreign nationals or delays with immigration processing.

PROCEED WITH CAUTION!

Without citizenship or a permanent resident green card, Canadians will likely be required to put down at least 30% on any loans they acquire from a conventional US lender, if they get one at all.

There are a few relatively simple things Canadians can do to work around these rules. For example, you can buy residential real estate property through a company to which lenders may feel more comfortable lending money. Another strategy is to provide a copy of your immigration paperwork up front. The matter of disclosing your US status up front applies if you are a US citizen, have applied or are in the process of applying for a green card, or have a work visa such as an E-2 or a Trade NAFTA (TN) visa under the North American Free Trade Agreement (NAFTA). (E-2 and TN visas are discussed below.) Some lenders accept a copy of the visa plate pasted into your passport or the card stapled to the passport as evidence of your immigration status, even though it merely confirms you are not a US citizen nor a permanent resident.

Other Canadians experience some success by presenting a lender with US tax returns showing US income earned in the States; this could also help convince a US lender of your intent to pay your loan. If your US deals are contingent on American financing, you may also want to talk to your lawyer about pursuing more complicated strategies. As always, where there is a will, there is a way.

You'll want to keep in mind these three practical considerations when you grapple with the decisions you'll need to make when you conduct cross-border business and then face issues related to citizenship:

1. Make Honesty Your Only Policy

With all of the interest in US residential real estate investment, a lot of Canadians are entering the US on fact-finding missions. They're going into the US for a closer look at the market, but may or may not buy property. When asked the reason for your entry into the US, you could tell border authorities that you are entering the county "on business" and say that you are "going to talk about real estate" if asked for more information. You do not have to say you are looking at distressed properties or foreclosures.

If you've entered the United States on a pleasure trip and find a property you want to buy as an investment, you can make an offer on the property. Just remember that you may not qualify for US financing. Until Canadian or US financing is in place, be careful what you assume about your status!

The central issue with US financing appears to be plain old-fashioned xenophobia, otherwise known as your basic dislike of foreigners. This is less personal than systemic, so never think you can "talk your way" past anyone, from border authorities to bankers.

As always, aim to work within the system and make honesty your only policy.

2. Consider Getting a Green Card

If US financing is a deal breaker, or becomes a deal breaker as you grow your US investment portfolio, you may want to consider getting a green card. But be careful. A green card exposes Canadians to US tax on worldwide income. That's right. Profits from any of your Canadian businesses may be taxable in the US.

And there are other implications, too. Under current law, all male US citizens must register with Selective Service, including those who hold a green card, which signals permanent resident status. The Selective Service System maintains information on citizens potentially subject to military conscription.

For more information about green cards and immigration processes, please visit the US Citizenship and Immigration Services website at www.uscis.gov.

3. Perform Cross-Border Management

Although it can be very complicated to manage US properties from Canada, there may not be any legal issues related to managing a US portfolio from north of the 49th parallel if your "work" involves collecting rents or hiring contractors like plumbers and other tradespeople to complete upgrades and repairs.

That changes if US customs officials get the impression that you are doing things that deprive US citizens of jobs. This is more likely to be a problem when you are managing multiple properties. If this is an issue, you should explore an E-2 or TN work visa.

Available only to "treaty nations" (which include Canada), the E-2 visa allows individuals to enter and work in the US based on an investment they control inside the US. This visa is renewable in three-year increments so long as the applicant remains in business.

Under NAFTA, Canadians can also apply for a work permit at a port of entry. To qualify for a TN work permit, you need to enter the US to work in a profession listed in NAFTA.

ADDITIONAL INFORMATION

For more information on how to acquire an E-2 or TN work permit, visit www. travel.state.gov/visa.

Note: To be eligible for a TN work permit, you must hold a university degree in the field where you plan to work in the US, have a valid passport, be able to show proof of employment and seek TN designation for a profession recognized by NAFTA. Experience may be required in addition to a degree and some professions list an alternative to a university degree.

For a detailed list of professions, go to www.consular.canada.usembassy.gov/ nafta_professions.asp.

If you are university educated and want to pursue a TN designation to qualify your US immigration status, talk to a cross-border lawyer about how you might qualify under one of the listed professions.

PROCEED WITH ENTHUSIASM!

If your immigration status is holding you back, enlist the help of a cross-border legal specialist.

Insure Your Investment.
Carry Property Insurance

Canadian real estate investors have to take property insurance seriously if they buy a personal residence or investment property in the US. But how do you know that you're working with a reputable insurance agent and that you are carrying enough insurance? Here are a series of things US real estate investor Jamie Richardson tells me we need to think about to properly and adequately insure our real estate investments.

Find an Agent Who Can Shop Around

Ask the agent questions about her history insuring investment properties or second homes for Canadians. I see some real advantages to working with an insurance agent who is capable of writing policies through several different insurance companies. Since different companies offer different insurance packages, I think this type of agent is more familiar with market options and is in a better position to review several insurance options before making a recommendation.

That agent should also have experience writing policies for the type of home you need to insure. If you are dealing with single-family homes or multi-family homes, make sure this agent knows what you really need. She should be able to anticipate your questions—and present options and scenarios you didn't even consider.

Areas of Coverage

Because I'm focusing on the rent-and-hold real estate investment market and know that some of you are also looking at buying a second home in the US that may be vacant part of the year, I want to zero in on those markets. My insurance insiders tell me you need to focus on the following coverage areas:

- Dwelling
- Other structures
- Personal property
- Loss of use
- Liability
- Medical payments to others
- Replacement cost value and actual cost value

Dwelling

This aspect of the insurance policy applies to "permanently attached" items, so it typically covers your house and the attached structures and fixtures in the house, such as built-in appliances, plumbing, heating, permanently installed air conditioning systems and electrical wiring. For example, a dishwasher is considered to be "hardwired" to the property and is therefore covered under this coverage. Using the same rationale, some policies will not consider a refrigerator to be covered under the Dwelling portion of a policy because it is not permanently attached to the property. (The refrigerator may be covered under the Personal Property portion of the property.)

Other Structures

"Other structures" are detached structures such as garages, storage sheds and fences. If your property has a storage shed, you need a policy that covers it. This is an area where the wrong assumption can cost you a whole lot of money. Make sure the agent you're talking to has all the information she needs.

Personal Property

This part of your policy typically covers personal property, including the contents of your home and other personal items owned by you or the family members who live with you. This protection can be based on actual cash value or replacement cost. If you are the landlord, you should strongly encourage your tenants to get renter's insurance. Without it, their personal property will not be covered in the event of insurable property loss.

Loss of Use

This covers loss of rental income because of an insurable loss. Let's say your tenant starts a kitchen fire while cooking and the property sustains extensive damage such that the home is no longer habitable. The "loss of use" coverage will cover the loss of rent while the property is being renovated. This sustains cash flow.

Should the fire occur in your personal second home, "loss of use" coverage will cover the cost of additional living expenses for you and your family while the property is being renovated.

Liability

Personal liability coverage protects you against a claim or lawsuit resulting from bodily injury or property damage caused to others by an accident on your property. Canadians who own rental property or a second home in the United States must take this coverage seriously. This same issue was emphasized in Part 4 regarding the legal fundamentals of investing. Liability insurance is a critical part of your asset protection plan.

Medical Payments to Others

This pays medical expenses for persons accidentally injured on your property. Considering you now own property in the world's most litigious society, medical payment coverage is another very important way to protect your business.

 SOLD

Property insurance is one area where cheaper is definitely not better. Some states set relatively low limits for insurance coverage. Don't be taken in. You need good advice about how much insurance is enough. Do ask if an umbrella policy makes sense. This is in addition to other insurance and goes "over top" property insurance, automobile insurance and workers' compensation insurance, for example.

A NOTE ABOUT THE SECOND HOME

Insurance insiders tell me that a second home can typically be insured under a standard homeowner's policy, which generally offers the best coverage at the best rate. But if you own a second home that you live in for several months of the year, and then decide to rent it during the other months, you must notify your agent.

The minute you have a tenant in your property, your homeowner's policy will not cover you completely should you have a loss.

Replacement Cost Value and Actual Cash Value

Replacement Cost Value (RCV) is based on what it would cost you to replace an item or structure. Actual Cash Value (ACV) is what you might expect to pay for the item, as is. While RCV is based on the item or structure's pre-loss condition, ACV is replacement cost minus depreciation. So be careful. Let's take a look at an example of what could happen.

Says a windstorm or hurricane destroys the roof on your property. The roof was 10 years old and cost $8,000 when it was originally installed. It's going to cost $10,000 to have a new roof installed with roofing material of like kind and quality, such as three-tab shingles with a 20-year life expectancy.

Under an ACV policy, the insurance company is going to determine the depreciation and subtract it from the replacement cost. Using an industry standard calculation that says three-tab shingles depreciate 5% a year, the insurance company will issue a draft for $5,000 for a new roof.

REPLACING THOSE SHINGLES

10-year-old roof that depreciates 5% a year = 50% depreciation withheld

$10,000 cost of new roof − $5,000 depreciation = $5,000 ACV to be paid by insurance company

Under an RCV policy, the insurance company would compensate you $10,000 for the new roof. Of course, this means RCV increases the cost of an insurance policy, but if you ever need to file a claim, you'll be glad you chose this option. That peace of mind is even more important when your investment property or second home is located a long way away—and in a different country, to boot!

Read Your Policy

Make insurance a cornerstone of your due diligence. Too many people do not read their policies until after they have a loss and need to make a claim. Do your homework up front and avoid nasty surprises!

Making a Claim

To understand the value of a good insurance policy, it's helpful to look at what happens when you need to make a claim. Here's a quick checklist of what you need to do.

- ☐ Notify your agent immediately. You will want to call and put the agent on notice even if you are unsure if you will make a claim.

- ☐ Take pictures and/or video to document all damages.

- ☐ If you need to do any temporary repairs so that you don't incur additional damages, do them.

- ☐ Be sure to take pictures of the temporary repairs and keep all of your receipts.

- ☐ An adjustor from the insurance company will contact you and arrange to inspect the damage. After the adjustor inspects the damages, he will determine what he believes to be the cost of the repairs.

- ☐ Get three independent bids for the repairs, and compare them to the insurance company estimate.

- ☐ If the insurance adjustor estimated the repairs accurately, you will get a settlement to complete the repairs.

The Settlement

The insurance company will generally issue a settlement in one of two ways. The company will either give you a check in the amount they believe the repairs will cost, or will send you their estimate with a Sworn Proof of Loss statement that you will need to sign, have notarized and send back to the insurance company before you are issued any payment for the loss.

PROCEED WITH CAUTION!

Be Careful What You Sign

When you sign this Sworn Proof of Loss, you acknowledge that the repairs will cost no more than the insurance company's original estimate. You therefore have no recourse if the repairs cost more or if any additional damage is found.

If your estimates are higher than the estimate used by the insurance company, do not sign the Sworn Proof of Loss statement, which is your prerogative. Instead, submit to the insurance company three estimates with a letter. The letter should state that the insurance company's estimate is low given your own estimates. Ask the company to review the attached three estimates and to issue a settlement based on the actual costs found in the three estimates submitted. Insurers will typically settle based on the lowest of the three submitted estimates.

Location, Location, Location!

Like automobile insurance, the price of property insurance is determined largely by where you live. Hence, the insurance premium for a $150,000 home in one city in Florida will not be the same as a house in another city, let alone another state.

Some of this is because of severe weather like hurricanes, tornadoes and earthquakes. For example, hurricanes are a reality in Florida and premiums will be higher depending on your property's proximity to the coast. The US Weather Service estimates Jacksonville to be the least likely coastal city to experience hurricane-force winds in any given year. In Jacksonville, the probability is rated at 1 in 50. In Miami it's 1 in 7 thanks to its proximity to the Gulf Stream, which obviously means a higher premium in the latter city. In California, insurance is affected by earthquakes.

My point here is that you need to talk to your insurance agent to ensure you are fully covered should you have a loss.

MYTH OR FACT

Myth: Insurance in Florida is far higher than in most states in the US.

Fact: This is not the case. Insurance in southern Florida is higher because of the increased risk of hurricanes but that's not an issue in the northern part of the state.

Insurance premiums can affect your investment's cash flow. Since insurance is one area with few "global" truths, get your information from knowledgeable local agents.

41

Carry Insurance Beyond the Property Line.

Medical, Auto and Third-Party Liability: Are You Covered?

Canadians traveling to the US as investors or snowbirds must also make sure they carry adequate medical, automobile and third-party liability insurance, all of which protect them when unforeseen events put their Canadian and US assets at risk. When discussing this coverage with an insurer, make honesty your best policy. Sean Walker, a Canadian insurance specialist I know, says you must make sure you know the following:

- How long will you be away?
- Do you plan to travel often to the US?
- Are you taking your own vehicle or renting?
- Are you staying at a hotel or rental home?

Medical Insurance

Did you know that typical inpatient costs at US hospitals tally more than US$10,000 per night? Most Canadians know that treatment in the US is expensive, but many do not realize just how expensive it is. If you're still not convinced that medical coverage is absolutely necessary, consider one of the stories a US insurance industry colleague shared with me.

A 72-year-old Canadian man took a two-week trip to North Carolina. On the last day of his trip he fainted and was taken to hospital, where doctors treated him for atrial fibrillation. An air ambulance was arranged to return him to Ontario, at a cost of almost C$13,000. This trip included door-to-door service, with ambulance transport to the US airport and then from the Ontario airport to the hospital. The US hospital stay and air ambulance trip added up to more than C$100,000 and it was covered fully by his travel medical insurance.

I've heard Canadian snowbirds and some investors say they deliberately skip medical insurance because of the added expense. I urge you to be safe versus sorry and to shop around. The policy that covered this 72-year-old Ontario resident cost $150. Here are a few other considerations to keep in mind.

Kind of Trip

Travel medical insurance can be purchased for single trips, or for multiple trips over the course of a year. The multi-trip plans usually offer coverage for trips up to a specified length of time such as one week, two weeks, one month or six months. It usually pays to go this route if you plan on three trips over the course of a year. Those planning one longer trip are usually better off with the single-trip option.

Financial Coverage

Typically policies are issued for either $2 million or $5 million. They should cover emergency treatment of accidents or illness, including ambulance costs, hospital and doctors' fees, prescription drugs and rental of medical devices like crutches.

Make sure that it covers things such as air evacuations, the cost of bringing family members to your bedside, and living expenses for family while you remain hospitalized. Also, ensure it includes repatriation; you want to make sure that if you die while in the US, your body is returned to Canada for burial.

Know the Rules for Pre-Existing Conditions

Coverage may still be available if you have a pre-existing condition. You may need to complete a medical questionnaire, but there are very few conditions that can't be covered, especially if the condition has been stable for the last six months.

Be mindful of the details, because some policies won't cover any pre-existing conditions and the definitions of what constitutes a pre-existing condition may vary from company to company.

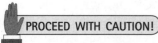 PROCEED WITH CAUTION!

Simply displaying symptoms of an illness is often enough to exclude coverage, even if a diagnosis hasn't been made!

Premiums, Deductibles and Payment Arrangements

Premiums are often based on a combination of your age and your length of travel. Ask your local insurance broker for a breakdown of packages available to you and find out your coverage deductible and the payment arrangements. Will the insurance company pay the hospital directly or will you need to pay and wait for reimbursement?

Automobile Insurance

Automobile insurers want to know where you're going and for how long. If you are taking your own vehicle, notify your local insurance carrier and the local licensing office as well as the licensing department in the state you are going to visit.

Because provincial laws vary, you need to ask your local insurer about specific requirements. For example, I live in British Columbia where the law says that a vehicle out of the province for vacation purposes does not require any additional coverage. But if you are traveling with the purpose of investing in real estate, the trip is not a vacation, it's business. In BC, I'd be required to change the territory my vehicle is licensed in if I am gone more than 30 days.

Some US states may require that you license your vehicle in their state if you are going to remain there for an extended period of time. Do your research.

(PROCEED WITH CAUTION!)

Mind the Rules

If you are required to license your vehicle in the US and don't, your Canadian license won't be valid and your Canadian insurance won't help if there's trouble.

Rental Cars

Be extra vigilant if renting a car while you're away. A lot of automobile renters pay the renter way too much for insurance, or don't take the rental agency's "extra coverage" because they think their credit card will protect them.

While some credit cards have sufficient coverage, most do not. They generally provide you with a collision damage waiver only. This does not include any liability or theft coverage, nor does it cover loss of use/income for the time that repairs are being done. These are all things you are responsible for when you sign the rental contract.

You can eliminate these issues by buying rental car insurance as an add-on to your regular car insurance, or as a stand-alone policy.

Third-Party Liability Insurance

Third-party liability insurance is another area fraught with misunder-standing. This coverage protects you for damages done to others. A limit of at least C$3 million to C$5 million is advisable in and outside Canada. Never forget that a lot of Americans do not have adequate health insurance. If an accident happens and the court decides *you* caused it, the plaintiff will be after you to cover their medical bills. This is definitely one fight you want your insurance company to handle!

As Canadian courts are awarding ever-higher amounts of money to plaintiffs, third-party liability coverage is no longer a luxury—it's a personal and profes-sional fact of life.

Third-party liability can also be critical if you're in a motor vehicle accident in one of the many states that does not require its motorists to carry insurance or in one that follows some kind of an insurance hybrid approach. For example, while New Hampshire and Virginia do not require insurance at all, California and New Jersey require insurance but set very low minimum limits. Again, that puts your assets at considerable risk, and underlines the importance of carrying adequate liability and medical insur-ance to make sure that you don't run into any problems after an accident.

Ask your local insurer about the rules in the states you plan to spend time in—or drive through. You can get special coverage for "underinsured drivers" that will cover you in states where coverage is not mandatory or is too low.

42

Familiarize Yourself With US Mortgage Financing.

Having Your Documents in Order Gets You Off to a Good Start

Fundamental #9 reviewed the complications of getting a US bank to loan Canadians money to buy US investment real estate. With the help of US real estate investment consultant Wendy Fedoruk, I am going to reiterate below some of the key points about private financing and hard-money lenders.

First, the US loan process is relatively simple if you want to buy a second home, and that's what many Canadian real estate investors would like to do while they're doing business. Second, the large and stable lenders in the US are more than happy to provide second-home mortgages for Canadians. The typical down payment required in the US is 20% to 35% and interest rates are usually 0.25 or 0.5 above the rate for US nationals. On average you can expect to get interest rates between 5% and 6.5%.

Loan Application

To apply for a mortgage in the US you need to have all of your financial papers in order. At the beginning of the process, the bank will request

- T4 slips from the last two years and your last two pay stubs
- T1 returns for the last one or two years
- Your most recent 60-day history of checking and savings accounts and all RRSP statements or any other investments that you own (all pages)
- A list of your lines of credit, with balances available
- Your most recent mortgage statement or rent receipt

- A copy of your tax bill for all real estate owned (to verify the tax amount)

- A list of vehicle payments

- Your Social Insurance Number (to check your credit history)

- Legible copies of your passport

The bank will pull your Canadian credit history and arrive at a score. The score required to proceed with the loan differs by institution. There are two Canadian credit reporting agencies that you can contact to check your rating: Equifax Canada (equifax.ca) and TransUnion (tuc.ca).

It takes some time to gather all the information but buyers who take all of this data to their first meetings will find it greatly expedites the process.

 SOLD

Check your own credit score before you borrow money. It's not uncommon for problems with a credit score to be related to issues with mistaken identity or situations you could explain. Clean up these issues before they're used against you.

 US LOAN APPLICATION TIPS

- Use a black pen on all documents that are being faxed or scanned.

- Expect your interest rate to fluctuate until you have a property under contract, because this is how the American system works.

- At the very end of the full approval process, just before the deal closes, you will need to act quickly to meet the bank's deadlines. All documents and passports must be notarized and couriered back to the title company within a 24-hour period. Anticipate this time crunch and leave a day free to get this done.

- Apply for a US checking account and credit card through your US bank after the mortgage is approved or when you are next in the US. The credit card will not be a regular credit card because you do not have established credit in the US. You will be able to use it like a debit card to access cash or cover incidentals. This is a great way to build your US credit history a little more quickly.

Investor Loans

A few US institutions will provide investor loans for Canadians. These will have higher interest rates and down payment requirements than a second-home loan. To reiterate points from Fundamental #9, your investor financing options will likely occur outside the traditional banking system. Here are some of your options.

Private Financing

This money is backed by individuals or organizations that lend to investors. They will check your credit and review your portfolio, but may be willing to work with a lower credit score than would be required by a traditional lender. The down payment is usually 25% to 30% and interest rates hover around 10% to 12%. Also, expect a one-time up-front fee of 1% to 3% of the loan.

Hard-Money Lenders

Hard-money lenders are private investors who focus on the value of the property. These are really asset-based loans, so the borrower's credit score is not important. Some auction lenders will lend within 24 hours but it normally takes a week because they won't lend before a property has been fully inspected. Hard-money lenders will lend up to 70%. Interest rates are usually between 15% and 18% and the setup fee is between 1% and 5%. Investors use this for bridge financing and for fix-and-flip projects.

PROCEED WITH CAUTION!

Understand What You're Getting Into

The hard-money lending pool teems with sharks. Remember, this loan isn't about believing in you, it's about believing in your property. These lenders have taken a close look at your property and know they can make their money back if they have to take back the property for non-payment of the loan. It's not uncommon for hard-money lenders to want all of their money back within 12 months.

Investors who want to swim in this pool must be very careful. The fix-and-sell market is tough. If you've borrowed heavily to buy and renovate a property and it doesn't sell, you could lose both the property and your cash.

Buy US Real Estate Property With Other People's Money.

Look For Ways to Help Other Canadians Make Money

Having looked at some of the issues in Fundamental #42, it's easy to see that financing US real estate investment property with funds from US institutions is complicated if you live on the north side of the 49th parallel. Some Canadian investors will avoid all of the potential hassles by using their own money to finance their first properties. Others will bring in other investors who have money to invest, but no inclination to do the work. In the real estate investment business, when they work together that's called a joint-venture deal and that's what I want to talk about now.

Canadian real estate and joint-venture guru Don Campbell tells me that in a joint-venture deal, one partner (you) finds the deal and has the expertise to make it work, while another partner or partners puts up all or part of the cash in return for the investment opportunity. Many Canadian investors use a 50/50 co-venture to acquire real estate where one person is the money partner and the other is the property expert. The money partner lets the property expert handle the day-to-day operations associated with running the business.

Bringing other people's money into your real estate deals opens a lot of great opportunities for Canadian investors who want to use that money to leverage their own funds and expertise. Before I address some of the main things you need to think about if you decide to bring other investors into your US deals, I want to remind you that to really make this process work you've got to pay even closer attention to your due diligence and make sure you're buying into the "right deal." This is critical because a successful deal is the best way to attract even more funds to your investment business!

SOLD

Nothing screams *"Success!"* like a real estate investment deal that makes money for you and your partners. Co-venturers who see their investments pay off are more likely to increase their investment and send other investors your way.

Beyond sticking to sound real estate fundamentals that help you acquire cash-flowing buy-and-hold properties with long-term equity appreciation, you want to pay close attention to "who" you bring into your deals. I know you are in business to make money. That aside, you must understand that

- You cannot work with everyone
- You do not have to work with everyone

My argument is simple. The US market for distressed property is hot, and while Canadians are aware there is money to be made, a lot of them do not know how to do it! For that reason, savvy Canadian real estate investors who view the US foreclosure market as ripe for the picking can become what the industry calls "money magnets" if they can show other people that their investments make money. If that's what you want to do, you must also be able to show less-informed potential investors that you know *why* your investments work—and that's why you are in charge. For example, you can show them how you find deeply discounted properties and then renovate them efficiently, effectively and economically; buy properties in areas with strong rental demand and a rising market for first-time homebuyers; keep your units rented, etc.—and that you can put their money to work in the same way.

 PROCEED WITH ENTHUSIASM!

Showing what you have done already is a good way to show potential investors what you plan to do in the future.

Begin With People You Know

Being able to attract co-venture money does not mean you must bring into your deals all of the money that comes your way. This is very important because it can make or break your business.

Don Campbell tells me that he structures his co-venture deals to make sure that both parties win when the deal works out; but during the process he maintains control of the deal and the decisions made around it. I like that approach because it puts the investor—who's doing the work—in charge.

He's also fussy about who he partners with and always does background checks on potential partners. Whether family, friends or business associates, it is very important to him to really know who he is going into business with.

Something very important to take away from this discussion is the fact that when you create joint ventures, no matter who the other party is, you must treat it like a business relationship when discussing or dealing with property issues. For example, legal agreements should be written and completed, regular meetings should be held to discuss any property issues and these topics cannot be allowed to enter into any family get-togethers. Always require the other party to get their own independent legal and accounting advice before signing any of the agreements. Now, although Don only invests in Canada, I suggest that you do the exact same, if not even more, if you are investing in the US with Canadian partners.

It's important to treat these relationships very seriously, you are in a trust situation where you are investing other people's money alongside yours. If you wouldn't invest in the deal with your own money, never invest in it with someone else's. It's also recommended that you "design the divorce in advance"—before you get into a joint-venture agreement, make sure you and the other party truly understand what each person's role is to be, how the profits and cash flow will be divided during and at the end of the relationship and, just as importantly, how you are going to deal with the situation if one party does not perform its duties or is not able to wait until the agreed-upon sale time. It is much easier to come to an agreement before there is any real money on the table. A well-written agreement will protect your interests should the partnership or deal encounter issues. For example, you need to know what might happen if your joint venturer gets divorced or dies and you need to have a plan in place should your exit strategy need to change because of a shift in the real estate cycle.

Before you buy your first property with your new partner, create an agreed-upon spreadsheet that will be used to divide the profits. Use your accountant to ensure that all of the taxes, dividends and expenses are included in the calculation. Both partners must agree that this will be the template, so there are no disputes in the future. This spreadsheet becomes an integral part of your joint-venture agreement.

Keep Your Advisors Informed

As you and your investors will be relying on trusted tax and legal advisors, you will need to budget for these expenses at the beginning. Engage them early in the process and keep them informed along the way. You will need a legal agreement that clearly defines the relationship and what happens as the deal proceeds. Your tax advisor also needs to know the details of your joint-venture deal as both parties will have to file the appropriate reports with the Canada Revenue Agency (CRA) every year, whether there were any profits achieved or not. Under Canadian tax law, you cannot put strategies in place retroactively!

 PROCEED WITH CAUTION!

Never, ever put someone else's money into a deal that you are not 100% sure of or one that you wouldn't put your own money into!

Arrange Pest Inspections for Your Real Estate Purchases.

Don't Get Caught With Unexpected "Guests"

Hiring a qualified pest inspector is one piece of due diligence a lot of Canadian real estate investors don't even know about when they start looking at buy-and-hold property in the US. And that's a shame, because across North America there are a number of serious insect pests that cause substantial economic damage to residential dwellings, costing homeowners billions of dollars a year in property repairs and pest control.

In fact, entomologist Ray Reuter says that going into a US real estate deal without a quality pest inspection leaves you wide open to future issues and can drastically affect your return on investment through problems keeping good tenants and unexpected cash calls to deal with structural damage or extermination.

With bedbug infestations across the US up 500% in recent years, some states have introduced legislation that requires landlords to pay the entire cost of exterminating these particular pests. Others require similar action under laws about getting rid of certain pests, including rats, mice, roaches, ants and bedbugs.

 SOLD

If you're not sure about a landlord's responsibility for pest control costs, check out the local tenants' association or the municipal and state landlord tenant laws. In Florida, pest control is listed under Obligations of the Landlord.

Subterranean Termites

One pest that causes a great deal of damage and is now common throughout most of the US is the infamous subterranean or Formosan termite. Warmer areas in the southeastern US are seriously affected by termites, including

Florida, Georgia and Louisiana, as well as some parts of California. The population diminishes as you move north and west, but moderate to heavy populations are reported in Nevada, Arizona, New Mexico, Texas, Oklahoma, Kansas, Missouri, Tennessee, Kentucky, the Carolinas and a few other midwestern states.

The subterranean termite is the most villainous wood-destroying pest in the country and costs the US roughly $2 billion a year for treatment and repairs, much of which directly affects homeowners and investors.

In most US real estate markets, the serious economic damage exacted by sub-terranean termites makes the cost of a quality pest inspection worthwhile.

Carpenter Ants and Bedbugs

Two other pests you'll want to watch out for are carpenter ants and bed-bugs, which are deemed the "hottest" bug issue of the day. Both of these pests cause damage to homes, but on different fronts. Carpenter ants are similar to subterranean termites because they cause direct damage to the structure of a property. Bedbugs don't necessarily cause economic damage to the home, but they are costly to remove and can cause physical discom-fort and/or psychological distress. In fact, people across North America are even using websites like The Bedbug Registry (bedbugregistry.com) to check bedbug infestation reports before booking a hotel room—or renting an apartment. Both of these insects are difficult for the untrained eye to notice and both can cost substantial amounts of cash to eradicate.

A quality pest inspector is inexpensive insurance against buying a prob-lem. But the key word here is *quality*, because pest control operators are definitely not all the same. Before flipping through the Yellow Pages or doing a Google search and picking the company with the cheapest price or the best-looking ad, do your homework on what the industry offers. While many investors and homeowners cut corners when it comes to pest control, a good pest control operator is well worth any price premium they might charge.

Here are some steps to consider before you hire a pest control specialist:

Go Pro

Look for companies belonging to professional organizations and state and/or government-run programs. In the US you'll want to verify the company is licensed with the governing body, such as the USDA, and has membership in the National Pest Management Association and any state-run organizations like the Kentucky Pest Management Association or Pest Control Operators of California.

Membership with such organizations shows a company is serious about continued learning, has potential access to the latest management tools and techniques available and has access to fellow operators when they need outside assistance.

The world of pest management is continually changing as new techniques are introduced, new chemical compounds are unveiled and some pesticides are pulled from the market. Make sure you're hiring a company that's current with industry norms.

Ask About Control Measures

Call a few companies to discuss the techniques they use when dealing with a particular pest. If the answers vary widely, call a local university with an entomology program or pest management extension service to get help with narrowing down the most effective techniques. You can also find a wealth of information on college websites, including those for the University of Kentucky, University of California Riverside, University of California Davis, Ohio State and University of Maryland.

Check References

Service provider references are critical. Ask to talk to clients whose properties had similar pest issues as yours so you can follow up to see if the problem was remedied and if things are still going well. Keep in mind that insects are unpredictable and reinfestations are not always the fault of the pest control expert; some insects will come back because of the environment where you live or because of the human dweller's lifestyle habits.

Look for a Warranty

Most quality companies in the area of pest control issues will offer a guarantee on the services provided. The warranties vary from company to company and depend on the pest being dealt with, so do read the fine print. Discuss the warranty options with all operators you contact, compare your options and factor a warranty into your final selection of service provider.

PROCEED WITH CAUTION!

Bedbugs Are Special

Because of the nature of the pest and the limited control methods available, warranties are a little different when dealing with bedbugs. With bedbugs it is almost always necessary (and good practice) to have a follow-up inspection. Most quality operators will tell you that up front and provide a solid explanation as to why it is needed.

Be Mindful of Sales and Marketing Tactics

Some companies can get your money before you know what's going on. Be smart: take your time and educate yourself before hiring an operator.

You may never come across a pest control problem in your real estate journey, but this is an area where performing some early due diligence can help you avoid serious cash calls. While some knowledge of problem insects is valuable, always hire a professional to do a quality inspection so you know what pests you're dealing with, where they are in the structure and where future problems or re-infestations are most likely to occur.

SOLD

A good pest control operator saves you time, money and a whole lot of headaches! Avoid the DIY approach using products you can pick up in the local store. You will probably end up doing more harm than good—and still have to hire a professional exterminator.

Decide Whether You're Buying a Lifestyle or an Investment.

Can Part-Time Home/Part-Time Rental Work?

A lot of the current interest by Canadians in US real estate markets has strong ties to the snowbird community, that group of retired and semi-retired Canadians who routinely migrate south to warmer American locales to escape the colder winter temperatures of their home country. Over the last couple of years, these seasonal US residents have noticed the dramatic proliferation of Foreclosure and For Sale signs and a growing number are asking if they should be treating their routine US holiday homes as investment opportunities. The answer is a resounding maybe!

This book zeroes in on Canadian real estate investors whose familiarity with real estate markets tells them this is a particularly good time to expand their portfolios to include some buy-and-hold rental properties in the United States. That focus is deliberate, as I aim to bring these investors up to speed on some important issues they may not expect to face. By reviewing the fundamentals of this market, I'm providing novice investors with some sound how-to investment principles.

The Snowbird Complication

But what about those snowbirds? With residential real estate prices at deep discounts, can they reasonably expect to buy a US property, use it personally for part of the year and then rent it out the rest of the time? Well, if this is what you're thinking of doing, I recommend extreme caution.

First, residential real estate is a major purchase, and yet I see too many Canadians buying vacation property with this "investment" focus but without a clue about what's really at stake. It's like a "field of dreams" strategy, so let me be clear: just because you buy it does not mean vacationers will come.

I'm not saying this strategy cannot work. But it won't work unless you treat it like a business strategy and have a solid marketing plan in place to make sure the property meets your revenue projections.

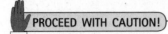

PROCEED WITH CAUTION!

Don't Confuse Lifestyle and Investment

American banks will lend Canadians money to buy a vacation home, but be aware that investor loans are tougher to get because the US banks know that real estate investment looks easier than it really is.

Think about what that means. The US lender is banking on your ability to meet a second-home payment. They think you have what it takes to make those payments. If you're buying that home because you think someone else (a renter) is going to make those payments, be careful. This strategy is not an investment if it puts your lifestyle at risk!

There are several key reasons why US vacation homes are not as easy to market as some Canadians expect. As so many of the Canadians I talk to do not realize why this is the case, I want to highlight some of those issues here, beginning with the fact that people looking for US vacation property currently have a great deal of choice. Why would they stay in your two-bedroom condo in an age 50-plus gated community when they may be able to rent a house with its own pool—a place beside an ocean beach?

Timing is another concern that many people fail to incorporate into their vacation-home investment dreams. For all of the differences between the Canadian and US climates, our summers and winters follow a remarkably similar path. If you plan to use the vacation property during the coldest Canadian months—aka, a prime winter vacation period—who's going to rent it during the off-season? And there can be other problems, too. For example, the southern US may be beautiful in the fall but that's also prime hurricane season. In other parts of the United States, tornado season coincides with prime summer vacation periods.

You should also think about property management, because seasonal contracts are difficult to set up and tough to maintain. It makes sense to factor quality property management fees into a buy-and-hold investment's cash-flow strategy. But if your place is only rented a few weeks of the year, how will you handle ongoing maintenance or repair issues, let alone make sure the place is properly cleaned between vacation tenants? You can hire property managers, but if the property's not renting the way you figured it might, that may not be an affordable option.

Remember, too, that all of your other property expenses, from insurance to taxes and utilities, will need to be paid regardless of whether the place is rented six months of the year or two weeks.

A Longer-Term Strategy

Anyone who knows me knows I'm all about the big picture and in real estate that equates to the long-term strategy. If you read through Part 6 of this book, you'll have a better sense of what it really means to set your business and personal goals. Let's say that you do a good job of goal planning and you know you want to retire in five to 10 years. With that mind, you are looking for an investment that will help make that possible. In the meantime, you don't want to live entirely for the future (which may never come), but might want to break up the last years of your working life with a few special vacations.

In the short term, Canadians in this situation may want to look at buying a US buy-and-hold rental property with positive cash flow. These houses should be located in a community characterized by predicted capital appreciation and an increase in first-time homeowners. As you're looking ahead and enjoying life now, you could use the cash flow to fund those vacations.

Down the road, several other options will open up. You could use that rental as your second home, leverage it to buy a second home or sell it and use the proceeds to buy that vacation home.

Imagine—instead of tying yourself to an investment strategy premised on risk, you've used real estate investment fundamentals to create future wealth and some pretty exciting pre- and post-retirement options.

 MYTH OR FACT

Myth: Throngs of Canadians are looking to vacation in a US property.

Fact: As markets go, this market is pretty saturated. Before you buy a vacation home with plans to rent it out for part of the year, check on what's happening with the market in the community where you plan to buy.

Looking for Investments in a Foreign Location
An Investor Talks About Why He Likes the US Market

Craig Chandler lives in Australia and has been investing in US real estate for many years. He's developed his real estate investing niche over time and his experience as a foreigner in the US market has much to offer Canadians who are looking at buying distressed property in that country.

First and foremost, Craig sees value in finding an investment niche. For him, it's residential houses in blue-collar neighborhoods located in desirable towns where people will want to live and retire. "There needs to be strong employment in multiple industries so jobs are not reliant on one industry," notes Craig. "I prefer blue-collar areas as they are more afford-able to buy and the yield, as a percentage of purchase price, is much higher than more expensive properties. This means they cash flow better. Also, if this type of tenant loses their job, they are more likely to find another job a lot quicker than a white-collar worker will, especially in an economic downturn."

Because he knows people like to live near the water, he also focuses on coastal areas. Beyond that, Craig narrows his investment property search by applying the following search criteria.

Desirable Area and Climate

"I look for reasons people will want to live or retire in an area. Climate can play a large part in this. I personally prefer areas in warmer climates, mainly in coastal areas. Florida and California would be good examples ... as well as warmer areas such as Arizona and Nevada."

Craig was on the lookout for investment properties in coastal areas of the US because of how this desire to live near the water impacts real estate in his home country of Australia, where property markets are affected by what's called the "seachange." The word describes the movement of Australians, many of them baby boomers, from cities to coastal areas where they retire or work remotely. "I have done very well following this trend and investing in property in many of these coastal towns."

He's also watched how demographic movements like the seachange affect a region, as growing populations in these areas tend to have a positive effect on local infrastructure, employment and other lifestyle amenities.

"In more recent times in Australia we have also seen what has become known as the 'treechange.' This is basically the same as the seachange but instead of moving to coastal areas, people are moving to country or regional areas with more trees," explains Craig. Again, their key motivation is the search for better lifestyles. Real estate investors who are watching that trend can also target areas where this kind of demographic shift can have a positive impact on the stability of a market.

Multiple Employment Opportunities

"I'm a big believer in having multiple streams of income, which is another reason I love investing in residential property," notes Craig, who applies that same logic to his investment markets. "When I look to invest in an area, I like to know that there are multiple streams of employment available. I'm not a fan of buying in towns that have only a few major forms of industry." If those industries downsize or relocate, there is a significant impact on the area's economy, with limited options for newly unemployed workers.

"In Australia we have many mining towns that have high yields on residential property because of the shortage of available properties for rent and also the fact that miners have a high rate of pay and can pay much higher rent than in similar areas that don't have mines. Many people have done very well in these towns, but as a long-term investor, I worry about what will happen to values and rents if the mining industry hits a downturn," explains Craig.

Towns that are desirable for retirement and tourism also have a host of service industries to cater to their residents, including medical services, entertainment and trades involved with building and ongoing maintenance. Agriculture can be a primary employer in many of these areas and educational institutions like universities also generate stable employment.

Craig also keeps an eye out for lower-taxed states and cities, as these will attract business investment. (Some might even offer incentives for this.) "It's not hard to research what employment opportunities are available in an area, and it's also easy to find out what other industries are likely to come," says Craig.

He values the tourism component of a community because he knows that many retired people will retire to a community where they've spent holidays. "This all creates employment opportunities."

Infrastructure

Part of his assessment considers the existing infrastructure. "Many years ago I was looking at a deal in what was then a sleepy-looking coastal town half an hour from one of our capital cities. This area had a bit of a stigma attached to it over previous years but had great priced property and high rental yields. When I drove there, I noticed that all the foreshore areas were being landscaped and that bicycle and walking tracks were being constructed. I have a background in the nursery industry and noticed that the plants being planted were expensive varieties—not run-of-the-mill plants usually planted by local governments. The more I looked around, the more plans for new buildings, roads, etc. I saw."

Knowing that infrastructure encourages stable housing markets, Craig purchased several properties in the area "and it has proven to be one of my better investment areas. The funny thing was people from surrounding areas couldn't see the wood from the trees and didn't see the potential."

Multiple Recreational Activities

Craig also looks at recreational opportunities as a criteria for zeroing in on a real estate investment market. "When looking for desirable areas I also look at what recreational activities are available. In warm coastal climates you might have things like fishing, surfing, boating, golf, etc. Other areas might have activities like hiking, trail riding, cycling and horseback riding. The more there is to do in an area, the more desirable it will be to live there," says Craig. "If investing in or near tourist areas, you will mostly find that there are a wide range of recreation choices."

High Rental Yields and Demand

With distressed property at historic highs across the United States, Craig has been intrigued by advertisements he's seen that claim spectacular rental returns. "I even see ads in Australia trying to get people to invest in the USA with claims of yields as high as 20% and purchase prices of $30,000."

Ever the skeptic, Craig looks behind those numbers and says most properties are located in areas where it's tough for an investor to make any money.

He tells prospective investors to exercise a great deal of care when deciding where their investment money should go. "Just make sure there is plenty of rental demand in the areas you are looking at. Speak to a few property managers to check that they will be able to rent your property. Make sure you talk to someone independent of who is trying to sell you the property; just go on the Net or look in the Yellow Pages to find some other property managers."

Also check that the amount of rent you are being told you will receive is realistic in the market you are looking at. Craig gets this kind of information from local property managers, then crunches his own numbers on a lower rent than quoted, "just to be on the safe side."

Buying Houses Below Replacement Cost

Like a lot of investors, Craig likes to buy existing houses well below replacement cost so he's not competing for the same tenants who might be interested in renting a new house. As the newer places will cost more to rent, Craig protects the value of his investment property by making sure renters will find it more affordable.

And he never compromises on insurance. "Always insure your house for the full replacement value, even if this is much higher than what you paid for it. If your house burns down you need to be able to replace it!" insists Craig.

Investing in Different Countries

Experienced real estate investors don't have to leave their home countries to find deals that work. But with a lot of the world's economies in an economic downturn, Craig says it can make a lot of sense to invest in foreign countries as a way to take advantage of market opportunities and spread your risk.

"When an economy is doing really well, quite often the deals are not too easy to find," says Craig. "This may be a good time to use some of your funds from that area to invest into another that may be at a low point but has the potential to really grow over time. With the prices and yields currently available in the USA, I believe now is a great time to do this."

Here are three more reasons Craig sees particular advantage in the current US market:

1. Currency exchange

As this book was being written, the Canadian and Australian dollars were very high against the US dollar. "As a Canadian, that means you need a lot fewer Canadian dollars than you did in the past to buy US real estate," notes Craig. Better still, if the Canadian dollar drops back in value against the US dollar, "you stand to make a substantial gain on the currency exchange regardless of whether the property has risen in value or not."

2. Inflation and real estate

Craig also likes the way real estate is basically indexed to inflation. This means real estate prices, even those having weathered a significant market downturn, will appreciate over time. Over the long term, real estate prices and rents increase, but your mortgage decreases. This delivers increased equity and more rental income to pay down the mortgage a lot faster.

The thing with buying positive cash-flow real estate is that even if the value does fall, cash-flow rents will pay the mortgage so you can ride out the bad times. That makes current opportunities even more important, as a market downturn "can be a great time to add more properties to your portfolio," says Craig. He also sees positive cash-flow properties as an effective hedge against future inflation.

3. International travel

Foreign travel can be an interesting and fun by-product of investing in different areas and countries. "Another thing I love about real estate investing is that you can learn new things and pick up new ideas no matter where you go," shares Craig. A big believer in networking, he jumps at the chance to spend time with other real estate investors. "I network with investors from all over the USA, Canada, New Zealand, and Asia and Australia."

How to Make Investing Work for You: What You Really Need to Know

"Your confidence today will detemine your success tomorrow."

—Philip McKernan

PART

6

Apply the Right Mind-Set to Foreign Investments.

Develop the Confidence to Take Action

I have worked with many real estate investors and business professionals in my private and group mentoring efforts over the last several years. It is apparent to me that many successful individuals have a mind-set that is quite different from the masses. By "mind-set," I mean that they approach life with a certain set of assumptions that less-successful people do not hold, and those assumptions enable them to apply certain analytical strategies to real-world behaviors. In the end, they are simply better able to make decisions that positively affect their professional and personal lives.

This is a topic that I have been speaking about more and more to investor and real estate groups around the would. As I write this I have just come back from New Zealand, where I spoke about nothing other than mind-set for an entire weekend event. I share this because when I landed in Auckland and met the event organizer to interview him about his expectations and his clients' needs, I asked him about the real challenges facing New Zealand real estate investors today. It was soon apparent to me that no speaker on the agenda was addressing the one thing that these investors needed most. In fairness, many of the investors at the event could not necessarily have articulated that need. From my perspective, they longed for inner-game material—but few of them knew how to ask for it!

The inability to express that need has deep roots in the recent recession experienced in many parts of the world. People in New Zealand, as in Canada and the US, are still reeling from the effects of this event. And those effects aren't felt just financially, but have psychological implications as well.

I wanted to write this book because I realized that Canadian real estate investors are watching property markets in the neighboring US and are looking for tried-and-true investment strategies. My goal was to write a book solidly based on the real estate fundamentals that good investors could put into action. But alongside all of the core fundamentals with their strategies, tips and cautions, I also recognized that giving this information without asking you to consider your mind-set is a lot like giving you a car without a steering wheel.

Leave a Little Room for Your GUT

Let's get something clear right now: if you are human and have a pulse, taking the emotion out of the deal is impossible! I know this goes against much of the teaching about investing in the world today and appears to run counter to Fundamental #16: Dial Up the Intellect (Dial Down the Emotions), but let me explain. My point here is that if you are human, you can't expect to remove all emotion from your real estate deals.

I write this knowing that over the last decade investors and entrepreneurs of all stripes have been pushed to take the "feelings" out of the deal process. I think we do that at our peril. I am not saying to hell with the due diligence, accounting packages, spreadsheets and property inspections. I am not saying it's okay to "go with your gut" and toss deal research to the side. But I do believe there is some merit to "feeling the deal."

In my experience, there have been times when I did all the due diligence and was intellectually satisfied that the figures added up to a sound investment deal, but I still had gut-level concerns. Looking back on the times when I stuck with the deal and ignored those feelings, it seems like those deals never went as well as I had anticipated; even when you could argue they worked out financially, there were problems.

I suggest that while real estate analysis has its place, it should not replace your inner guidance system. While I generally don't like acronyms, I've broken my no-acronym rule and sometimes talk about the value of GUT.

G—Guidance from within
U—U have the answers
T—Trust yourself

My own experience with GUT and a real estate deal goes back to my first-ever investment property. It was a semi-derelict cottage on the west coast of Ireland, one mile from the town of Ennis. I spotted the cottage by complete accident while on a drive with my wife, and on a whim we pulled up and got out of my car on a wet and cold winter day. The experience sticks in my mind because when I stopped the car, my wife desperately needed a bathroom and was less than pleased with the delay. When I jumped back in the car five minutes later with that "Dad, can we buy a puppy?" look and suggested we buy the cottage, she assumed I was joking. I convinced her to get out and have a look, but I couldn't get so much as a maybe (or a smile!) from Pauline.

"It would look great after the renovation," I cajoled. (I now realize that I was working from a completely different mind-set. I could visualize how the property would look after the fixing up we'd do.)

"Renovation, what renovation? Why would the owner even bother trying to renovate this piece of crap?" was my wife's response.

Thinking I wasn't clearly explaining myself, I tried again. "No . . . I mean, how it will look after we renovate it."

To make a long story short, we did buy it at auction after a huge battle with the only other nutter willing to buy a semi-derelict cottage with rats in it. Looking back, that purchase made no sense from a commercial perspective. It was not the ideal first investment property but we renovated it, put tenants in it, managed to create great cash flow and capitalized on the equity. The negative components of the deal aside, that property was responsible for many of the other properties we subsequently bought.

On the other hand, I also remember buying a property in South Africa through a guy I did not have a good feeling about. Having been told by people I trusted that he was credible, I ignored my GUT feelings. My lack of trust in my own inner guidance system cost me a lot of money and caused even more stress. In hindsight, I recognize that US investment guru Warren Buffett knew exactly what he was talking about when he said:

"You can't make a good deal with a bad person."

I Am Passionate About Real Estate

When I'm mentoring and training real estate investors and professionals, I often hear them say they are "passionate about real estate." I used to politely ask why and begin to explore why the person believed that to be true. My real questions revolved around how someone can be *passionate* about bricks and mortar.

More recently, I have been somewhat bolder in my approach and I actually suggest that the person is not, indeed, passionate about real estate. This is generally met with some resistance but when we take the time to drill down to find out why a person thinks he or she is passionate about real estate, the individual usually realizes that what they're really passionate about is what real estate can represent, or help them get. And there are lots of good reasons to be passionate about that. These include the freedom to choose what you do with your time, time off work, extra cash flow and the chance to give back to society.

What I really like is that almost all of the time it turns out their real passions are linked to family, spirituality or a desire to give back so they can help someone else achieve their goals.

I share this because I want you to be very clear on "why" you are buying real estate in the first place. This clarity will help you develop the mind-set that will allow you to be more focused and in turn, more successful. It will also give you a mental edge to bounce back from the experiences you get on days when things don't seem to be going right. Again, let's be honest. Real estate offers its fair share of challenges. But so does life in general! My work shows me time and again that investors who have a clear understanding of why they invest are better able to get back up, dust themselves off and move on when a situation knocks them down. In this business, that kind of resilience is a virtue!

Conquer Your Fear

There is no shortage of fear in the world right now and it doesn't look like it's going to disappear for a while. Fear is a powerful and potent force and it must be taken on, not ignored. I encourage the people I mentor to forget about trying to control fear. Instead, I say, "look fear in the eye and invite it to dinner." What I mean by this is that you need to try to understand where that fear comes from.

For example, if you read an article that is telling you the economy is about to crash and you become fearful, it's most likely that this fear is less about the economy and more about some underlying dialogue going on in your head. It is important to understand the difference so you can start to build awareness of what is actually going on. I am fascinated by how there seems to be more fear around when there are more opportunities to buy great deals. I think this is why it is so important to understand the real estate cycle discussed in Fundamental #10. What I want you to realize is that fear costs us personally and financially because it has the tendency to stifle our ability to take action. Remember what I said about the mind-set of successful people? I would argue that they can approach life with a different set of assumptions because they meet their fears head-on!

The following diagram shows what happens if you let the Ring of Fear control your ability to make decisions. Use this diagram to address your fears—and stop the cycle!

The Ring of Fear

Source: philipmckernan.com

Lack of Clarity

A lack of clarity or direction is quite common even with the most successful investors. They may appear to have confidence and exude a sense of knowing "exactly what I am doing and where I am going," but inside they are lost. Without a clear direction of where you are going and a good understanding of why you are investing, it's easy to move from a lack of clarity to uncertainty.

Uncertainty

When you are uncertain, you are open to manipulation by messages in the media and those around you. This does not mean you need to be absolutely certain in every aspect of your life, but when it comes to money and investing it is critical to have some clear direction. Now, more than ever, it is also critical to have a strategy.

Fear

Fear is not the issue. The issue is where that fear comes from. You need to figure out what's causing the fear to show itself. If you dig behind the scenes you will see that it's a feeling of uncertainty that represents instability.

Confidence

Fear and confidence are directly and proportionately related. The more fear you experience, the less confidence you have available to you. Imagine you are in a plane 30,000 feet above sea level and you have two fuel tanks, one on each wing. In one tank you have fear and the other, confidence. It's not a bad thing to have fear; fear can, in fact, be useful. What you want to aim for is a balanced amount of fuel from each so that your actions are the right mix of confidence and caution.

Inaction

Many people allow fear to grow to the point that they are paralyzed. When this happens, it's like their fuel tank of confidence runs dry and they are no longer able to act. Doing nothing is fine if that is a real choice you've made, and not a result of inaction brought about by fear. I can decide not to pull the trigger on a deal. I can decide to wait for a better deal when I feel pressured to make a decision too quickly.

Momentum

The inevitable result of being caught up in the Ring of Fear is that your journey as a real estate investor will come to a halt, perhaps even before it's launched! The most tragic part of this situation is not the immediate loss of income, but the chance to have invested in your future. The world is full of people with regrets. When you let fear keep you from taking action, it becomes the assassin of your dreams.

Get Your "Whys" in Focus

How do you take those first steps towards achieving your dreams? Start by getting clear on the "whys" of what you want to do. I am convinced that this step forms the foundation that most people forget to build. Your future starts today. What's holding you back?

Be Clear About Why You Want to Buy US Real Estate.

Get Your Personal Goals Straight

I like to start my seminars by asking people if they're clear about their personal goals. A lot of people think they understand exactly what I'm asking—until I dig a little deeper. That's when the wheels fall off the proverbial wagon. Let me apply that strategy here and ask you to think about the following three questions:

1. Why are you thinking of buying real estate?

2. Why are you looking south of 49?

3. Why do you invest at all?

My whole premise with this book is to show you how to use core fundamentals to make US real estate investments work. The subject makes sense because there is no doubt that there are some incredible real estate opportunities in the US right now, and some market insiders are describing the current US market downturn as a kind of "perfect storm" for investors. As they see it, these same conditions are not likely to come around again for a very long time, if ever.

But is the fact you *can* invest in US real estate enough? And does the fact that now is a particularly good time for Canadian real estate investors (or Canadians who want to be real estate investors) mean you should rush south and pick up a deal or perhaps many deals?

For some, the answer is an easy yes. Others want to see if buying US properties would fit their bigger picture, their long-term investment strategy. I think there is some logic to proceeding with care, which is why I proposed those three "why" questions.

Answering the "Why" Helps Set the "How"

Real estate is like driving a fast car—it's exciting. It can also be quite dangerous if you don't know the car you're driving and you're not familiar with the road ahead. But while a car will generally cost you money, real estate will, almost always, appreciate in value. As well, a car is not likely to make you money after you buy it. In contrast, a cash-flowing property can pay your bills, provide cash for your next deal and back future deals with equity.

My point is that long before you figure out what kind of real estate property you are going to buy in the US and long before you map out the road ahead, you need to determine why you are in the car in the first place. Once you know that, it's relatively easy to look at the type of vehicle (investment) that best suits you. While you may decide to buy a vintage car that's slow and steady, you could also opt for a Formula 1 race car that's all about speed and making the best time on your money as possible. Others may say to hell with both strategies and buy the Hummer. For them, it's all about going big or going home!

Goal Setting Is Harder Than You Think

I am a business and personal mentor and I work in an educational field where I've seen people invited, motivated, pushed, cajoled and even coerced into feeling guilty about their lack of goal-setting prowess. They are asked how they can possibly know what it is they want to do in life if they can't articulate specific goals and, ideally, big, huge and massive goals. Isn't achieving these goals what success is all about?

Building on that same logic, people are increasingly pressured to have goals for every aspect of their lives. You might need investor, business, education, family, parenting, coaching, volunteering and even spiritual goals. As I write this, I can honestly say it tires me out to think about the work involved in developing all of those goals. It's really overwhelming.

How do I know that? Because I bought into those über-goal-making strategies for several years and I am here to tell you:

Traditional goal setting does not work!

The problem isn't that we don't need goals. We do. The problem is that because we aren't developing the right goals, we're wasting a whole lot of time pursuing the wrong ones! Let me show you what I mean. One statistic that's been widely thrown around for many years is that 97% of the world's population does not sit down and write down their goals. That implies that only 3% does. Others tell me that 3% of the world's population controls 97% of the wealth. The problem with numbers like these (and the people who think there is a natural connection between the figures) is that some people read them and believe that setting goals is enough to set them on the road for material success. Once those goals are written down, you just grab a pint of Guinness and wait for the money to roll in. Yeah, right! I can tell you with complete sincerity that it takes work to develop goals—and way more work to implement them. But that isn't even my main issue with traditional goal setting.

Having traveled to about 60 countries around the globe and having done business in many of those countries, I am not convinced that the 97% who do not set traditional goals are really missing out, but perhaps not for the reasons some people might think. I have pursued the finest coffee beans in Guatemala and Indonesia, gone in search of the best wines in distant lands like Argentina and Australia and spent time is rural villages and orphanages in Sri Lanka and the Amazon jungle. Many of the people I have encountered on these journeys are far from wealthy. Many of them actually have very little, yet it's rare to meet children in these countries who are not smiling from one side of their little faces to the other.

I am not trying to compare us to them, or to suggest that it is not important for us to set goals or attain more wealth. I just want to put into perspective the fact that life should not be all about setting goals to attain more. Success can be relative, and when it includes personal happiness, the success must be measured differently. Having said that, my central argument here is that the lack of goals is not the real challenge for the people I'm asked to mentor. In the end, I think the real issue is that they haven't been taught how to set appropriate goals.

This comes from my experience leading mentoring workshops and having people ask me to show them how to set goals and how to think big. First, I don't think we need any more ways to set goals because I think we are already goal-setting kings and queens. And second, I think that efforts to teach us to "think big" miss the mark.

I'm going to look at both issues in the next fundamental, where I challenge you to recognize how you can fine-tune your goals and hone a business strategy that balances your investment and personal goals. In the meantime, I want you to be clear about *why* you want to invest in US real estate. Even the best investment market has risks. Figure out which investment vehicle you really want to drive and be honest about how that decision will affect your life. I'm fond of saying:

Success is manufactured in the mind, while happiness is cultivated in the soul.

48

Learn to Believe Big.

Your Goals Tell the Real Story

I ended the last fundamental by saying we don't need more ways to set goals. What we do need is a better understanding of why the goals we set should reflect what we are really trying to do. I also tried to warn you to be wary of anyone who tells you to "think big." With this fundamental, I want to give you a new way to understand how your goals are affected by the way you think. As far as I'm concerned, you don't need to think big, you need to "believe big." And to do that well, you need to understand the difference between the two.

Believe Big

Close your eyes. Go on, close them. Think of the house you live in. As soon as you have it in your mind, think of a house that you'd really, really like to live in. Perhaps a friend owns it, or maybe it's a house you drive past every day. My point is that it's not hard to think big. Believing big is the real challenge. With that in mind, ask yourself these questions:

- Do I truly believe I could live in that house?

- Do I deserve to live in that house?

- Do I believe I deserve to live in that house?

- Do I even want to live in that damn house anyway?

I want you to understand that most people approach goal setting the wrong way because they begin the process by asking the wrong questions. When I am not delivering workshops or speeches, or spending time in the media promoting my books, I spend a great deal of time thinking. When I say a great deal of time, I mean a great deal of time. I like to take entrepreneurial or philanthropic concepts, philosophical ideas and commonly held beliefs and question them against my inner guidance system (GUT). I then rebuild these ideas as simply as possible so I can teach them. I've done that with the whole goal-setting and thinking-big issues.

Keep It Real: Authentic Goals Matter

With experience and study, I now approach questions about goal setting very differently. Part of that comes from having asked hundreds of my clients about the goals they have set. As I studied their answers, I uncovered a staggering but scary fact. That is:

When I first met them, all of my clients had goals that did not belong to them.

Yikes! Where did their goals come from, then? It turns out they had goals that came from society, friends, family and peers. While there's nothing inherently wrong with being influenced by people we care about or admire, the fundamental truth of this approach is that it leads people to adopt goals they do not really buy into. Remember when I asked you to think about that big house? Well, when my clients focused on their goals— their "big ideas"—it turned out they were often chasing the wrong thing. They'd been conditioned to believe some goals were worth adopting by virtue of the fact that others valued those goals. This is a problem, because if you don't really want to meet the goals you've set, it's darn near impossible to approach them with a "believe big" attitude.

And what's worse than not having any goals? I would say it's holding on to a set of goals you don't believe in. This type of behavior leads individuals to make choices they do not want to make. Worse, many sacrifice peace of mind by doggedly pursuing activities that cause them more stress than comfort. Let me show you how that can work in real life.

The Wrong Goals Hold You Back

A couple once approached me to do some private mentoring. One of the goals they wanted to achieve involved real estate investing and they told me they wanted to purchase 50 properties over the next three to five years. My first thought was, "That's an interesting number!" Whenever I see big round numbers, I want to know what's behind them; especially if we're talking financial numbers like $50,000, $100,000 or $1 million. I look behind the number because I generally find these numbers have no real basis in the real world. We pull them from the sky because they sound good.

 SOLD

Do you have real estate investment goals tied to specific numbers? What's behind those numbers? Does the number impede or support what you really want to do with or accomplish during your life?

When I ask, "Why is that number important?" I typically get a "what?" answer. And that is very interesting. Instead of being able to tell me why they wanted to buy 50 properties, this couple told me they needed a certain amount of dollars in a certain number of years. Again, the people I mentor are often very specific and many tell me they need the money from their investments "to be in a financial position to live the life we want." Again, that sounds logical, or so I used to think.

I now know that it's really important to get people to look at their answers more honestly. "So, what is your life like now?" and "Are you doing what you want to do?" are the questions they need to answer. It turned out this couple was not so happy. They were having major disagreements and not sleeping well. They both had jobs they hated and they were continuously beating themselves and each other up for not "achieving more, faster."

It also turned out they had already bought three properties in one year and were feeling a great deal of pressure to buy more even though they weren't really sure those first three were performing as well as they should be. Without really knowing it, they had basically committed to keeping their heads down and their noses to the grindstone for the next three to five years—but were wickedly uncomfortable with what that meant!

I know Dr. Spock would tell you that their property-buying business goal was logically in step with what they wanted to do in the future. But I'm not Spock and I would argue that their choices weren't just economically dangerous, they were potentially insane.

Calculate the Social Invoice

What I've learned from working with people like this couple is that the whole "make hay while the sun shines" strategy probably only makes sense if you're a farmer with livestock to feed. For most of the rest of us, the sun shines pretty much every day, even though we don't necessarily see things that way. (I would argue that's why so many of the economically poor people I've met around the world are happy in comparison to my fellow North Americans. These people practice gratitude for what they have instead of focusing on what they're missing.) On the real estate property front, most investors who take on something as intense as buying 50 properties in a short period of time would find themselves entangled in an all-consuming task. By the time my couple lifted their heads in five years, a lot of what they thought they were working towards could be gone!

I say this because I don't think this couple really wanted to wait five years before they enjoyed their lives. But when they decided to make 50 properties their goal, they lost sight of what that meant they would have to give up. Here, "thinking big" compromised their ability to believe big. My lessons here are pretty old-school.

Real Estate Investment Goal Setting Rules

1. **Real estate investment, like life, doesn't work like a switch.**

   Most people can't be totally focused on one enterprise for five years, then turn off the tap and get back to doing the things they love to do with the people they want to do those things with.

2. **The world changes and so do the people in it.**

   Five years is a long time. Think of your own family and friends. Where will your spouse, your children, your parents, your siblings and your business partners be in five years?

3. **You will change, too.**

   Experience changes who we are. Time makes us older and smarter— or older and more obtuse. You can put experience to work, or turn your back on its lessons and take no responsibility for the decisions you made.

I like to apply what I call the "social invoice" to this part of the discussion. Hindsight is a great thing and some of mine comes from having watched thousands of my fellow Irishmen and women fall into the trap of the "make hay" syndrome during the economic success story known as the Celtic Tiger. Over a 14-year period from 1993 to 2007, Ireland went from being one of the poorest countries in Europe to the second wealthiest country in the world. At first glance, this was great for the country. But I would say that we also paid a huge social invoice for the new obsession with acquiring more.

So why is that relevant to you and your plans to buy US investment property? Because the consequences of being too focused on the perceived rewards of investing carries a real cost. Canadians, for the most part, have not experienced the current economic downturn the way the rest of the world has. This puts a lot of Canadians in an economic position to invest in real estate. That's good. At the same time, I want you to remember to ask what your real goals are. Real estate investment is an enterprise best focused on long-term wealth, not short-term profit. That means it does not need to be a full-time obsession. You can enjoy the sunshine and make hay, but you can also enjoy the sunshine for its own sake.

Slow Down, Enjoy the Ride

Driving fast gives some people a great adrenaline rush. I've see that same flush of excitement in real estate investors and people who want to invest in real estate, when they get caught up in the notion that buying real estate is something they have to do quickly lest they miss out on current opportunities. I'm not sure who coined the term "speed kills," but it applies here, too. My main take-home lesson is that you should pursue wealth and happiness at the same time.

I'll illustrate that with the story of two Canadian investors, Mr. Rabbit and Mr. Tortoise. Mr. Tortoise sets out to acquire a nice US portfolio, focusing on one deal at a time. He loves the mantra, "Slow and steady wins the race." Mr. Rabbit sets out to blaze a trail and command the race. He is looking at deals every week and his mantra is "Slow and steady, my ass!"

Their different approaches allow them both to build a real estate portfolio. Mr. Tortoise finds a good deal with strong cash flow and a bonus—it's well situated to gain some equity. He closes the deal and commits to getting this property set up and running well before he starts looking for the next one. He goes to bed at night knowing that smart real estate investors who stick to the core fundamentals can make money in any market. He knows the current US foreclosure market looks good. He also knows there will be plenty of opportunities for investors like him for several years to come.

Mr. Rabbit, on the other hand, has a different strategy. He has an offer on one property and is considering an offer on another when he gets a phone call on a third. One of the potential deals isn't located in the same state as his first property, but he loves the discounted price.

Mr. Rabbit hasn't been home for dinner at six for a week and he hasn't been sleeping well. ("When you live in Eastern Canada and are investing in the Western USA, time management takes on a whole new meaning!" he says with a laugh.) He believes that sleep is for the weak, so he'll persevere. Once he's on American ground and doing deals, his cell phone will be burning a hole in his ear and he'll put pedal to the metal as he moves from house to house and bank to bank trying to make it all work.

Mr. Tortoise is at home after having dinner with the family when he starts to contemplate his next purchase. He's on the Internet scouting neighborhoods and looking for real estate agents who know the REO market in those neighborhoods. He knows the importance of solid research and a reliable investment team.

Back in the US, Mr. Rabbit finally closes on all three properties and suddenly feels the impact of that lack of sleep. He's been living off fast food, and the raw stress of handling so many details at once catches up to him. Pushing fatigue aside, a few days later he is convinced that his first deal is a corker as it's bringing in great cash flow. The second property is bringing in good cash flow, too, but by the second month in, he realizes it's not located in a great area and that it's not likely to keep a qualified tenant. He's annoyed. He was told the area was a good one but it turns out there has been very little growth historically. ("Note to self," says Mr. Rabbit. "In the future, when people give me information, I need to check it out.")

A few months later, Mr. Tortoise is still basking in the cash flow of his single purchase and is poking around the US market for another buy. Mr. Rabbit's life shows a new level of stress. The third property is a problem. It's been really hard to rent even though Mr. Rabbit has dropped the rent twice. He recently found out the electrical system is not up to code and he'll have to upgrade the system at considerable cost. ("Second note to self: What were you thinking? The contractor warned me about the electrical system! It seems like all the other roofs on the street are also being redone. I wonder if that's a coincidence or if I should have had the roof looked at more closely, too?")

Sticking to his guns, Mr. Rabbit is determined to make these properties work. After all, he bought them because they fit his investment goals—and if they don't, he's a failure. He tells other would-be investors about the discounted prices and insists he was right to buy with haste because he would have lost the properties if he hadn't moved so quickly. "I'm poised to lose money on two of these properties every month, but this is just temporary. Besides, I got them for a bargain!"

A small voice urges him to take a second look at what's going wrong, but he pushes it aside. His goal was to buy property quickly and he did it.

"That's good, right?" Mr. Rabbit is so determined to think big he leaves no room to look at whether he even believes his actions have moved him in that direction.

The ugly truth about this real estate twist on a storybook fable is that Mr. Rabbit is completely confused about why he is investing. Even though he's poised to lose a whole lot of money, he still thinks his investment strategy is on track. In reality, Mr. Rabbit's Formula 1 approach is about to be overtaken by a vintage model.

In contrast, Mr. Tortoise knew the kind of life he wanted to lead. He also knew he wanted to invest in real estate because it was a good way to support his long-term wealth-building goals. As he strolls towards his second property, Mr. Tortoise is calm and collected. As Mr. Rabbit races towards property No. 4, he teeters on the edge of financial (and physiological) disaster.

If this all sounds silly, read the story again. I guarantee you this situation is being reenacted in several American states at this very moment.

 **MYTH OR FACT**

Myth: Goal setting is an essential component of success.

Fact: The wrong goals can do more harm than good!

Choose Your Mentors Wisely.

Keep Your Investor Life Cycle Moving in the Right Direction

So how do we learn to "believe big"? For a lot of real estate investors, myself included, that process begins with a business coach or mentor. This does not have to be someone you pay for support but it does need to be someone you trust and someone who believes in you. It also needs to be someone who knows how you view the mentor/mentee relationship and knows that you have certain expectations about what you want to accomplish.

In fairness, you can't expect an altruistic mentor to be in a position to make your business and personal issues an ongoing top priority. On the other hand, if you're not sure that you will always need to be linked to a specific mentor, you may want to shape the relationship around a particular period of time, say six or 12 months. That can help you and the mentor focus on particular milestones.

A good business mentor and coach should be familiar with what you're trying to do but does not need to be engaged in the same enterprise. Further to that, I am absolutely adamant that you should only work with a mentor who is physically, emotionally and financially independent from the outcome of the business and personal decisions you might make under their tutelage. This can be a deal breaker in the real estate business, where some mentors are directly tied to investments.

As well, a mentor or coach must be willing to challenge your responses to very specific questions. This is how we develop what I would call "real knowledge." On the business front, the people who take action based on real knowledge can create amazing results and avoid many pitfalls. How do they do it? They do it by following sound investment fundamentals—and by committing to an investment strategy that's been tested and retested by others already in the business. For many, that means hooking up with a mentor.

Much of this book has been devoted to why the US market for single-family homes is looking so good right now. I've talked about what the distressed property market is and how Canadian investors can take advantage of the discounted prices available in communities with sound rental market fundamentals.

All of that good news aside, I am concerned that a lot of investors are moving into this market without being clear about why they want to invest in this particular market. Here are a few of the things I've recently heard when talking to Canadians who are thinking about taking some of their investment money south.

- "Well, it's obvious. The US housing prices are down and the Canadian dollar is strong."
- "Real estate is the best asset class in the world to build wealth."
- "I want to build enough wealth for the future so I don't have to work after I am 60."
- "I want to ensure I have freedom when my investments mature."

Every one of those statements makes sense. But until these individuals take a deeper look at what's really behind their desire to invest in this market, their motivation to invest in US property remains suspect and, by default, a riskier proposition. Is the currency exchange rate really a good reason to invest in real estate? Real estate is the best asset class in the world to build wealth, but do you realize that it's not risk free? What do you plan to do after you're 60? What does freedom mean? You want the freedom to do what?

Clarity Builds Confidence

Why is clarity so important? Because it's a great foundation for confidence. I work with real estate investors and business owners to help them understand what they really mean when they say they want to invest in real estate, build their businesses and get more from life. Together, we develop clarity about their goals and that clarity builds confidence by helping them identify exactly what they need to do to achieve those goals.

As discussed in the goal-setting fundamentals (#46 and #47), the people who approach me for mentoring are often focused on the wrong thing. They want to buy more doors and make more money and they think they need a mentor to help them with the challenges that presents. I tell them they're wrong. They may need a mentor to tell them that more doors may be a poor focus for their lives!

> The best mentors are individuals who know what you face (they are experienced real estate investors, for example) but are not connected to the outcome. That is, they have no emotional, physical or financial interests to gain from the decisions you make.

In the previous fundamental, we met Mr. Tortoise and Mr. Rabbit. I now want you to meet John. He's looking for a mentor and his story illustrates the things I want you to keep in mind when you're looking for the "right fit" with a business or life mentor.

John's Story

John is a real estate investor who felt like he was stuck. He was struggling to "get more" real estate in his portfolio and to raise the necessary joint venture money he needed to grow his real estate business.

John was under so much pressure that he put his passion for sailing on hold while he made hay with his Formula 1 approach to investing. (Sound familiar?) Unfortunately, the less he did to mentally unwind, the more panic set in and he was in a downward spiral of stress. He was unhappy, unhealthy and generally felt like the world was moving against him. Because he had little or no peace of mind, there was a sense of desperation in his voice and demeanor. Although he didn't realize it, he was communicating that desperation at meetings with potential joint-venture partners and every time he came up empty, the downward spiral sped up.

John told me that he had read 14 real estate investment books over the last eight months. He thought that showed his determination to "make it big" and he had defined success in real estate as buying enough properties to leave his day job. Without realizing it, John had bought into a brand of real estate philosophy that says you cannot be a successful investor if you continue to work for someone else. My frank response to that is, "Bullshit!" Let me tell you this: entrepreneurship is totally overrated.

John came to my Braveheart Retreat and we began to dig a little deeper and ask the hard questions we tend to stay away from. He slowly started to open up about his life and the fact that he quite liked his job. He found that difficult to admit because it went against the grain of what he was telling himself about people who worked for others. It turned out that John got lots of time off and was paid very well. More than that, he genuinely enjoyed his work and felt a sincere sense of pride in what he did.

Given the space, encouragement and above all the permission to personally consider what was really going on under the surface, John realized that some of his entrepreneurial desire was fueled by memories of what happened to his family when his own father lost his job many years earlier. John couldn't shake the feeling that the same thing would happen to him if he stayed working for someone else. As he saw it, his dad's job loss contributed to his father's alcohol problems and the end of his parents' marriage.

Do you see what happened here? John had chosen real estate investment as a kind of personal savior. Unfortunately, that engine was being driven by fears he had never faced—and those fears were actually keeping him from enjoying what his life already offered. The more he focused on finding the magic tips, tricks and strategies he thought he needed to grow his real estate portfolio, the more he missed out on the fact that he wasn't really pursuing his dreams so much as he was running from his nightmares!

In the end, John decided to stay at his job and continued to allow real estate to be a part of his life. With the stress of "I must get more property" gone, he is attracting more joint-venture partners. Most importantly, he is enjoying what he does have in his life as opposed to constantly striving towards what he mistakenly thought he was missing.

The Investor Lifestyle Disconnect

Please take a moment to look over the following questions. Ask yourself if you are experiencing any of this in your business or real estate investments. Do you

- Get disillusioned with real estate?
- Question if the direction you are going fits?
- Think you are not achieving the goals you set?
- Get frustrated at yourself and others in the business?
- Find it challenging to motivate yourself or your team?
- Think some days feel like chaos?
- Feel you are "close" to real estate investment success and find yourself frustrated by your inability to figure out the missing link?
- Get overwhelmed?
- Think you and your team are not on the same page?

- Find that some days feel like you are only steps from the whole thing falling apart?

- Think you're just not enjoying the whole business?

- Feel the team is not doing the job it needs to do?

- Find it hard to jump to the next level?

- Lack a crystal clear strategy?

- Feel isolated?

- Want to buy real estate but are not sure where to start?

- Think you got screwed by someone before and worry it might happen again?

I guarantee—and that is a word I rarely use—that if you are experiencing any of the challenges I listed above, there is a serious disconnect in what I call the Investor Life Cycle. But take heart! This is the most common issue in the real estate investment business. Even though a lot of property investors are not familiar with this cycle, every investor can benefit from understanding how it works.

Investor Life Cycle

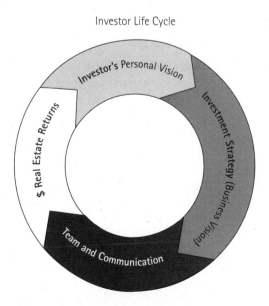

Source: philipmckernan.com

The Investor Life Cycle

Don't fret if there's a disconnect in your Investor Life Cycle. You can determine where the disconnect is, and get back on track. Start by asking yourself

1. Is my personal vision clear? YES or NO

2. Is my business vision clear? YES or NO

3. Does it support my personal vision? YES or NO

4. Do I have the right team in place to pull this off and does my team know and support my business vision? YES or NO

5. Do I have the funds available or access to funds to acquire the portfolio I want, or do I have the cash flow? YES or NO

Be honest with your answers and seek a yes or no. Every time you try to make an in-between answer work, you cloud the results. This gives you a temporary out—and aggravates a long-term problem.

Answering these questions helps investors figure out where the disconnect in their cycle is located. In other words, where on the Investor Life Cycle diagram does the lack of clarity begin for you? Ideally, you should start with the money as your point of reference, then go counterclockwise around the circle. Remember: every time you give a gray answer, it disconnects the positive flow of the cycle.

This exercise will help you pinpoint areas where some things are going well and others are not. It's good to recognize that some areas need more work. For example, in my experience many investors believe their team is working perfectly. If that's true, would you have problems with vacancies, issues finding deals that work and hassles with joint-venture partners? Be honest.

 PROCEED WITH CAUTION!)──────────────────────

Make Honesty a Priority

Do you remember the investing fundamental that said you will probably need to fire more property managers than you hire? When investors don't accept that they've made a bad hiring decision, it costs them. That makes it a great example of how your own lack of honesty can wreak havoc with a functioning Investor Life Cycle.

An authentic business vision must support your personal vision. If honest communication complicates your efforts to build the right team for your strategy, this will affect the team's focus and your business's net financial results.

When many gurus talk about the power of hiring a coach or mentor, they often cite Tiger Woods as someone who has benefited from outside assistance. What people looking for a mentor need to realize is that Tiger was not coached by a five-time Masters winner or someone who has won British Opens back-to-back. In fact, Butch Harmon is one of the most well-known golf coaches to work with Tiger and he has only one PGA win under his belt. What Butch offered Tiger obviously went far beyond his expertise on the fairway or green.

I share this because I want you to be careful to not let pride or fear of the unknown confuse your quest to find a great mentor. What you need is someone who understands your game, and is able to support, push and challenge you to reach your own vision of greatness.

This person must believe in you and in what you want to do.

 **MYTH OR FACT**

Myth: Your mentor must have done what it is you want to do.

Fact: Your mentor must know how to help you do what you want to do!

The
Real
World

Going From Fast Track to Right Track

Philip McKernan Shares the Stories of Two
Investors Who Risked What Really Matters

Ian Szabo and Chantal and Dorien Menard are the kind of real estate investors who attract a lot of attention from others who want to replicate their success. Beyond all the good news about cash flow and long-term appreciation, however, are two stories that serve as cautionary tales for other real estate investors. I share these stories here to illustrate that the "issue" isn't real estate investment, it's the way real estate investment can keep your eyes on the wrong prize. Ian, Chantal and Dorien are great examples of how investors can get so caught up in "doing everything right" that they put at risk what really matters in their lives. These are good examples of what I mean when I challenge people to be really honest about their business choices. There are a lot of people out there doing the wrong things for the wrong reasons. My main point here is that if something's not working, you need to commit to finding out what is really going on.

Off the Tracks

Ian Szabo knows exactly what it's like to be on the fast track to real estate investment success and realize that the "big plan" you thought you were in charge of has seized control of your life train—and is speeding you towards a place you never wanted to be.

Ian's story is characterized by the take-charge vitality of youth. Now 32, he spent 10 years in the highly competitive world of professional cuisine. A young chef who represented his country on a Culinary Team Canada in the 1990s, Ian was an executive sous chef with a team of more than 150 employees when he turned his back on job with a $10-million budget and set up a construction firm called PLP Contracting in Whitby, Ontario, northeast of Toronto.

A couple of years earlier, Ian and two other friends had each plunked down $10,000 on a rental property in a nearby city. In retrospect, that investment had all the hallmarks of a bad deal with the wrong property. But Ian was a quick learner. While he wouldn't buy that property again, the experience whetted his appetite for real estate investment using sound investment fundamentals.

When he launched PLP, the young investor planned to augment the money he made in renovations by buying properties in need of significant renovation that he could fix up and rent out for a few years before flipping them back onto the resale market. It was hard work, but compared to his culinary commitments it meant fewer hours away from his young wife and a chance to invest in the creation of long-term wealth.

Ian had been doing that for about a year before he first heard me speak about the disconnect between people's expressed goals and what they really wanted to value and accomplish in their lives. Two years after that, Ian's life spiraling out of control, he contacted me for help. The economy was still firing on all burners but the young investor was having trouble swinging the kind of joint-venture deals that would propel his business to the next level. The ensuing frustration was taking its toll on the people he cared about most, but Ian felt powerless in the face of his business and personal woes. He wondered how he could work harder.

Identifying the Real Issue

What Ian learned next changed his life. Always ahead-of-the-pack and striving towards a definition of success characterized by what he could eventually own, Ian realized that he wasn't being honest about how his personal life was affecting his business. Behind the scenes, he and his wife were struggling with fertility issues that were slowly but surely exacting a heavy emotional and economic toll on their relationship. No matter how hard Ian worked on his business, he and his wife weren't able to have the family they longed for. He could work more hours to make more money to pay for more fertility treatments, but he could never promise success. For a guy used to being in control, the situation was devastating.

"I was using real estate as my goal and saw it as the driving force for what I wanted to do and it pretty well crippled my life. Now, real estate is here to look after my life and my family," says Ian.

Now less focused on how he will make money, Ian's recommitted to taking care of himself and his wife, and the change has transformed his business. In addition to buying what he calls "ugly houses" to renovate and rent, Ian's renovation expertise has caught the attention of several top Canadian home TV shows and magazines, where he has found a new niche in educating other investors about what to look for in the renovations field. Convinced that his partners need to be people he actually wants to work with, he's more likely to wait for investing partners to come to him—and they are.

While he's not investing in US distressed property yet, Ian admits the raw numbers are alluring. "They're renovating houses for pretty much the same amount I'm paying in Canada, but they're buying these properties for unbelievably low prices. I can't help but be interested, but I'm cautious. What I do from now on has to support my real goals and values."

Bridging the Best Asset Class With Honest Goals

Half a country away, Chantal and Dorien Menard reached a similar conclusion and realized their business goals were not serving them well. More importantly, the goals didn't even "belong" to the couple. But whereas Ian looked to me for my coaching expertise because he knew he was in trouble, the Menards initially sought my help to kick their business up a notch. When they began working with me as their mentor, their initial plan was to use my expertise to close on several real estate joint ventures and grow their portfolio. "We are part of a strong networking group and we felt we should do what every other sophisticated investor was doing," recalls Chantal.

By then, the couple knew how many properties they wanted to buy, they had a definite time frame in mind and, best of all, they had developed a grand vision of how they would work hard for five years and then reap a huge financial reward.

When Chantal spoke with me in late 2008, she and Dorien had two young children. Living in Fort McMurray, Alberta, where Dorien is a specialized pressure welder in the oilsands industry, the couple owned three townhouse condominiums in Fort McMurray and had just bought two in northeast Edmonton. Because Edmonton was deemed the country's hottest residential real estate market and had strong economic fundamentals, the Menards felt compelled to get a piece of that market, too, thinking it was wise to diversify their real estate portfolio.

One of their first assignments with me was to get clear on a five-year vision. After spending hours fine-tuning her vision, Chantal had developed a plan that was all about living the dream of "financial freedom, making ridiculous cash flow, owning an absurd amount of properties and living a life of luxury and ease." She wasn't too impressed when I began to challenge the details. In her own words, "I was pissed off."

But her vision quickly changed when I took the couple through a few very powerful exercises, including one called a "have versus want" assignment. Since then, they've completed the same exercise several times and Chantal insists their answers have not changed over time—they are shockingly clear-cut. "It turns out everything we *really* wanted in our life, and what's important at a core level, things like health, lots of quality time with our family, strong meaningful relationships, spending lots of time at our vacation property and on our passions, were all things we already have today."

Looking back, Chantal is grateful she and Dorien learned this lesson when they did. "It's a lesson many investors learn the hard way, by jeopardizing and in some cases losing what they already have and value most in order to chase bigger and better dreams that do not serve the individual or the people surrounding them."

Living in a city largely untouched by the economic gloom that transformed the US real estate market, the Menards now realize their portfolio should focus on Fort McMurray itself, where oilsands development is holding strong. Because they know that market, have a strong team in place and have all the contacts they need, their real estate business there has experienced tremendous success. When I asked them, "Why complicate your lives by trying to diversify your portfolio when you've identified a goldmine and your system really works?" they realized I was right. The Fort McMurray business was a perfect fit with their decision to have Chantal work from home while their kids are young and she can spend more time with them. In the Menards' case, all three of their Fort McMurray properties were rented via long-term leases to corporations.

Getting real about what they truly wanted prompted the Menards to shift their rental business to the rent-to-own market. In May of 2010 they began to convert their properties in Fort McMurray to rent-to-own leases and became affiliated with a successful rent-to-own company. "Giving families a place they can call their own and build their own equity has been extremely gratifying. This is a very expensive place to live," explains Chantal. "Even if a couple has great jobs, it's hard to pay $42,000 a year in rent, buy groceries and save for a down payment when the average price of a home is over $600,000."

The switch to rent-to-own has many benefits for them. "We are no longer bothered by property management and maintenance of our properties, we know exactly what the selling price is at the onset of the lease, we have long-term three-year leases and most importantly we are helping families achieve home ownership," says Chantal.

"It's funny but as soon as we made these huge discoveries about what we actually wanted and stopped trying so hard to do what everybody else was doing, that's when great opportunities began to fall right into our lap."

The Menards plan "to take the money we make from those sales and reinvest it in Fort McMurray real estate. It means a lot to provide another family with home ownership, but it's a sound business strategy, too," says Chantal.

Staying Close to Home

Given their remote location in northern Alberta, Chantal admits that investing in the US distressed property market doesn't make sense for them right now, especially since their updated long-term vision is all about protecting and enhancing what they've already got.

"Listen, at the end of the day I will always believe that buying and holding long-term real estate with strong economic fundamentals is the best asset class in the world. We are not done with real estate investing; we are just making sure that our investments really support what we want to do."

With her young daughter and son, ages three and two, napping nearby, Chantal says the timely end to their previous preoccupation with buying numerous properties in a specific period of time helped her and Dorien realize their dream of owning a vacation property was already in reach.

In 2009, they bought a vacation property on Lac La Biche in the boreal forest of northeastern Alberta. Two-and-a-half hours from home, the recreation property is also where both of their families have roots. "I feel like it doesn't matter where we might move in the future. This place is like our home base that will always be here. The memories we have here are priceless and that's what life should really be about," says Chantal.

Thinking back on her initial reaction to my challenge, she's now grateful for my help putting their business and personal goals into a healthy perspective. "To achieve real happiness, we didn't have to increase our net worth by billions of dollars" and own a particular number of doors.

Back in Whitby, Ian Szabo is similarly appreciative of how an outsider helped him turn his life around. Ian sticks with his business coach precisely because he and I share the same basic values and "Philip can cut through the crap when I'm speaking and bring me back to what really matters. He challenges everything."

As Ian sees it, that's made him a better businessman. More importantly, it's made him a better husband. "I'm back to doing the things that I want to do and working with the people I want to work with. It's incredible."

HOW TO TEMPER YOUR VISION WITH FACTS

It makes sense to spend some time thinking about and then writing down a long-term vision of what you want your life to look like. But I want to challenge you to keep it real.

I encourage my clients to attach budget numbers to their vision strategies, a task that leaves some of them literally gasping for breath.

Chantal Menard admits she spent a lot of time developing her vision and was really pleased with its level of detail. Factoring in actual budget numbers flipped that vision on its head. "It wasn't just how much money we needed to get what we thought we wanted. I was shocked to realize how much money it was going to take to keep it all going. And for what? We already have exactly what we want. I was inviting trouble when I thought I was 'planning' for peace and comfort!"

Contributors Resource Page

I have built strong relationships with a number of key US real estate market experts and I am especially grateful for the assistance of the following key contributors:

Part 1: Jim Sheils, Florida

An author, speaker and international real estate investor, Jim specializes in single-family home acquisitions in northeast Florida.
www.jacksonvillerealestatewealth.com

Part 2: Brian Scrone, Florida

A real estate investor and trainer whose specialties include property management, raising capital, and renovations, Brian is based in Florida.
www.jacksonvillerealestatewealth.com

Part 3: Tom Wheelwright, Arizona

Tom devises innovative tax, business and wealth strategies for sophisticated investors and business owners. Tom is also a real estate investor.
www.provisionwealth.com

Part 4: James Burns, California

An asset protection and tax attorney and experienced real estate investor, James is also an author and speaker.
www.jamesgburns.com

Other Contributors

Drew Betts, Vancouver, BC, real estate investor
(*http://drewbetts.ca*)

Don Campbell, joint venture specialist, REIN Canada
(*www.reincanada.com*)

Craig Chandler, Australia, real estate investor

Wendy L. Fedoruk, US Real Estate Investment Consultant
(*www.usproperty101.com*)

Greg Head, Calgary, Alberta, real estate investor
(*www.tellmethetime.com*)

Chantal & Dorian Menard, Fort McMurray, Alberta, real estate investors

Ray Reuter, entomologist, REIN Canada
(*www.reincanada.com*)

Jamie Richardson, real estate investor
(*www.jacksonvillerealestatewealth.com*)

Ian Szabo, Toronto, Ontario, real estate investor
(*www.plpcontracting.com*)

Sean Walker, Vancouver, BC, insurance specialist
(*www.fawcettinsurance.com*)

Jim Yager, Partner, International Executive Services,
KPMG LLP, Toronto, Ontario,
International Executive Tax Services Group

 UPDATES

For updates on information found in this book,
please visit Philip McKernan's website:

www.firesale49.com

More Support for You!

We have made every effort to equip you with all the necessary information required to complete a real estate transaction in the US. The reality is, however, that you may want some additional support that is pertinent to your personal circumstances. If you would like some in-the-trenches experience with our team of experts, Real Estate 49 will provide you with the following:

- US Real Estate Resources
- Tools to Build Your Team Directory
- Expert Advice
- Backstage Training
- Real Estate Tools
- Real Estate Mentoring

www.realestate49.com

PHILIP McKERNAN
SPEAKER - MENTOR - TRAINER

Mindset for Success

The difference between the wealthy and the poor is not that they have more strategies, tricks or tools. It's that the wealthy use differently one tool that we all have: mindset. The fact that you purchased this book will give you an edge in real estate; however, if you don't cultivate the right mindset then most likely it will sit on the shelf next to your other wealth-building books and gather dust.

Through his mentoring programs, Philip will help you

- gain clarity
- overcome your obstacles
- cultivate your confidence
- conquer your fears
- become self aware
- create an authentic vision
- live your passion

www.philipmckernan.com

Stay Connected

FIRE SALE WEBSITE

www.firesale49.com

FACEBOOK

www.facebook.com/philipmckernaninc

VIDEO BLOG

www.philipmckernan.tv

TWITTER

www.twitter.com/philipmckernan

PHILIP'S WEBSITE

www.philipmckernan.com

SOUTH OF 49 BOOK

www.southof49.com

**FREE Real Estate 49
e-News. Sign Up at
www.realestate49.com**

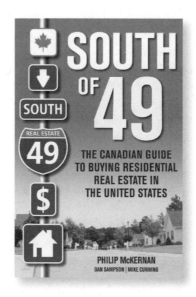

About the Author

Philip McKernan's interest in real estate was nurtured in his native land, Ireland, but he is a student of the global village and currently makes his home in the beautiful city of Vancouver, British Columbia.

Having traveled the world to source a variety of business opportunities, Philip developed a natural interest in the places people live, an entrepreneurial curiosity for how the real estate market differs from country to country and a sophisticated approach to helping people make real estate investments in and outside of their home countries.

Much of Philip's interest in the US real estate market is driven by the opportunities that market presents to investors north of the 49th parallel. But his experience goes well beyond that market: today, Philip's real estate investments include properties in Ireland, the United Kingdom, France, Finland, South Africa and North America.

An internationally respected and sought-after keynote speaker, Philip routinely speaks to Canadian, US, UK and Australasian forums on developing the right mindset to succeed in real estate and life in general. He is also a frequent contributor in the media internationally and domestically, including BNN, Global, CTV, CityTV, *Toronto Star*, *Canadian Business* and *Canadian Real Estate Magazine*.

Through his mentoring business, Philip runs various workshops, training programs, retreats and real estate mentoring programs to assist real estate investors and professionals to overcome obstacles, gain clarity, manage fear, cultivate confidence and take the action to realize their dreams.

Philip's first book *South of 49: The Canadian Guide to Buying Residential Real Estate in the United States* was released in late 2009.

For more information, visit www.philipmckernan.com.